Ida Fisher has been widowed twice. The concept for *The Widow's Guide to Life* evolved from her frustration with the lack of one central source to supply information specifically for widows. Through dealing with the pain of her own losses, she learned that the death of a spouse could be viewed as a beginning, not an end—that there is life-affirmation in becoming self-responsible—and that life can be enriched through the realization of one's own personal power.

To her first career as wife and mother she added a second as a university administrator. In her third career she conducts seminars and workshops for widows. She is forming a nationwide network of widows' mutual support groups.

Byron Lane, PhD, is a psychologist, organizational consultant and Professor of Behavioral Science in the School of Business and Management, Pepperdine University, Malibu, California. He is the author of *How to Free Yourself in a Business of Your Own,* also published by Prentice-Hall.

THE WIDOW'S GUIDE TO LIFE

How to adjust/How to grow

IDA FISHER
BYRON LANE

A SPECTRUM BOOK

PRENTICE-HALL, INC. *Englewood Cliffs, New Jersey 07632*

Library of Congress Cataloging in Publication Data

FISHER, IDA.
    The widow's guide to life.

    (A Spectrum Book)
    Bibliography: p.
    Includes index.
    1. Widows—United States—Life skills guides.
I. Lane, Byron, joint author. II. Title.
HQ1058.5.U5F58   646.7'00880654   80-28110
ISBN 0-13-959452-3
ISBN 0-13-959445-0 (pbk.)

© 1981 by Prentice-Hall, Inc., Englewood Cliffs, New Jersey 07632

A SPECTRUM BOOK

All rights reserved.
No part of this book may be reproduced
in any form or by any means
without permission in writing from the publisher

10 9 8 7 6 5 4 3 2 1

Printed in the United States of America

Cover design by Al Pisano
Manufacturing buyer: Barbara A. Frick

PRENTICE-HALL INTERNATIONAL, INC., *London*
PRENTICE-HALL OF AUSTRALIA PTY. LIMITED, *Sydney*
PRENTICE-HALL OF CANADA, LTD., *Toronto*
PRENTICE-HALL OF INDIA PRIVATE LIMITED, *New Delhi*
PRENTICE-HALL OF JAPAN, INC., *Tokyo*
PRENTICE-HALL OF SOUTHEAST ASIA PTE. LTD., *Singapore*
WHITEHALL BOOKS LIMITED, *Wellington, New Zealand*

To the women in our families . . .
   Annie
   Beatrice
   Gail
   Ilana
   Janet
   Joan
   Judy
   Lauren
   Lisa
   Lynn

Contents

Preface   xiii

Acknowledgments   xv

PART I
TRANSITIONING: ENDING THE OLD LIFE   1

1
Experiencing, Changing, Accepting   3
   Grief and Mourning   4
   Rituals   6
   Alone Is Not Loneliness   7
   Stress   8
   Children and Family   8

viii   Contents

2
Personal and Financial Affairs   12
    A Timetable and Checklist   13
    Funeral and Memorial Services   15
    When and How to Pay Bills   18
    Filing Insurance Claims   19
    Disposition of Personal Effects   21
    Establishing Personal Credit   22
    Closing Employment Affairs   24
    Planning a Budget   27
    Recordkeeping   31

3
Handling Your Legal Affairs   35
    About Attorneys   35
    Selecting an Attorney   36
    Alternate Forms of Legal Assistance   38
    Your Part in the Legal Process   38
    Preparing a New Will   40

4
Dealing with the Social Security Administration   43
    How to Apply   43
    Benefits and Eligibility   44
    Social Security Tips   45
    Medicare   46
    Medicaid   49
    Supplemental Security Income (SSI)   50

5
Veterans Administration Benefits   53
    Widows' Benefits   53
    National Service Life Insurance   55
    VA Benefit Tips   55

6
Dealing with the Internal Revenue Service   57
    Individual Income Tax—Form 1040   58
    Fiduciary (Estate Income) Tax—Form 1041   61
    Estate Tax—Form 706   62

Contents   ix

7
Working with State and Local Agencies　　65
　　Taxes　66
　　Transferring Titles　68
　　Obtaining Vital Documents　70

8
Working with Specialists　　72
　　Accountant　72
　　Insurance Person　74
　　Stockbroker　80

9
Choosing a Financial Institution　　86
　　Safety　86
　　Interest on Savings Accounts　87
　　Ownership of Savings Accounts　88
　　Checking Accounts　88
　　Services　89
　　Trust Departments　91
　　The Human side of Financial Institutions　92

PART II
TRANSITIONING: BEGINNING A NEW LIFE　　95

10
Establishing Your Identity　　97
　　Freedom from Roles　98
　　Coming Into Your Own　98
　　Selfness versus Selfishness　101
　　Aloneness versus Loneliness　101
　　Power of Positive Thought　102
　　Goal Setting　103

11
Of Men and Sex　　106
　　Twenty Sexual Positions　106
　　Going It Alone—Masturbation　107

x Contents

    Not Going It Alone—How to Find a Man   108
    Alternatives to Marriage   110
    Remarriage   111

12
The Holistic Way to Health   113
    Exercise   114
    Nutrition   115
    Deep Relaxation   116
    Psychological Well-Being   118
    The Fully Human Being   119

13
Managing Money   125
    How Much Are You Worth?   126
    Investments   128
    Pitfalls and Pratfalls   132
    Estate Planning   133
    Inflation   135

14
Life Planning   138
    A Personal Workshop Overview   140
    Personal Workshop Procedures   142

15
Career Planning   150
    Entering or Reentering the Job Market   151
    Men's Jobs for Women   152
    Temporary Agency Employment   153
    Time-Sharing Jobs   153
    Create Your Own Job   154
    Out of the Closet   156
    The Single Working Mother   157
    Job Finding and Getting Tips   158
    Where to Find Help   160
    Career Planning Personal Workshop   161

16
Housing Options — 166
Choosing a Location   167
The Interior Environment   168
Living Alone   168
Living with Others   169
Renting an Apartment   170
Home Ownership   171
Condominiums and Co-ops   173
Leisure (Retirement) Communities   173
Retirement Homes   174
Mobile Homes   174

17
New Vistas — 177
Recreation and Travel   177
Back to School   183
Volunteer Work   187

18
Support Systems — 194
Individual Person Support   195
Support Places   197
Support Groups   197

Index — 203

Preface

Within you is the ability to move on to a new and different but rewarding life—this book supplies the tools you need to tap into your own power. Learn how to cope with every real and imagined obstacle in the way of your making a successful transition. Understand how to create a life of fulfillment and high-level wellness.

If you're reading this shortly after your husband's death, you'll want to take advantage of the timetable that tells you what you need to do right now, and what you can safely put off until you feel more able. If you are years into your transition you may be tempted to skip some chapters. Don't. You'll be surprised at the parts of your process you missed and may wish to consider now.

Concerns about handling your finances are covered from many perspectives. See yourself grow tall as you go eyeball to eyeball with lawyers, accountants, Social Security administrators, VA representatives and tax agents. Discover how much you're *really* worth, how to budget your expenses, and how to increase your income through knowledgeable investing. Then, learn how to choose the financial institution that will serve you while you're saving.

Perhaps most important of all, begin to establish your new identity as you realize that you can have two full lives in one lifetime. Enjoy the satisfaction that comes with the knowledge that you don't *need* a man in your life, and that having one may depend on how well you let go. Rediscover your body as part of the new you, and learn how to maintain it at levels of wellness you never thought possible.

Enjoy yourself as you do your career and life planning in simple steps that will put you surely and firmly on the path to becoming productive and fulfilled. Find out about a vast array of housing options and how your choice affects every part of your day. Explore new vistas in recreation, travel, schooling, and volunteer work. Finally, connect with your support system—the people who will share with you in your sorrow and in your joy.

Virtually everything you want to know about your new life is covered here. In addition to the text, at the end of each chapter there are books to read, pamphlets you can send for, and organizations you can contact for additional assistance.

You'll find that your experiences have much in common with those of other women, and that you can go beyond hope to promise. You *can* handle your own affairs, you *can* establish a new identity that is yours alone, you *can* be sexually satisfied, you *can* achieve super health, you *can* have a rewarding career, and you *can* find and be with people who will join with you in celebrating your uniqueness. There are many paths to the new, rewarding life, but if you wish to make a successful transition you must manage your home life, sex life, and work life to suit who you *are,* not who you *were,* and in the process discover who you can become.

Acknowledgments

We appreciate our very own support group of people who are both expert advisers and loving friends. Each of them read chapters and gave us feedback that sometimes caused an "ouch," but always made an improvement—Nadine and Israel Levy, Reggie and Warren Schmidt, Ellie Pope, Sylvia Weber, Iris Mink, Leonard Colene.

Then there are those members of the group who supplied another kind of support—the caring that told us we could do it, even when we weren't sure we could—Edith and Bob Tannenbaum, Jane Shedlin.

At the beginning of Chapter 14 we say a bit about Arthur Shedlin, but here's a bit more—the chapter on Life Planning would not have been written without his help.

Stephen Bosustow shared the material that he collected about the problems of the widower. Fred Case put us in the capable hands of Michael Hunter at Prentice-Hall. Phyllis Solow gave us valuable insight about mutual support groups through her work with widows in the Los Angeles area.

All writers have people behind the scenes who make them look good, and we have two of the best—Vicky Lichtenstein who, through her editing, makes it look as though we can spell, punctuate, and use proper grammar. And Joann Medora, who drops her husband, daughter, and dogs in order to get our typing out on time.

Blessings on all of you.

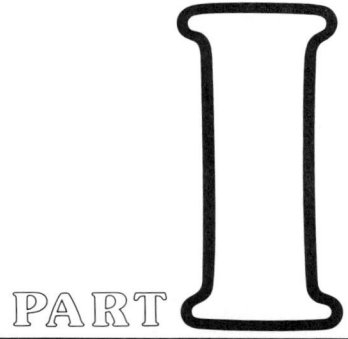

PART I

TRANSITIONING: ENDING THE OLD LIFE

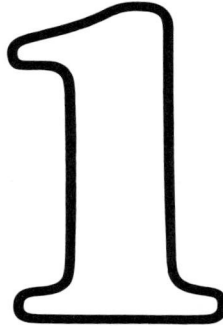

Experiencing, Changing, Accepting

"Next to burglars, mice, and green worms, every normal girl fears a widow. Courtships have been upset and expected proposals have vanished into thin air, simply because a widow has come into the game. . . . A widow has all the freedom of a girl, combined with the liberty of a married woman. She has the secure social position of a matron without the drawbacks of a husband. She is nearer absolute independence than other women are ever known to be." Myrtle Reed wrote these lines in *The Spinster's Book,* published in 1901.

The current view of widowhood is quite different, from the perspective of both the widow and of society. In Myrtle Reed's time, the turn of the century, the death rate for men and women was about the same. By the 1920s, there were two widows for every widower. Life expectancy for women continues to increase much faster than for men and, moving into the 1980s, 85 percent of the women in America will spend the last years of their lives alone.

In not so olden India, it was the wife's duty to immolate herself on her husband's funeral pyre. Some American women still see themselves as an extension of their husband and perform this ritual symbolically, believing that their life has come to an end. If this were to continue, we could expect that the upwards of half a million women who become widows each year would be living without hope, without spirit, and without contribution to the growth of their family and the nation.

Fortunately, there's a dramatically changing national consciousness that is encouraging all women to establish their own separate identities. In the new reality, women must look to themselves, not to their relationships, for their security. They must be prepared for two distinct and, hopefully, equally rewarding phases of their lives.

Significant loss has the potential for being either a growth-producing or life-denying experience. While the pain of separation is acute and real, the positive way to approach this harshest of life's transitions is by a reaffirmation of your own life. It involves a willingness to grow and the courage to be. The path is not easy, but it will lead you "nearer absolute independence than other women are ever known to be."

GRIEF AND MOURNING

Marriage, birth, parenting, divorce—for all of these adult passages there is some preparation available. Not so for death. Preparation for our own dying and for the deaths of those we love is not part of the American model. Even in prolonged illness, the reality of the end comes as a shock. While the pioneering works of Elisabeth Kubler-Ross and others are educating us in more effective ways of dealing with death, it will be some time before we accept dying as an extension of living.

One of the myths perpetuated in our country is that "holding oneself together" or "keeping a stiff upper lip" is a desirable trait and a show of strength and fortitude. The photographs of Jacqueline Kennedy after the death of President Kennedy evoke almost universal admiration. Yet, clinical studies of optimal psychological health tell us that the opposite is true. No woman can hold herself together permanently. The pressure will cause ruptures in totally inappropriate ways—anger at friends who have living husbands, withdrawal, and other behavior that results in self-destruction or isolation. In order to have a beginning of your new life, there must be an ending of the old, so experiencing grief becomes a healing and transitioning process. A psychologist would term it "doing good grief work." This does not mean that you should manufacture grief, but do not hold it back. Your long-term good health and reentry into a new and rewarding life will be enhanced by allowing yourself to give full vent to your feelings.

You can understand the importance of the grieving period and of allowing yourself to experience it fully if you can see it as the bridge between two parts of your life. In a way, the time you spend in the grieving process is actually building the bridge that will bring you to the new life sound and without harm.

You will find that the life you had together provides many strengths you can rely on. You will also experience the feeling of loss—of holes in your life. One of the major tasks of the grieving process is to find ways to fill in those holes.

The grieving process has no specific time limit. You will gradually feel more whole as time goes on, but you may expect short periods of feeling the pain again. Grieving is not like the flu—it doesn't just go away. Similarly, down periods are not to be viewed as relapses—they're simply part of the process.

Without attempting to control the duration of the total grieving process, you may wish to exert some control over shorter, interim time periods. Consciously take a break, make contact with the world around you and do something pleasurable or productive. These short rests will allow you to utilize the process of grieving for your highest interest, without having it consume you.

Your physician may prescribe medication to help you sleep. Certainly, in the early stages, you will need rest to recharge your energy in order to go on. When you feel able, it is a good idea to discontinue the medication. Ordinarily, pain killers mask pain while the body heals; but in this case, they work just the opposite, covering up aches that must be experienced as part of the recovery process.

Studies on grief have shown specific phases that you may go through. While we've identified them in sequence, you may not necessarily experience all of them, or have them in any order. You may even have an in-out feeling, swinging from out of control to being frozen in time and space. Our purpose in pointing out the stages of grief is so you may take comfort in knowing that what you are experiencing is not unique, it is common to nearly everyone.

Disbelief/Denial. Even though the fact of death is obvious, your mind/body may not accept the reality. This is a protective device, allowing your system to accept the information slowly, in appropriate doses. Understanding this, you can allow yourself to stay with whatever is happening.

Numbness. This is a continuation of your protective devices. While your support system, in the form of family and friends, is gathering, you may handle necessary details of your life in a robotlike fashion, without feeling fully connected.

Disorganization and Forgetfulness. Even though you may normally be in control of your life, at this stage you may forget things easily and find it difficult to do simple tasks. This phase may come and go, interweaving with other phases. You may also find yourself being confused, looking for direction, or trying to find meaning in your bereavement. When your organism reaches out for help and finds it no longer available, it is natural to expect some disorientation.

Aloneness. When your system opens up, the lonely feelings come through strongly. We discuss this in more detail later in the chapter. Remember that this is not an endless phase. It, too, will find resolution in time.

Anger. "Why me?" is the question that arises. You may be angry at your husband for leaving you, angry at friends who have not been hurt, angry at God. You may feel cheated, or that you have been treated unfairly. Since anger is not socially acceptable behavior in our culture, you may not have this part of your process so favorably received. Even so, it is important not to try to make your anger "logical"—just let yourself be and experience everything, anger included.

Guilt. This is one experience you can do without. Guilt over things you failed to do properly or neglected to do is an energy drain for no real purpose. It is unlikely that you can gain absolute control over guilt feelings at this time, but you might try not being so hard on yourself.

Depression. As the impact of your loss comes fully over you, depression is a common experience. Part of this comes from feeling sorry for yourself and the life that you must now reorder. Without denying the feeling, you may find it helpful to actually begin the necessary work of reintegrating your life. Activity is an antidote to depression.

Idealizing. At some time, you may begin to remember your husband in ways that never really were, often as all-perfect. Acknowledging his negative as well as positive traits, to remember him as a normal human being, will help you move through the grief process without setbacks.

Envy, Pointlessness, Emptiness. These are other feelings you may experience. It's perfectly understandable that you would feel envious of a loving couple holding hands, or that you would feel empty, or that your life seems pointless. Just notice any of these feelings and allow them to be.

Whenever someone close to you dies, you grieve not only for your loss—in a sense you grieve for yourself as you are confronted with your own mortality. If you're willing to see this and acknowledge that you're not immortal, it may give you some positive direction for creating your new lifestyle.

RITUALS

Grief is a physical relief. It is the body opening up the channels so your life energy may flow freely. The recognition of this natural flow is not a new discovery; it dates to antiquity. Many of the ancient customs surrounding death have been ritualized for our religions. In some sophisticated urban circles, it has become very "cool" to ignore tradition and do things in a "modern way."

Just as cutting off the free flow of grief leaves unfinished business to crop up later in your life, so denial of rituals from your heritage may impede the healing process. Rituals are important in marshaling support systems and confronting the reality of death.

While there are wide variations among Protestants in the treatment of death, Catholic and Jewish rituals are more clearly defined. In the Orthodox Jewish tradition, there is a heavy emotional period called "Shiva" (literally, seven), in which the bereaved stays at home for seven days following the funeral. During this period, as if to exemplify the continuation of life, friends and relatives pay condolence calls.

> Ann M. was raised in a reformed Jewish home, one where rituals such as Shiva are not practiced. It is unlikely that she would even be familiar with the many ritual aspects of Shiva. Many months after her husband died, in a discussion with friends, she came to realize that in a totally subconscious way she had performed many aspects of the ritual. As she described it, "For whatever reasons, I chose not to leave the house for a week. It seemed to be okay, so I wore no shoes, and I found myself sitting on the floor most of the time. My connection with the world was through the memorial candle that someone had brought me, and that continued to burn for seven days."

The Catholic wake is a vigil in which neighbors and friends sustain the family through the grief process. They pay their respects to the deceased and join one another in an expression of faith through prayer and joyous celebration of life.

ALONE IS NOT LONELINESS

Some view a glass as half empty, while others view it as half full. Recent studies have shown that your views can strongly influence what happens in your life. Since how you look at things is very much your own choice and can be changed with effort, this suggests some interesting possibilities.

If you believe that a relationship is everything, then it follows that without the relationship you are nothing. That's the half-empty view. If you view yourself as having a total and valuable identity within a relationship, when the relationship ends you can move on to *a new and different but rewarding life*. That's the half-full view, allowing you to get on with the job of filling yourself up.

Aloneness is a reality—a state of being. *Loneliness* is a self-induced state. It can be perpetuated or changed, as you choose. It's tempting to remain in the now half-filled house, with its securities and memories. It's very fearful to move out into the world as a single.

No one wants a third or odd person at a gathering of friends. That's one view. Realizing the importance of your being and how much you add to a group is another view. The former will keep you immobilized, the latter contributes to your reentry into life.

If all of this sounds very difficult now, it really isn't. It's simply a matter of making up your mind that you can be as fully alive unconnected as you were connected.

STRESS

Drs. Thomas H. Holmes and Richard H. Rahe have identified death of a spouse as the life experience producing the greatest stress. The significance of this is in the relationship between stress and illness. Each of us experiences stress as part of our daily lives. It is the dis-stress, the part that our bodies can't handle, that makes us ill.

This is probably the most important time in your life to pay attention to your body. You may experience many warning signals such as a change in your sleep pattern, forgetfulness, or, at the extreme, the sense of "losing you mind."

In a later chapter, *The Holistic Way to Health,* we deal with general health practices. Some, such as autogenic training and meditation, are particularly helpful in stress reduction. But, for the moment, consider not adding additional stress factors to those you are already experiencing. Major changes such as moving or taking a new job are high on the stress list.

Earlier we spoke about drugs masking the necessary process of grief. Your physician may prescribe tranquilizers, and certainly this is okay initially. However, continued use of drugs may keep you from becoming an aware participant in your own healing process.

The most effective healers and stress reducers at this point in your life are time, tears, and talk. While death heightens the awareness of the importance of each moment of time, it is acceptable to allow yourself to actually "waste time." This means pleasuring yourself, being in the moment, giving yourself permission to *not* perform duties. Find loving people with whom you can talk, and don't shut off the tears when they come. If you can just let go for a while, nature's healing process will take over, helping you to avoid stress-related illness and speeding you on your way to a healthy new life.

CHILDREN AND FAMILY

It is part of our tradition to shield children from the trauma of death. Current studies in this area suggest a more natural flow to the relationship between parent and child in the sharing of loss. Since attempts at hiding facts or deception of any kind are always sensed by children, being open and honest is preferable. Secretiveness arises from the notion that children simply can't handle death; yet children, because they have not been negatively conditioned, often handle death better than adults.

You need to be open about your grief, and there is no reason not to share. Depending on your child's age, there will be limits of understanding, but the reality is that you need each other and this is not a time to close off any part of your being together.

With the subject of death in our culture finally coming out of the closet, some of our better high schools are offering classes in death and dying. Students are learning to prepare for the inevitability of death. This offers great hope for a changing view of death—integrating it into our life process rather than externalizing death as something that is not a part of life. If you are fortunate enough to have a youth with such an education in your home, you can learn much that will assist your own passage.

Your family can be one of the most important aids in your rebirthing process. The being and sharing with each other, the acceptance of reality, the exchange of love, is important to each of you as an individual and to all of you as an interrelated unit.

In this chapter, we have looked at death and separation as a beginning of a reaffirmation of life. We have seen it not as an ending but as a new beginning. All of our struggling over modern ways of viewing separation brings a smile as Myrtle Reed, from 1901, informs us, "When the time of parting comes, for there is always that turning in the road, the sadness is not so great because we must go on alone. Life grows beautiful after a time and even wholly sweet, when a man and a woman have so lived and loved and worked together. . . ."

ADDITIONAL INFORMATION

Grief and Mourning
Books

Herman Feifel (Editor). *The Meaning of Death.* McGraw-Hill, 1959. Articles on many aspects of death. An early work bringing the subject of death and bereavement into open discussion.

Earl A. Grollman (Editor). *Concerning Death: A Practical Guide for the Living.* Beacon Press, 1974. Covers grief, religious, medical, and social issues.

Elisabeth Kubler-Ross. *Death: The Final Stage of Growth.* Prentice-Hall, 1975. If you have an interest in death as a transition, this book by a seminal researcher in the field is a must.

Stanley Keleman. *Living Your Dying.* Random House, 1974. A new approach to realizing the value of life by accepting death in daily doses.

C. M. Parkes. *Bereavement: Studies of Grief in Adult Life.* International Universities Press, 1972. An important book from the leading international authority on bereavement.

Roberta Temes. *Living with an Empty Chair: A Guide Through Grief.* Mandala, 1977. A combination of the psychological and practical to help you understand the bereavement process and the stages of grief and mourning.

M. V. Kamath. *Philosophy of Death and Dying.* Himalayan Institute, 1979. A clear, highly informative study of the experience of death and dying. Included are the thoughts and reflections of fifty-five famous men and women during their experience of dying.

Lynn Caine. *Widow.* Bantam Books, 1974. A candid sharing of one woman's experience. Save if for a day when you're feeling good. It's weepy, but important material.

Alone Is Not Loneliness

Books

James A. Peterson and Michael L. Briley. *Widows and Widowhood: A Creative Approach to Being Alone.* Associated Press, 1977. Deals thoughtfully with the emotional aspects of widowhood, particularly aloneness and family issues.

Patricia O'Brien. *The Woman Alone.* Quadrangle/The New York Times Book Co., 1973. An upbeat look at the worthwhile struggle to be who you are and like it, even though alone.

Alfred A. Lewis and Barrie Berns. *Three Out of Four Wives: Widowhood in America.* Macmillan, 1975. An angry expose on the plight of the American widow. You'll recognize issues such as financial insecurity, sexual deprivation, loneliness, and uncertainty about the future. Offers some sound advice about a successful reentry.

Children and Family

Books

Earl E. Grollman. *Talking About Death: A Dialogue Between Parent and Child.* Beacon Press, 1975. Helpful information for communicating with young children on the subject of death.

Jim and Janet Egleson. *Parents Without Partners.* E. P. Dutton and Company, 1961. Pages 113–131, Newly Widowed, are still relevant today. Covers issues of single parenting, the PWP concept (working with other single parents). Good insight into the feelings of children who have only one parent.

Franki and Barbara Sternberg. *If I Die and When I Do: Exploring Death with Young People.* Prentice-Hall, 1980. Moving account in their own words of how children experience death in our culture.

Rose Zeligs. *Children's Experience with Death.* Charles C Thomas, 1974. Don't read this for pleasure (it's heavy), but contains solid information on how adolescents deal with death, particularly that of a parent.

General Information

The Widowed Persons Service of the American Association of Retired Persons, AARP/AIM/NRTA, 1909 K Street, N.W. Washington, D.C. 20049, provides information on programs in your community; and two helpful booklets—*Your Retirement Widowhood Guide* and *On Being Alone* by James A. Peterson.

Parents Without Partners. A national organization that provides support through sharing problems of single parenting. Check with local telephone directory assistance for chapter nearest you, or write: Parents Without Partners, International, 7910 Woodmont Avenue, Washington, D.C. 20014.

Personal and Financial Affairs

A Note on Competency

There are no experts. Our many months of seeking information from and checking the work of government agencies and private professionals leaves us appalled at the extent of the incompetency we encountered. We have experienced asking questions of as many as four workers in one government agency, and getting four different answers. In all our researching, we have seldom talked to two people in the same agency and received the same answer.

In our interviews with many widows, we hear the same stories—"my accountant never told me," or "my lawyer didn't know." Part of this is due to the complexity of the system, and on occasion it is due to downright incompetency.

It is *not* our purpose to sit in judgment on anyone. It *is* our purpose to warn you that much of the "factual" information you will get may be unreliable. That leaves it clearly up to you to learn as much as possible about your own affairs, wherever possible take charge or take over, and never allow someone to assume responsibility for you.

A TIMETABLE AND CHECKLIST

Throughout the book we speak of taking responsibility for your own life, becoming actively involved in all the decisions that affect you, and moving positively ahead into a new way of being. The list that follows is intended to clearly outline all of the affairs that most probably will need to be handled. Some must be done immediately in order to comply with the law, or to protect yourself financially. Others can be deferred for weeks or months. This is *not* an exact timetable. It can be altered to suit individual circumstances. It *is* a structure you can lean on in three ways:

1. You can see at a glance the full spectrum of collecting, organizing, and deciding what you must do in the first year of your new life.
2. Those tasks that may be safely deferred are clearly indicated. We hope this is anxiety-relieving.
3. Where necessary each item is cross referenced to a particular chapter or page, so you can look for explicit direction. If you don't find all the information you need, go to the end of that chapter and consult the "Additional Information" guide.

Immediately

Make funeral or memorial service arrangements. Page 15, this chapter.

Within the First Two Weeks

Change a checking and savings account to your name. This can be handled by your bank or savings and loan, and funds to handle your immediate needs can be released without legal red tape. See Chapter 7, page 69.

Establish an estate bank account to handle funds received in your husband's name. See Chapter 3, page 39.

Notify insurance companies. See page 20, this chapter.

Contact your local Social Security Administration office and begin benefit proceedings. See Chapter 4.

Contact the Veterans Administration and begin benefit proceedings. See Chapter 5.

Notify your husband's employer and/or business associates. Also, notify any associations with which he was affiliated. Check each for possible benefits. See page 24, this chapter.

Within the First Four Weeks

Select an attorney. See Chapter 3.

File your husband's will. If there is no will, the court should be notified. If the will is in your safety deposit box, ask your bank official to grant you entry for just this item. See Chapter 3, page 39.

Petition for appointment as administrator or executor of the estate. See Chapter 3, page 39.

Pay some immediate bills, but do *not* pay major items or medical bills. See page 18, this chapter.

Develop your support systems. See Chapter 18, page 194 through page 200.

After the First Month

Begin probate. See Chapter 3, page 39.

File insurance claims. See page 19, this chapter.

Pay necessary medical and hospital bills. See page 18, this chapter.

Start process of closing out self-employment business affairs. See page 26, this chapter.

Plan an interim budget. See page 27, this chapter.

Begin the disposition of your husband's personal effects. See page 21, this chapter.

Within Six Months

Select an accountant. See Chapter 8.

Transfer title on home and/or other real property. See Chapter 7, page 68.

Transfer title on all savings accounts. See Chapter 6, page 69 and Chapter 7, page 88.

Transfer title on all automotive vehicles. See Chapter 7, page 68.

Review your interim budget. See page 28, this chapter.

Establish personal credit. See page 22, this chapter.

Change or cancel charge accounts and credit cards. See page 23, this chapter.

Change beneficiaries on any of *your* life insurance, pension plans, retirement plans, etc., that had your husband as beneficiary.

Change name on homeowner's, auto, and other insurance policies.

Change name on utility billings—gas, water, electricity, telephone.

Order change in telephone directory listing. It is wise to use your first initial, rather than a name that would indicate you're a woman alone.

Begin reaching out. Invite friends for lunch or dinner. Investigate classes or programs of interest. See Chapter 17.

Contact support groups. See Chapter 18, page 197.

Start working on your physical and psychological health. See Chapter 12.

Prepare a new will. See Chapter 3, page 40.

After Six Months

Begin the process of establishing your new identity. See Chapter 10.

File federal and state individual income tax returns. (Note: if your husband's death occurred in the last two or three months of the year, you can file for an extension to allow yourself at least six months before you attempt this job.) See Chapter 6, page 58 and Chapter 7, page 66.

File a federal estate tax return, if required. See Chapter 6, page 62.

File a state inheritance tax return, if required. See Chapter 7, page 67.

File federal and state fiduciary tax returns if you established an estate account. See Chapter 6, page 61 and Chapter 7, page 66.

Transfer title on stocks, bonds, and other assets. See Chapter 6, page 62 and Chapter 8, page 82.

Close probate. See Chapter 3, page 40.

Plan your financial future. See Chapter 13.

Begin your life and career planning. See Chapters 14 and 15.

Consider new housing arrangements. See Chapter 16.

Begin your journey into new vistas—education, travel, volunteer work. See Chapter 17.

FUNERAL AND MEMORIAL SERVICES

If the information contained in this section is no longer needed in the death of your husband, you may want to read it later on for consideration in planning arrangements for yourself.

Any discussion of funerals has two aspects—emotional and financial. Most often the subject is dealt with at an emotionally charged time, which means that the financial aspects take on lesser importance. This situation is tailor-made for those funeral directors whose sole interest is in making money, rather than carrying out the wishes of you and your deceased husband. As a result of many questionable business practices in the funeral industry, there is growing public inquiry about the high cost of dying.

Let's begin by looking at the purpose of funerals, then at determining the proper cost, and finally at ways to arrive at a decision that best fits your wishes and needs.

Why Funerals?

Basically, funerals are institutionalized ways of putting death into perspective. There are a variety of religious and cultural views of funerals, but in our modern society it is primarily a process of closure. In its finest form, it is the celebration of a life now ended, an expression of the ongoingness of human existence, and a release of the family and friends to go forward with their own lives.

An alternative to funerals, and serving the same purpose, is a memorial service. It may be held days or weeks after the death in a home, garden, church, or public place. Memorial services are becoming increasingly acceptable as a less stressful, less costly, and equally authentic way of saying goodbye.

Financial Aspects of Funerals

Most traditional funerals cost over $2,000 and can easily go to $10,000. Over $6 billion is spent annually in the United States on funerals. Yet, you can spend as little as $250 if you choose. The Federal Trade Commission in a recent study has warned that, at a time when you are most vulnerable, you may be approached by what is known in the trade as a "grief counselor." In reality, he is a salesman for the mortuary and his job is to sell you an elaborate funeral, often beyond your financial capabilities.

Although we are making progress, in our society death is still viewed as a taboo subject, and much of what is involved in the American funeral ritual supports that denial. At a point when everything that is happening already feels unreal, the unscrupulous funeral parlor can use your vulnerability to its economic advantage. Elaborately lined coffins, cosmetics, and even the artificial carpeting that covers the raw earth, help to perpetuate the unrealness of death.

Caught between your grief and love for your husband, you may join many other widows in arranging for a funeral that could be the largest single expenditure of your lifetime. One way of assuring yourself a low-cost service (low cost does not necessarily mean low quality) is to join one of the proliferating memorial societies. There are now over 150 in the United States and Canada. Their main purpose is to provide, through a membership plan, services of local morticians who provide simple arrangements at modest costs. You may even join such a plan after a death and immediately before making funeral arrangements. Membership fees are low, usually in the range of $5 for an individual, $10 for a family. They are typically nonprofit associations, and the fees cover only organizational expenses. Even if you look at the membership cost as a referral fee, you will be amazed at the possible savings.

With a memorial society, you are not limited to the type of arrangement you select. If you prefer more elaborate services, you can still benefit by going through a funeral society. Ways to contact these organizations are shown at the end of the chapter.

Even if you know a funeral director (also known as mortician, undertaker, or embalmer) you can trust, you should know what is, or is not, legally required. For example, embalming is rarely required by law. Direct cremation is possible without the casket, bypassing both the mortuary and the cemetary. As you can imagine, the funeral industry does what it can to suppress this type of information.

Be aware that both the Social Security Administration and the Veterans Administration provide burial allowances. Chances are excellent that you will qualify for one or both. The amounts are such that it is possible to make dignified arrangements with no additional costs to you. See Chapters 4 and 5 for details.

Making the Best Decision for You

A costly, elaborate funeral is not necessarily a sign of love or respect, and it may jeopardize your financial future and your children's as well. Try not to make arrangements that will expiate any guilt you may have, impress your family and friends, or prove to your husband how much you loved him. Elaborate funerals for people of modest means are becoming a thing of the past, with simplicity and honesty becoming more accepted.

You will need to deal with some of these issues:

- Selection of the casket.
- Should the body be open to view?
- What about flowers?
- Should there be interment (ground burial), cremation, or entombment (above ground burial)?
- What type of service—humanistic or religious?
- What cemetery should you choose?
- Should there be a memorial marker?

Consider alternatives to a traditional funeral such as immediate cremation, with memorial services at a later time when relatives and friends can conveniently gather.

For some, a nonplanned, spontaneous get-together to share feelings is helpful. You may want to consider establishing a living memorial by planting trees or shrubs, setting up a scholarship fund, or simply mailing printed eulogies to friends and relatives. There are no rules, and it is possible to be creatively caring, even at such a time.

Whatever your decision, make it the right one for you. Consider children and other family members, but if conflict arises over what is best, make the first autonomous choice of your new life—be good to yourself.

After all the arrangements are handled and you are freshly in touch with your feelings, you might wish to make some notes for the future that you can later turn into plans. Drawing on your present experience, you may wish to provide instructions about your own funeral or memorial service, relieving your children or family of the decision-making burden. This is a most loving and caring thing to do.

WHEN AND HOW TO PAY BILLS

It doesn't matter how much skill you may have at handling bill payments or how unskilled or disorganized you may be, the trauma of death is the great equalizer and, unless you are the rare exception, you will find that the small stack of unpaid bills looks like it rests at the top of Mt. Everest.

In one sense, your state of shock may help you financially, for the best thing to do about most bills during the first few weeks is nothing. There is a very sound reason for this—some payments may be covered by insurance policies that are unknown to you at the moment. For example, many auto loans are covered by insurance that automatically pays off the entire loan when the owner dies. The same with mortgages. Check to see if you have mortgage insurance; you may find that your home loan is paid off. Even things like credit union loans, regular credit cards, and other major purchases could be covered. So, it is wise to let bills like this wait until you recover your equilbrium, and then check for possible coverage.

The same with medical bills. Many are covered by insurance, Medicare, or other policies. A phone call to your creditors (if you don't feel up to it, ask for help from friends and relatives) will practically always make available the time you need to explore your coverage. Most people really do understand.

At a time when the mountain looks more approachable, you will be able to begin paying some of those bills. At this point, pay attention to two aspects of your task. 1) Analyze each payment—the amount, to whom payable, and what bank account you want to use. 2) Keep accurate, retrievable records.

Again, before you make a payment, be sure it is not covered by insurance. Then, decide if it should be paid through your personal account or the estate account (see Chapter 6). This allocation may affect your taxes.

Being a good recordkeeper is very simple. Here is our "handy-dandy, anyone-can-do-it" record-keeping system.

Create one folder with the title "Bills Payable." As bills come in, simply place them in this folder. Create a second folder with the title, "Personal Bills Paid (Date) to (Date)." And a third folder titled "Estate Account Bills Paid (Date) to (Date)." Only pay bills at specified periods. The first and fifteenth of the month are good choices. Payments on these dates will keep you current, and make bill-paying more palatable.

When you're ready to make payments, take out the unpaid bills, examine each and decide if it is an estate bill or a personal bill. On the estate account bills, write your rationale for assigning it to the estate on the bill itself or on a slip of paper you attach to the bill. You may be required some years hence to explain to an IRS agent why you made this choice. Don't leave it to your memory. Our accountant's helpful saying of the year is, "Whatever you do, leave tracks."

Now, pick a pile and start making payments. Always pay by check. It becomes a receipt for payment. As you complete the check, write on the face of the bill the date of payment, the check number, and the amount; note if it is a partial payment or add any other information you might need to jog your memory later. Get the check ready to mail, and put the paid bill into its proper folder. That's the whole system. Your check register will cross-reference with the bill, and the bill will have all the details of the transaction. Once again, organization triumphs over sloth.

FILING INSURANCE CLAIMS

Money owed to you by insurance companies may well represent a sizeable portion of your estate, will often cover the majority of medical bills, and may cover your payments on major items such as an automobile. Accurate, organized, early filing of claims also represents an immediate source of cash. When dealing with insurance companies, these are some rules to be explored:

- Check every imaginable source to make sure you have not overlooked any coverage.
- Never take no for an answer on a medical insurance claim until someone (hopefully not you) drops from exhaustion.
- Make a pal in the insurance company and then work with her/him exclusively.
- File early, accurately, and claim everything.
- Remember that no one will offer you anything. You must ask.

Filing Life Insurance Claims

Begin by checking every possible place for life insurance benefits. *There are millions of dollars in benefits in the coffers of life insurance companies that are unpaid because no one filed a claim.*

In addition to the policies you find in the safety deposit box or in your husband's file, try these places:

- Check your husband's business. Partnerships and corporations often carry insurance on the life of executives. Some pension plans contain life insurance. Many trade unions provide life insurance. We know of

several cases where life insurance coverage is hidden in a medical insurance policy.
- Business associations, fraternal associations, clubs, and alumni groups often provide life insurance.
- If your husband died in an accident, his credit card insurance may provide automatic coverage.
- Auto accidents covered by casualty insurance frequently have death benefits.
- Work-related deaths may be covered by Workmen's Compensation benefits.
- If you believe there may be coverage (old checks showing payment to an insurance company are a good clue), write the company for verification or a duplicate policy.
- Sometimes disability policies provide death benefits.
- Never assume that a policy has lapsed. Check.

Next, check Social Security for lump-sum death benefits (see Chapter 4) and the Veterans Administration for lump-sum and extended benefits (see Chapter 5).

Now, with all policies in hand, you are ready to file claims. Contact the insurance company by mail or your representative by phone. Request claim forms and the procedure for expediting claims. In all cases, you will be required to furnish a certified copy of the death certificate. Typically, simply providing the policy number on the claim form is adequate, but you may be required to return the policy itself. Be sure to send policies by Certified or Registered mail so that you have a receipt.

You will find that most companies will make payment within two or three weeks of receiving the completed claim. Along with payment, or in a later mail, you should receive a Form 712 Life Insurance Statement for a Decedent, which is to be filed with Federal Estate Tax Form 706. Retain this form, even though you think you may not have to file a return, until all matters involving your husband's death have been settled.

Filing Medical Insurance Claims

Using the same checklist for life insurance, gather any medical insurance policies. Check them for time limitations on submission of claims. Wherever possible, have the doctors and hospital process the claims. They're experts and can save you a great deal of work. Watch for areas where you have double or supplemental coverage so that claims get filed with *all* the companies that provide coverage for you. *Don't pay the doctors and hospitals and wait to be reimbursed by the insurance company.* They might urge you to pay first, but we urge you to take care of yourself. The doctors and hospitals can handle stress right now better than you. There just may be complications, and it's not uncommon for medical insurance companies to take up to a year to settle claims.

Never, never take no for an answer on any medical claim. Often, claims are rejected for improper documentation, and it's simply a matter of clarification. If you believe you should receive payment and the insurance company says no, learn the name of one person at the company whom you can speak to personally. Contact him/her and learn the procedure to resubmit, or the reason for rejection. Once you understand the reason for refusal, you can figure out ways to get paid. Persistence really pays off here. *The assertive person gets more money from medical insurance companies.* While most insurance matters are handled by computers, there are still live human beings out there, and you can find one to help you. If you don't feel up to it, find the most persuasive member of your family and enlist her/his aid.

Also, remember that many medical insurance policies include a portion known as "Major Medical." Usually, beyond basic hospital coverage (or without your being hospitalized), this portion pays 80 percent of bills for doctors, drugs, rental of special equipment, ambulance service, etc. It's surprising how many people don't know of this coverage in their policies. If you don't file, they won't pay. One good rule is to file for *everything.* If it isn't covered, they'll disallow it. It is better to have filed and lost than never to have filed at all.

Medicare claims are no different than any private policy claim. The Medicare carrier should be handled as you would another company. Don't be intimidated by thinking you are dealing with the U.S. Government.

DISPOSITION OF PERSONAL EFFECTS

This is one of the most individual, touchy, let's-not-talk-about-it subjects of all. There are complex emotional and financial considerations around what to do with clothes, jewelry, hobby materials, and even the contents of the medicine cabinet.

Whatever way you choose to go about reordering the contents of your home to accommodate your new single life is okay, as long as it suits you and your feelings. Advice from friends and family, however well intentioned, is best ignored.

As with all decisions at this time, *don't rush.* Wait until you feel up to the task. If family wants to join in, they can be supportive and helpful as long as you control the disposition of everything.

Within your range of choices, there are two extremes that might cause difficulty in your eventual readjustment—making an immediate clean sweep, or postponing any action indefinitely.

> When Jane G.'s husband died, she decided to shape up, be brave, and get going. Out with the old, in with the new. She disposed of everything that belonged to her husband and packed away pictures and all the treasures from their marriage. She sold her home, moved into an apartment, and promptly left on a trip to the Orient.

Jane's internal, perhaps subconscious decision was to avoid the pain of her loss by not dealing with it. Unfortunately, *anything* that we don't deal with in our lives, particularly a traumatic event, doesn't simply disappear; it stays inside us in some form that will later show up as physical illness, depression, poor social adjustment, or any one of a hundred ways that keep us from living fully.

> Sally P. simply could not bear to move any of her husband's possessions. She lived in a twilight zone, unable to deal with the reality of his death. Everything remained in place, ready for his return. An unsuspecting visitor to her home would assume that her husband had simply gone out for a walk.

It's quite apparent that both women are doing the same thing—avoiding dealing with the present reality. Whatever the pain, they would both be better off going fully through a period of grief and mourning, emerging whole, healthy, and ready to move on.

Assuming that you are ready to make a reasoned disposition of your husband's possessions, you might consider their end use. Charities make a wonderful choice. If friends or family can use things, that's fine, as long as you are comfortable seeing those articles being worn or used by someone else. There's certainly nothing wrong with keeping items that you can utilize or that have sentimental value.

Ugly as it may seem, taxation enters into your choices. Keep careful records of everything you give away or sell. When filing estate and inheritance tax returns, you will be required to show the value of personal effects. Items you give to charitable organizations are deductible on your income tax.

ESTABLISHING PERSONAL CREDIT

Since all plastic is a derivative of oil, it is interesting to contemplate what the credit card of the future will look like, once the flow of petroleum stops. Or, one might wonder about the effect on the energy crisis if everyone in the world started paying their bills with money.

If you're like most others, you have a bulging wallet, full of little plastic cards that will gain you access to parking places, buildings, the machine that dispenses traveler's checks, and all the goodies of your favorite department store, or the corner drugstore.

Only most of them are in your husband's name. What to do? Fortunately, the Equal Credit Opportunity Act of 1974 states that you may not be denied credit on the basis of sex or marital status. For the most part, the handling of cards currently in your possession is relatively simple. Those you don't want, simply cut in half, throw away, and forget about them. For the remainder, request that the companies issue new cards to you in your own name. You may elect to use Mary Smith, Mrs. Mary Smith, or Ms. Mary Smith, whichever suits you. Most good firms will comply without changing the account number or asking for verification of financial ability to support the account.

Before you file an application for new credit, it is wise to complete the transfers suggested in the preceding paragraph. This way, when you fill out a new form, you will be able to enter current charge accounts in the appropriate spaces.

You may be denied credit only if the issuing company decides that your income or financial picture does not warrant it. If you are refused credit, you have the right to know why. The Fair Credit Reporting Act gives you right of access to the information about you in credit bureau files. It's interesting to note that being on welfare is not a basis for denying credit. If you ever have problems in this area, refer to information at the end of this chapter or contact National Organization for Women (NOW) for public service groups who are working on these matters. Women's Centers in some universities and law schools also provide assistance and often counseling. Don't let a firm tell you you need a cosigner. They can't unless this is required of all similar applicants. It's important that you not be discriminated against financially because of your widowed status.

Pros and Cons of Credit Cards

In our credit-crazy society, most of us need one general-purpose credit card. It's virtually impossible to rent a car without a national credit card, and many hotels look askance when you try to pay by check. Wisely used, a credit card actually can save money. Let's say you buy something on the third of the month for $100 and charge it on your card. The bill arrives at the end of the month and is due in ten days. You pay it on the third of the month. You have had the use of $100 for one month with no charge whatsoever. You save whatever money the $100 in your savings account earned.

There's no question about the convenience of a credit card. It allows you to shop without the risk of carrying a lot of cash. You can purchase items when they are on sale and you are short of cash. You can order goods and even entertainment tickets by phone or mail. You pay many bills with one check, and you have good tax records.

After the one major card, you're on your own. There are multipurpose cards that require an annual fee and oil company and department store cards that are issued free to encourage your purchases.

On the other hand, credit cards can cause a whole array of problems. If you use the extended credit terms, you will pay interest rates from 18 percent on up. You may be tempted to buy things you do not need and cannot afford. If you are habitually late in making payments, you will incur additional charges.

If you have a lot of cards, they will add bulk and weight to your purse, causing it to wear out and need replacement more often. Your carrying arm will become longer than your other arm, pulling you off balance and requiring periodic, expensive chiropractic adjustment. Because of the risk of losing your cards, you may clutch your purse tightly to your bosom, making you hunchbacked. If you have ever seen a woman going through her credit card wad in a department store and analyzed the procedure, you will be amazed at the lost time by salespersons in waiting. This cost inevitably gets added to the price of the merchandise, which fuels inflation. Then, there's that thing about oil. . . .

On balance, it's a good idea to have one carefully monitored bank credit card and a few for the major department stores you frequent. Have fun!

To Borrow or Not to Borrow

Some pundits in the field recommend that you take out a small personal loan at the bank in order to establish a line of credit. They recommend you put the funds into your savings account. That way, the differential between interest received and interest paid is your cost for establishing a line of credit.

We think that's a lot of monkeying around, unless you have a specific purpose. Such credit lines are not meaningful where there's substantial collateral, as in the case of an auto or home purchase. However, if you're contemplating starting a business, this suddenly becomes an excellent way of getting known by your friendly banker.

Purchasing something on the installment plan and then making regular payments by personal check is legitimately helpful in the process of getting you something you want and also helps in establishing your credit. Whatever your choice, in any credit matter remember to borrow the least amount possible, repay promptly, and carry a light purse.

CLOSING EMPLOYMENT AFFAIRS

The information contained in this section is plainly mercenary. We want you to get everything that is coming to you and that your husband would have wanted for you from his employer, partner, or from the sole ownership of his business. While you may feel some inappropriateness about thinking money at this time, please don't. Anything that you don't claim now you won't have later, and when your head is a bit more clear, you'll be sorry.

There are also the usual nonmonetary rewards in taking care of yourself and in finding out that you really do have a good "business head."

Benefits Available from Public Employers

With rare exception, everyone employed in the public sector is covered by some sort of retirement or pension plan and possibly an annuity. You should check immediately to determine the provision of the plan for a surviving spouse. If your husband was eligible for retirement benefits (not necessarily actually retired) there may be a monthly allowance for you. If your husband was a pre-retiree, at the minimum you will get all of his vested interest (contribution plus interest) in the plan.

Many pension plans include life insurance for each member. There are usually several options in the payoff: lump sum, monthly payment for a specified period of time, or lifetime monthly payments. Many factors go into the choice of which payment is best for you. These include your age and physical condition matched against actuarial tables, other sources of income available to you, investment plans, inflation, and others. A good idea is to consult the organization's insurance counselor about all benefits including continuing medical coverage. He's anxious to help and has no stake in the matter other than your best interest.

Benefits Available from Private Employers

Private pension, profit sharing, retirement, life insurance, and annuity plans have as many variations as there are companies. Most firms feel a strong obligation to assist you in getting maximum benefits. If your husband belonged to a union, there may also be benefits provided. Where companies do not provide retirement plans, individuals may set up Individual Retirement Accounts (IRA). Your husband may have done this, and you are entitled to the proceeds.

Be sure to check with your husband's company to see if they provide for continuing medical coverage in some form for you and your dependents.

If your husband worked on a commission basis, there might be some problems in obtaining the entire amount due you. Most companies are scrupulously fair about this, but some firms may need double checking by you to assure fairness. Don't count on the company's benevolence. Check figures and compare with your husband's prior year earnings to be sure the amount offered you fits a pattern. Don't agree to a figure, and don't cash or deposit a check until you are certain the accounting is correct.

If you have a reasonably good picture of your husband's affairs, you will know what's right. If you do not, and a great deal of digging is required to come up with data (checking through order books, old records, and even with customers), let the firm know that you intend to submit your estimate of earnings to be matched with theirs. If a problem develops consult the Mediation Board of the U.S. Department of Labor in your local area for information on your rights and procedures to follow in contesting a settlement.

Self-Employment or Private Practice Decisions

If your husband had a wholly owned small business or private practice, you will need to decide very early whether you wish to continue to run the business yourself, hire or promote someone to run it, sell, or liquidate it. These are major decisions with serious financial and lifestyle implications. While you may wish to postpone such a decision, often you will find yourself unable to do so. Leases carry death provisions, private practices dry up rapidly, and businesses just do not run themselves.

It is just possible that your new identity is partly contained in the management of the enterprise, and you can plan how you will want it handled. If it should be sold or liquidated, you will need to move rapidly in order to conserve the value of assets. In any case, take advantage of your most trusted advisers to supply you with data that will aid your choice, but *you* make the final decision.

If your husband was in a partnership or corporation, you may not have any choice. A well-designed partnership has buy-out provisions, often covered by insurance, and you will simply be presented with a check for your husband's share of the business, based on the formula in the partnership arrangement.

Similarly, in a closed corporation the surviving stockholders usually buy out the interest of the deceased. This is not always the case, and if you are a good businessperson you may be asked to continue to represent your husband's share. In the rare case of no provision, you will have the same level of choice as indicated in the sole proprietorship.

Before you make any of the decisions available to you, consult Chapters 14 and 15 on life and career planning. This may help you decide what you want to do about your management skills and the degree of active participation you might wish to take in your husband's business. Also, consider the emotional implications connected with working your husband's business when he is no longer there.

Just as in employment, the privately owned small business may also provide benefits such as insurance, pension plans, etc. Many small business persons have Keogh retirement accounts, and you should check for this.

As a final note for everyone: be certain that you get all the salary payments owed your husband at the time of his death. Final payment should include accrued vacation time and possibly sick leave payment. Check credit unions for money on deposit and credit life insurance benefits. Remember that very little happens automatically. You must apply for practically all monies due you.

PLANNING A BUDGET

The first person who writes entertainingly on budgeting, capturing and retaining everyone's attention, should be awarded the Legion of Merit. Anyone who does this while addressing the subject to women who have been widowed just a short time should also receive the Croix de Guerre with four battlestars, kisses on both cheeks, and a permanent place in the Writer's Hall of Fame. Expecting to be recognized in some other fashion, we continue.

If you happen to be one of the persons whose number one headache-maker is figures, try to remember the brighter side of budgeting—it gives you a fair amount of control over your financial life. Control over your financial life is often the precursor to control over other aspects of your life.

Looking at it another way—show us someone who doesn't need to know about budgeting and we'll show you a rich person or a bum. If you're a rich person, kindly move on to the next chapter. The rest of you pay attention as we work on budgeting.

We suggest you approach the subject in two phases. The first should take into account the realities of the moment—that your mind is not functioning at full capacity and that it is not wise to add new stress to an already overstressed situation. In a reasonable period of time you can begin budgeting in earnest.

Phase I—Pre-Budgeting

For a little while, treat yourself gently. Remember that anything done can be undone with an eraser. You can alter your plan every few weeks, if necessary, to fit the evolving situation. You needn't remember everything. No matter what the figures tell you, or the urges you may have, resist these temptations:

- Quitting your job.
- Selling your house.
- Moving back with your family.
- Moving your residence anywhere.

When your life settles down, there is time for heavy decision-making. Begin your temporary budgeting by listing all your sources of income with amounts and due date. Try doing this in two categories, the first being regular repeating income such as salary, expected dividends, interest, insurance payments, Social Security payments, pension plan payments, and VA payments. The second category is lump sum payments, such as a business sale or insurance settlement. The recurring payments can be considered as regular disposable income, the latter as capital to be invested to increase your regular montly income. If you have real need at this time, do not hesitate to use capital resources, but plan to look at the whole process in a more comprehensive way later. (See Chapter 13.)

Next, start keeping a record of all your expenses. Check and credit card payments leave clear tracks. You may want to carry a small notebook to record cash payments. A little later you can use the actual totals to estimate future expenses.

At this time, you are not striving for accuracy; you are attempting to identify the categories in which you spend money, get a general idea of the amounts, and learn what it's like to have total control of your finances. Even if you shared in, or mostly controlled, this process during your husband's lifetime, you'll find it substantially different when you plan alone. If you do your fact gathering well, but without pushing, you will be in a good position to move into serious budgeting.

Phase II—Controlled Budgeting

Carefully worked-out money planning will give you a sense of personal responsibility, control over your life, and exhilaration as it all works out. Approach it as a positive move in your personal growth, not as a bore or drag on your time. If you set a goal to become a good money planner, you can achieve these results:

- You will have a total view of your financial resources, which is an important dimension of the total you.
- You will have a clear idea of how much you can spend for an item before you go shopping.
- You will get more for your money because you will see the necessity to become a "smart shopper."
- You will be able to clearly identify any deficiency in your income.
- You will be able to plan for inflationary tendencies in the economy.
- You will have the basic material for long-range financial planning.

A good budget will give you the large view (annually) and the short-range view (monthly). Income is most often considered on an annual basis, while the control of expenditures is most effectively done monthly. So, your paperwork will want to cover both. Many expense items, insurance premiums, auto licenses, and taxes get paid on an annual, semiannual, or quarterly basis on specific dates. Other major purchases such as clothing are made at random times. Planning for such payments requires setting money aside on a monthly basis, so the funds are available when the need occurs. This is best done through a savings account. We call this "future payments," and you might label this an FP savings account.

You'll find a complete Budget Planner at the end of this section. It provides for annual and monthly figures in just about every category you will encounter. Note also that there is a column for you to enter your *actual* expenditures to compare with budgeted amounts. Entering these figures from time to time will give you accurate information as to how well you are doing and aid you in revising the budget as need occurs.

To begin with, it's a good idea to duplicate the master copy of the Budget Planner. Have several copies made so you can revise and compare. A very important reality of our times is the inflationary spiral in our economy. This complicates your plans and your life, but it can't be ignored. Utilize the government cost-of-living figures that are published periodically to update your budget projections. This method of looking ahead won't change inflation, but it will reduce the shock to your system and keep you thinking about the best ways to reduce its impact. (We'd like to give you a clear answer to the problem of inflation, but we're still hunting for our own.)

With copies at the ready, enter all the figures, using the data you've previously compiled. If you're missing information, refer to checkbook registers and paid bills for the prior twelve months. Remember to leave room for unexpected expenses—the breakdown of the washing machine, unanticipated failure of your auto's transmission, the arrival of your favorite aunt who must be entertained. As you work with your projections and actual expenses, you'll soon learn how much to provide for the unprovidable. When all is done, remember that you have a guideline, not a rulebook. Juggling expense items is a challenging game; it helps you reorient your priorities and keeps you from going "budget buggy."

One additional thought: create a calendar of major expenditures for all nonrecurring expenses such as taxes, insurance, etc. This reminder will prevent nonpayment by oversight, and it will give you a view of heavy payment periods. You can even add birthdays to this calendar as a gift-giving reminder.

It's hard to resist giving pithy advice on budgeting:

- Don't buy things you don't need. (Isn't that fantastic. Bet you never heard it before.)
- Try not to be influenced by well-meaning friends who are anxious to cheer you up by helping you spend your money. (But do find an ill-intentioned friend now and then and do something outrageous.)
- Don't shop for food when you are hungry or tired. (Try the all-night stores at 5:00 A.M. and make some new friends.)
- Don't fall prey to door-to-door salesmen. (But if you do, select a tall, handsome man. You can cancel the contract within three days for a full refund. This Federal Trade Commission regulation was designed to encourage dalliance without danger.)
- Don't make major purchases until you have a good rapport with your budget. (Even then, the Brooklyn Bridge is a bad investment.)

We would like to close with a thought that was handed down to us through the generations. "When you're up to your waist in alligators, it's very difficult to remember that you came to drain the swamp."

30 THE WIDOW'S GUIDE TO LIFE

BUDGET PLANNER

Income		Estimated Annual	Estimated Monthly	Actual Monthly
Social Security		$	$	$
Pension Benefits				
Life Insurance Benefits				
Veterans Administration Benefits				
Annuity Benefits				
Savings Account Interest				
Stock Dividends				
Bond Interest				
Rental Property				
Salary (Net Check)				
Income from Business				
Other				
Total Income				
Expenses				
Housing				
Rent or Mortgage Payments				
Insurance (homeowners, tenant)	FP			
Property Taxes, Assessments	FP			
Maintenance (repairs, plumbing, etc.)				
Yardwork (gardner)				
Household Help				
Utilities				
Gas or Oil				
Electricity				
Telephone				
Water (and water softener)				
Garbage or Trash Collection				
Cable TV				
Food				
Grocery Purchases				
Restaurant Meals				
Transportation				
Public Transportation (bus fare, etc.)				
Car Pool				
Gas, Oil				
Repairs (maintenance)				
License and Registration				
Parking				
Insurance Premiums				
Automobile	FP			
Life	FP			
Health	FP			
Accident	FP			
Liability	FP			
Other	FP			

BUDGET PLANNER (continued)

Expenses		Estimated Annual	Estimated Monthly	Actual Monthly
Taxes				
Property	FP	_____	_____	_____
Other Local	FP	_____	_____	_____
Estimated Income (federal and state)	FP	_____	_____	_____
Installment or Loan Payments				
Automobile		_____	_____	_____
Furniture		_____	_____	_____
Department Stores		_____	_____	_____
Bank or Savings and Loan		_____	_____	_____
Credit Cards		_____	_____	_____
Charge Accounts		_____	_____	_____
Other		_____	_____	_____
Personal Maintenance				
Clothing Purchases	FP	_____	_____	_____
Laundry, Drycleaning and Repairs		_____	_____	_____
Hairdresser, Cosmetics		_____	_____	_____
Health Care (doctor, dentist, drugs, vitamins)		_____	_____	_____
Entertainment and Recreation				
Movies, Theater, Concerts, Sporting Events		_____	_____	_____
Hobbies		_____	_____	_____
Vacations	FP	_____	_____	_____
Self-Improvement				
Educational Expenses (classes)		_____	_____	_____
Books		_____	_____	_____
Magazines and Newspapers		_____	_____	_____
Contributions, Dues, and Gifts		_____	_____	_____
Child Care				
Babysitters, Nursery School Fees, Allowances		_____	_____	_____
Total Expenses		$_____	$_____	$_____
Total of All Monthly FP Items		$_____		

This is the amount to be put into the Future Payments (FP) savings account each month. If you have a credit union payroll deduction, this is part of your savings.

RECORDKEEPING

In the section When and How to Pay Bills, we included a simple system for control of personal payables. Under Planning a Budget, there are suggestions for recording income and expenses, as well as setting up a planning calendar.

These are additional suggestions for maintaining control of records, valuables, and money matters:

- Keep everything that relates to recordkeeping in one place. A fireproof file cabinet is best, but a set of drawers will do. It should contain your unpaid bills file, paid bills file, checkbook register, cancelled checks, tax statements, etc. If your insurance policies are in a safety deposit box, have a record of the policies by company, policy number, and amount in your file.
- Make a record of everything you carry in your wallet—credit cards, driver's license number, medical and insurance cards—and put it in your file at home. This is a real stress-reducer in case of loss.
- If you don't have a safety deposit box, obtain one. Many savings and loans provide one free with a minimum account. It should contain items that are difficult or impossible to replace: birth, death, marriage, divorce, adoption, and naturalization certificates or papers. Also, all securities (stocks and bonds), insurance policies and inventories (should you need to file a claim), a copy of your will (if the original of your will is in the safety deposit box, be sure that a family member or beneficiary has access to the box), deeds and titles to your home and other property, mortgages and promissory notes, military papers, savings passbooks or certificates, valuable jewelry, contracts, copyrights or patents, automobile title.

No one expects theft, fire, or vandalism, but being prepared is also providing a measure of security.

ADDITIONAL INFORMATION

Funeral or Memorial Services

Books

Funerals: Consumers' Last Rights. By the Editors of Consumer Reports. Pantheon, 1979. Guide to funerals and their alternatives, introducing a number of options in a sensitive manner. Includes appendices for state law variations, donor card forms, description of embalming procedures, and a list of VA cemeteries.

Yaffa Draznin. *How to Prepare for Death: A Practical Guide.* Hawthorn Books, Inc., 1976. Provides information for making decisions in death-related circumstances. Covers legal and financial issues. Contends that most of the trauma of death has a pragmatic base and deals with the practical aspects.

Elisabeth Kubler-Ross. *Death: The Final Stage of Growth.* Prentice-Hall, 1975. See section four on funerals.

Earl A. Grollman (Editor). *Concerning Death: A Practical Guide for the Living.* Beacon Press, 1974. Good coverage of the funeral and the funeral director, the selection of a cemetery, choosing a memorial marker, the pros and cons of cremation, and organ donation and transplantation.

Pamphlets

The Price of Death. Superintendent of Documents, U.S. Government Printing Office, Washington, D.C. 20402. ($1.05) Information from the Federal Trade Commission on how to make reasonably priced funeral arrangements.

The Continental Association of Funeral and Memorial Societies, 1828 L Street, N.W., Washington, D.C. 20036, will provide free of charge a booklet on how memorial societies work and how to find one in your area. They also publish *A Manual of Death Education and Simple Burial* which provides information on costs and other aspects of funeral arrangements and includes data on body and organ donations to medical schools. Cost is $2.00.

General Information

The St. Francis Burial and Counseling Society, 1768 Church Street, N.W., Washington, D.C. 20036. Information on funeral alternatives. This nonprofit organization came into being through one woman's quest for an inexpensive, simple coffin.

There is a likelihood that your state has an agency that regulates the funeral industry. Contact it for additional information.

Establishing Personal Credit

Pamphlets

The Credit Handbook for Women. American Express Company, Box 927, New York, New York 10010. (Free)

Women to Your Credit. Commercial Credit, 300 St. Paul Place, Baltimore, Maryland 21202. (Free)

U.S. Government Publications. Write to Consumer Information Center, Pueblo, Colorado 81009:
Shopping for Credit Can Save You Cash. #627G (Free) Comparison of cost of buying with loans, credit cards and revolving charge plans.
Where You Shop Is as Important as What You Buy, #628G (Free) Pros and cons of shopping at different types of stores.
Fair Credit Reporting Act. #676G (Free) Information on how to learn one's own credit rating and how to dispute incorrect information and have it removed.

34 THE WIDOW'S GUIDE TO LIFE

Equal Credit Opportunity Act. #526F (Free) Describes your right to credit and what to do if it is denied you.
Budgeting for the Family. #069G (90¢) Steps in developing a budget, includes section on credit.

General Information

Agencies to contact for assistance with credit discrimination:
   For credit card, retail store, or finance company problems:
      The Federal Trade Commission, Washington, D.C., or check your telephone directory for a local office.
      Associated Credit Bureau, Inc. 6767 Southwest Freeway, Houston, Texas 77036. Information on your credit record and rights.
   For problems with federally chartered banks:
      The Comptroller of Currency, Washington, D.C.
   For problems with state banks:
      Federal Reserve Bank in your local area.
   General problems:
      Your local district attorney's office.

Planning a Budget

Consumer Credit Counselors is a national organization which provides free counseling and budgeting services. There is a nominal fee for their debt management program. Check the white pages of your telephone directory for one in your area, or write the National Foundation for Consumer Credit, Federal Bar Building West, 1819 H Street, N.W., Washington, D.C. 20006.

Many banks, loan companies, savings and loans, and credit unions prepare information sheets and sample budget materials.

Recordkeeping

AIM's *Guide to Your Vital Papers and Where to Find Them* is an excellent record-keeping document. Write Action for Independent Maturity, AARP, 1909 K Street, N.W., Washington, D.C. 20049, for a free copy.

Keeping Family-Household Records—What to Discard. 638F. Available free from Consumer Information Center, Pueblo, Colorado 81009. What and where records should be kept.

Handling Your Legal Affairs

For most of us, the mention of legal action conjures up dark-robed magistrates scowling down from mahogany benches. The atmosphere seems solemn and leaden, the proceedings interminable and beyond our understanding. It is no wonder that ordinary citizens experience a great deal of anxiety when dealing with the complexities of the legal system. In order to clear the air and bring light to the proceedings, we hope to detoxify and demystify some of the legal proceedings connected with your transition.

ABOUT ATTORNEYS

Once upon a time, the word counselor was used interchangeably with the word attorney. People would put their affairs into the trustworthy care of a general lawyer who would watch out for the entire family evermore.

Unfortunately, the family counselor has gone the way of the family physician, and what remains is a legal profession composed primarily of specialists. Even more unfortunate is the changing image of the legal profession. Once viewed with great respect, ever increasing numbers of people view lawyers with distrust and suspicion.

Consider:

36 THE WIDOW'S GUIDE TO LIFE

- There are more laws and lawyers in the U.S. than in any nation in the world.
- One of the fastest growing branches of education is law. As more and more lawyers join the profession, they close ranks to help one another. The result is a proliferation of make-work practices that has pushed the price of legal assistance skyward.
- While the inability to translate a medical prescription creates minor anxiety, not being able to understand a contract you are signing creates a really irritating dependency. Many institutions are switching contractual language to plain English, but for the most part attorneys continue to use legalese, thereby distancing themselves from their clients.
- As competency continues to be challenged through malpractice suits, lawyers pile up mountains of paperwork to protect themselves. Most of it is indecipherable and adds enormously to the cost burden.
- Legal fees of $100 per hour are common and moving up.
- For probating a will, attorneys' fees are usually set by the state legislature. For example, in California, they are:
    On the first $15,000 of the estate, 4 percent or $600.
    On the next $85,000 of the estate, 3 percent or $2,550.
    On up to $900,000, 2 percent or $18,000.
    On all over $1,000,000, 1 percent.
  That translates to legal fees (not including court costs) of over $3,000 on an estate of $100,000.
- Many attorneys employ paralegal assistants who handle routine detail work. Theoretically, this should reduce your cost. It doesn't—you still pay the entire load.

SELECTING AN ATTORNEY

The extreme variation in fees and competency makes the choice of a lawyer a difficult affair. At a time when you really want someone to take over completely, it is necessary for you to coolly evaluate and make reasoned choices. Yet, to hope that all will turn out well is to take an unreasonable chance with your long-range interests. So, reach deep inside for your best "take charge" person and use some of these pointers to help:

- If you're fortunate enough to have a good relationship with an attorney of demonstrated long-term competency, hang onto him, cherish him, protect him, and keep him out of the cold and wet. Such persons are rare, indeed. Only be sure that his competency extends to the laws dealing with estate matters.

- Wherever possible, avoid relatives as your choice for an attorney. You may hesitate to question, ask for what you want, or to be part of the process. You may even consider it indelicate to inquire about fees and then be surprised to find that money runs thicker than blood.
- It's okay to shop around and interview lawyers. If you contact one who won't offer you a candid initial meeting without charge, it would be best not to consider him.
- You can ask for and get a written fee agreement in advance. Ask the local Bar Association if it has a prepared list of established fees, and use it as a guide. Remember, however, that probate fees need not go to the legal limit. You can reduce the fees further by doing some of the work yourself. You'll find tips on how to do this throughout the chapter.
- If you have a situation with more than a little complexity, you might just as well go for the best specialist in town. In this case, the established fees for probate become limitations that work for you.
- It's important that you feel trusting and are able to communicate easily with your attorney. If the "chemistry" between you is good, you'll find the relationship more satisfying. This is not the best time in your life to be struggling with someone you can't make contact with.
- Make sure your lawyer will be available to you. There are a lot of details that need to be addressed.
- Watch out for conflicts of interest. Your husband's business attorney who is representing his partner may not be a wise choice for you.
- There are places where you can get information about lawyers.
    The local Bar Association
    Law schools
    Lawyer referral services
    Professional contacts
    Recommendation of friends
    Bank officials
- The lawyer/client relationship is absolutely confidential, so cooperate and disclose everything that is relevant. Respect his time, but don't hesitate to ask questions.

We realize that our hard line on attorneys will cause some eyebrow raising, although several of our own lawyer friends have said we're not tough enough. Our position arises from the stream of horror stories we hear from widows. Our intention is not to condemn the entire legal profession—rather it is to point out a major hurdle to be faced if you want the handling of your legal affairs to go smoothly. We're not alone in this concern. No less an institution than *Time* magazine ran a cover story in 1979 lamenting the sad state of the legal profession.

Providing some basic information and places where you can go to check on attorneys reduces helplessness and dependency. We don't believe it's in your best interest to feel dumb and powerless in this relationship.

ALTERNATE FORMS OF LEGAL ASSISTANCE

The relaxation of advertising restrictions, through a Supreme Court decision, has accelerated innovation in legal practice. New legal groups provide minimal services and self-help materials, often at dramatically reduced costs. In Los Angeles, we have checked some organizations that have counterparts in other cities.

- Group legal assistance is now available, similar to group medical practice. For one annual fee, the participant receives unlimited phone consultation and assistance.
- The Law Store operates out of a shopping center. It provides kits for preparing your own will, various predesigned forms, and legal assistance on specific issues at reduced fees.
- The Legal Action Workshop has an attorney on the premises who passes out legal advice over the counter. Also available are prerecorded tapes covering standard situations.
- A legal clinic operates out of a drugstore. They use a computer for standardized issues, keeping costs to a minimum.
- Legal stationery stores have preprinted forms for wills, leases, property transfers, joint tenancy agreements, etc.
- Legal Aid Societies have some permanent staff, and adjunct lawyers are often on loan from large law firms. These are low, or no-cost services for those who qualify. Check your phone book under "Legal Aid" or inquire at the local Bar Association.
- Neighborhood legal offices are being established under federal grants. Others are being staffed and financed by law firms who assign partners and associates to the offices on a rotating basis. Fees are based on ability to pay.

YOUR PART IN THE LEGAL PROCESS

As we have discussed in an earlier chapter, allowing time for the mourning process is essential to your short-term health and to your long-term readjustment. It is also important to continue to assume responsibility for all facets of your life, including your personal affairs.

No matter what, you are going to be the central person in gathering the information required for the various legal processes. You may simply turn the material over to your attorney, or you may take an active part in each of the steps.

It is our view that you will be better off being a partner in the process or by taking the lead. No matter how well-intentioned those serving you may be, no one has the information you have; and no one knows better than you how to achieve the results you desire. Further, you can speed up your reentry, improve your knowledge of financial affairs, and save yourself a great deal of money by understanding the legal requirements and by being actively involved.

What follows is general information to guide you on your way. Each state has different laws and requirements. But, each state has one particular court that handles the matters that occur from the death of one of its citizens. So, for specific details, consult a clerk of this court. In California, it is known as Superior Court, in New York, Surrogates Court. It may also be known as Probate Court, Court of Wills, etc.

Where there is a will, someone must appear in court for the filing. In the absence of a will, property is distributed according to the laws of the state. On the assumption that there is a will and an estate that must be settled, here is information you will need and steps you must take:

- Initial filing of the will is a routine matter that includes verification of the signatures of witnesses to the will. It also involves appointment of an executor. In most cases, this will be yourself. Simple acceptance of the will is not an absolute. If you are not happy with the terms, you may elect against the will. All states guarantee that you will get a portion of the estate, but the percentage will vary, so the amount you are entitled to will dictate your course of action.
- Probate of the will is the legal process of protecting you, your heirs, and others who are affected. It involves proving that the will is valid. Not all wills need be probated. If all of your property is in joint tenancy (title to the property is clearly in both your and your husband's name) the probate process is not required. Additionally, most states require that only estates exceeding certain amounts be probated.
- Once the proceedings begin, the estate takes on an entity that is separate from your personal affairs. As executor, you will need to open a bank account to collect and deposit funds due the estate and to pay valid claims against the estate.
- Record all medical and funeral costs. If you paid any of these personally, they can be reimbursed to you from the estate account.
- If you need funds for your personal use until the estate is settled, you may petition the court for disbursement. This sounds like a fancy proce-

- dure. In fact, it is a simple, routine matter that is always granted if the request is reasonable and funds are available.
- The court will ask you to provide a record of all the assets of your husband's estate. This involves an inventory process. Be certain that you include everything.
- Ready for the monster? You have at least two, and possibly six, tax forms to file. The first two are common to everyone—federal and state income taxes. The estate itself is a separate entity and must file state and federal income tax (or fiduciary tax) returns. After the smoke blows away, you may need to file a federal estate tax return. And most states have an inheritance tax. (Nevada is a notable exception—they get you with the slot machines.)
- You may be required to handle a variety of other affairs such as trust arrangements, disbursement of specific bequests, and others. Ordinarily, you must present the court with an accounting of everything you have done, however it is possible to obtain a waiver. With the final stamp of approval from the state judiciary, you are able to take possession of the property.
- In some states, property that is held in joint tenancy, community property, and even some property that was held solely by your husband may be transferred to your name, often before the close of probate. Forms are available from your state controller or county treasurer. This is something you can do and save attorney's fees.
- A final tip—it may be advisable to waive any fee as administrator or executor of the estate. Such fees come out of the estate and then are taxable to you as ordinary income. If the fee amount remains in the estate, it may be taxed at a lower rate or not at all.

All of the foregoing has assumed that your husband left a will. In the absence of a will, you may still be able to administer the estate. Check with local authorities to determine how to proceed.

PREPARING A NEW WILL

By now, you know the importance of a will that clearly states your intent. If you don't have one, the state decides disposition of your estate. So, you'll want to begin right away to prepare your own will. Obviously it's important that your will be written in an acceptable form, observing legal requirements. If your assets are few and simple, a standard form may be purchased in a legal stationery store. *Don't* write your own will. It may not stand up in court.

Having an attorney write your will should not be an expensive procedure.

It is wise to ask for the charges in advance. Here are some ideas that will get what you want and at minimum cost:

- Think through and write down everything that you want to appear in your will. This will save your lawyer's time.
- Consider leaving information about disposal of very personal effects such as jewelry, furniture, artifacts, outside the will.
- A good witness to your will is a notary public. His signature is on file at the County Clerk's office. Note that a beneficiary should *never* be a witness. While some states require only two witnesses, others want three, so get three signatures and be safe.
- Never alter an original will. An addendum may be made by what is known as a codicil. A codicil should have everything, even the date, in your own handwriting, and it may need to be witnessed.
- Give serious thought to who will be executor of your estate. The experience you are presently having gives you an idea of the magnitude and frustration of this job.
- It makes good sense to specify your funeral arrangements. This takes a burden off your family.
- If you have minor children, a trust arrangement and guardianship is critical. Be aware of age factors when naming a guardian.
- There are new concepts not connected with the will that you may wish to consider: you can donate your organs to transplant banks or your body to medical science. Such a donation, properly signed and witnessed, is legally binding. It would be well to have your family understand and accept your wishes.
A new body of law is growing up around the "living will." This allows you to control the matter of prolonging your life artificially and unnecessarily should you be unconscious or unable to make statements judged "competent."

In no way is this chapter to be construed as legal advice—it is intended to outline some general rules and ways to proceed, based on the experiences of many widows.

ADDITIONAL INFORMATION

Books

Philip J. Hermann. *Do You Need a Lawyer?* Prentice-Hall, 1980. Help in deciding whether or not your legal problems require the services of a lawyer, and if they do, how to choose one that meets your needs and budget.

Barry M. Gallagher. *How to Hire a Lawyer: And Feel Good About It.* Delta Press, 1979. How to locate and evaluate a competent lawyer and how to obtain reasonable fees. Includes a Directory of State Bar Associations and a list of Public Law Firms and Organizations.

Joseph C. McGinn. *Lawyers: A Client's Manual.* Prentice-Hall, 1979. How to confidently and successfully deal with the legal profession, get free legal assistance and advice, save money on legal fees, find, hire, and dismiss a lawyer, and determine if you need one in the first place.

Pamphlet

You, the Law and Retirement. 080G U.S. Department of Health, Education and Welfare. Consumer Information Center, Pueblo, Colorado 81009. ($1.20) Helpful information, relevant for now as well as the future.

General Information

American Bar Association National Headquarters, 1155 East 60th Street, Chicago, Illinois 60637, will provide information on lawyer referral services in your area.

The Martindale-Hubbell Directory available in your library rates lawyers throughout the United States by age, education, specialty, and background.

Wherever there is paralegal training you will find condensed versions of state laws. For example, Lega-Books in California publishes the *Handbook of Probate Law.*

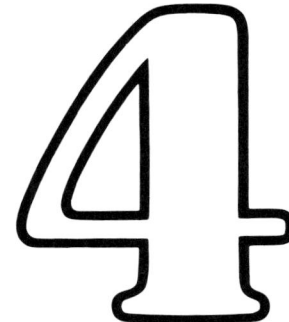

Dealing with the Social Security Administration

Dealing with the Social Security Administration can be a painful experience. Unquestionably, the representatives attempt to be helpful. Unfortunately, they are bureaucrats who are overworked, overquestioned, and very often overwhelmed. As a test, we attempted to get a series of questions answered over the phone. We began by making repeated calls to a local Social Security information center, each time speaking to a different person. Not only did we get different answers, we got different levels of competency. With one representative, it was even necessary for us to point out the proper brochure to be consulted. This test was repeated in other cities with similar results.

This does not mean that you won't get what you're entitled to, eventually. It does mean that you'll experience a lot of frustration unless you're prepared. It's vital to your financial security to file the proper forms, present the required evidence, and do all the nice things that one does to get along with Uncle Sam and his friendly workers.

HOW TO APPLY

There is no way to avoid making a personal appearance at the local Social Security Administration office. A representative must complete a lengthy form by asking you an incredible array of historical questions. The purpose in telling you all of this is not to raise your anxiety level—only that you be prepared and pick a day when you're feeling up to it. Unless you're very fortunate, it is likely that you will be interviewed by a representative whose priority is gathering information rather than being concerned about your feelings. Knowing this, go armed with all the information required, your best smile, and a full measure of patience.

Take with you:
- A certified copy of your husband's death certificate.
- Your husband's, yours, and all of your children's, Social Security numbers.
- A certified copy of your marriage certificate.
- A certified copy of your birth certificate.
- Certified copies of the birth certificates of all children under eighteen years of age or under twenty-two if a full-time student.
- Verification of your husband's earnings. This may be the most recent W-2 form, your latest income tax return, or a Social Security eligibility form.
- Naturalized citizens need proof of citizenship.

Not essential, but helpful in processing:
- A certified copy of your husband's birth certificate.
- Your husband's military discharge certificate. (Military service can be counted toward Social Security credit.)

The more documentation you furnish, the easier it will be to process your claim. This is a sampling of the type of questions you will be asked:

What is the birthplace of your husband's mother?

What is the birthplace of your husband's father?

What is your husband's mother's maiden name?

BENEFITS AND ELIGIBILITY

If your husband was eligible for Social Security (more than 90 percent of the men in the United States are), you are eligible for at least one type of benefit immediately, the $255 lump-sum death benefit. The balance of your benefits will fall under one of these categories:

- If you have dependent children who are under age eighteen or disabled, each of you is eligible for 75 percent of your husband's age sixty-five

benefits. For example, if your husband's benefits would be $400 per month, you and your child may each receive $300 per month. Your benefits cease when your child becomes eighteen, but his may continue until age twenty-two if he remains in school. There is a maximum for each family.
- If you are sixty or older, you may collect benefits immediately. If you elect to begin at age sixty, you will receive 71.5 percent of your husband's age sixty-five amount. If you wait to age sixty-one, it will be 5.7 percent higher, and so on, until age sixty-five when you will receive the full amount.
- If you are covered under your own benefits, you may collect yours or your husband's, whichever is higher. This option becomes available at age sixty-two.
- If you are at least fifty years old and disabled, you may receive 50 percent of your husband's age sixty-five benefits, if the disability occurred within seven years of your husband's death.
- If you don't fit any of the above categories, you are not eligible for benefits now but most probably will be in the future. If you would like to know the amount of these benefits, pick up a Request for Social Security Statement of Earnings card at the local Social Security Administration office and mail it in. Be aware that the amount quoted will increase over the years, as it is tied into the cost-of-living index.

SOCIAL SECURITY TIPS

- You are responsible for initiating any action. Nothing happens automatically. Allow ample lead time—the wheels of government move at the rate of a covered wagon. If you are a little late in filing, you may receive backpayments; but if you wait over twelve months, you lose out.
- If you earn wages over a specified annual amount, you are not eligible for benefits, or they may be reduced. Check this out carefully. If you're over seventy-two (it drops to age seventy in 1982), the rule does not apply, so this becomes a great time of life to start a new career.
- If you remarry, you lose your benefits—unless you're over sixty. Happily, this recent change in the law allows "senior citizens" the benefits of connubial bliss.
- To be eligible for death benefits, a widow must establish that she has been married at least nine months. The nine-month rule does not apply if death was accidental or if minor children are involved.
- A woman widowed more than once can elect benefits under either spouse's coverage—whichever is larger.

- Social Security benefits are not taxable.
- Most actuaries advise that you are better off taking reduced benefits early, if you are not working. The Social Security Administration also passes out this advice. Check with your financial adviser to see what's best for you.
- File Request for Social Security Statement of Earnings every three years. By law, after three years, three months and fifteen days, incorrect earnings statements need not be corrected. The law is not rigidly applied, but it's good protection to check the system regularly.
- In 1982, a new provision goes into effect for widows who are also eligible for a public agency pension. If the federal, state, or other local government pension is more than survivor's Social Security benefits, you cannot collect Social Security. If less, the provision will make up the difference between the public agency pension and Social Security. This amendment to the Social Security Act is highly controversial, and one of the nation's leading Social Security experts is urging a battle to prevent the enactment of this rule.

As Social Security costs continue to increase and the prevailing mood of the electorate is to decrease the size of government, a continual battle rages in Congress over changes in the act. These are proposed *reductions* in benefits that severely affect widows:

Elimination of the lump-sum death benefit.

Elimination of survivor benefits above the secondary level for children who are attending school full time.

Elimination of widows' benefits when the youngest child reaches age sixteen, instead of the current eighteen.

Elimination of survivor benefits for the families of persons who are not fully covered under Social Security.

Raise the age back up to seventy-two (it was lowered to seventy, effective 1982) for unlimited earnings and the collection of Social Security benefits.

Your possible benefits are endangered! Add your voice and/or help to your local political action group.

MEDICARE

Millions of older citizens are receiving billions of dollars annually in Medicare insurance benefits. Marvelous as this is, less than half of the medical costs for the elderly are actually covered by the Medicare program. With medical costs escalating even beyond those in other parts of the economy, the whole issue of health care becomes a major concern of our society. There is no way for us to deal with all of the complex aspects of government-assisted health care in this chapter, yet the subject needs your scrupulous attention. To provide the best coverage, we have chosen to point out the major concerns, lesser-known facts, and offer some views on how to maximize your benefits. Beyond that, the readings and other sources at the end of the chapter should provide valuable additional information.

Medicare—Part A, covering in-patient hospital care, is free for anyone sixty-five years of age, who is covered by Social Security. Let's be clear that "free" means only that you do not pay a premium. There is an annual deductible, and other payments for services are made on a fixed-fee schedule. Anyone age sixty-five, but not covered by Social Security, may purchase Medicare coverage.

Medicare—Part B is optional major medical coverage. It makes payments for doctors' services, out-patient hospital services, x-rays and a host of other services. You will be enrolled automatically in Part B when you obtain Part A although, since you must pay premiums on Part B, you may refuse coverage if you wish. While the amount of the premium fluctuates, it is a bargain by any insurance standard. It, too, carries a deductible and then pays 80 percent of services on a scheduled amount. Since Medicare schedules usually lag a year behind increases in charges, your actual coverage may be far less than 80 percent of the fee.

While this adds up to substantial benefits, it falls far below your real needs. It is important that you have supplemental coverage to fill in the Medicare gaps. The purchase of supplemental coverage is tricky. It is possible to get inadequate coverage, and it is equally possible to pay high premiums for practically no coverage at all. In any case, it is virtually impossible to get 100 percent coverage.

While there is additional assistance for widows with very low incomes through Medicaid (see the following section in this chapter) and other sources, health care could be the priority concern of your future. There are ways you can help yourself: in addition to purchasing insurance coverage and taking advantage of available benefits, you can join other widows by becoming an activist on two fronts. (1) Get involved in maintaining good health and preventing disease. We discuss this thoroughly in Chapter 12. (2) Join organizations that are working for comprehensive national health care. In the final analysis, this is the only way that adequate health care can be made available equally to all.

In our seminars with widows, these are responses to the most frequently raised questions on health care:

- Don't purchase duplicate or overlapping supplemental health care policies. Your primary need is to supplement Medicare—Part B. The hospitalization portion of Medicare is relatively adequate. Pick one comprehensive Medicare supplemental policy from a reputable company such as Blue Cross or Blue Shield, and do not buy any other health insurance.

- Medicare coverage is not automatic. You must activate the process by filing an application.
- If you want Part B of Medicare, you should file for it when you begin Part A. The premium rises each year that you wait, and after three years, you are no longer eligible. We urge you to take Part B. Inadequate though it may be, it is a far better value than anything else available.
- If you are a widow age fifty or above who has been severely disabled for at least two years, you are eligible for Medicare.
- Note that Medicare is available only through approved facilities. Make sure your hospital qualifies before you enter.
- Some doctors will lower their fees to match the Medicare schedule. You should discuss this with your physician in advance if possible. Shopping for a doctor who is not only competent but cooperative is your right.
- While a hospitalization benefit period under Medicare is ninety days, after you have been out of the hospital sixty days, you can reenter for a full benefit period. There is also a lifetime reserve of sixty days you can draw on for extended stays.
- From the above, it is readily apparent Medicare is short on coverage for catastrophic illness—the type that requires extensive hospitalization and expensive treatment. When purchasing your supplemental policy, bear this in mind and obtain maximum major medical coverage. If you must economize on premiums, consider a high deductible with high catastrophe coverage. You might have to pay some bills for ordinary illness, but a serious situation would not wipe out the resources of you and your family.
- Medicare is *not* handled directly by the government. Different organizations, called "carriers," have been selected by the federal government to process claims. Dealing with them is no different than dealing with any other insurance company, which means that you can complain when you believe you have been treated unfairly. Most people take the attitude, "Why fight city hall?" As a result, less than 1 percent of claims that are short-rated or turned down are appealed. Yet, an amazingly high percentage of those appealed are successful. Remember that the government works for *you*—you're the boss. If you need to appeal, start with the carrier. If that doesn't work, contact the Social Security office and get help. If your claim is on Part A, hospitalization, there is a recommended five-step procedure:

1. Request an explanation.
2. Request reconsideration.
3. Request a hearing. (If you must travel over seventy-five miles to the hearing, you'll even have your expenses reimbursed.)
4. Request a review.
5. Court action.

For Part B, just request a claim review and then a hearing. If you have questions about the appeal process, the Social Security office has a pamphlet with full explanation.

- An important consideration should be Health Maintenance Organizations (HMO). These are medical groups that stress preventative care. Generally, you pay a monthly fee which entitles you to complete health care: physical checkups, drugs, surgery, everything. The advantage here is that you can get any service you want, when you want it. A possible disadvantage is that you have limited choice in selecting your physician. The government is interested in promoting HMO's, and your Medicare may cover most of the fees for you to belong. Along with holistic health practices, we think this is a viable health-care option you should check out.

MEDICAID

Until now, we have been discussing federally-funded and federally-administered programs, uniform throughout the fifty states. While a portion of the funding on Medicaid comes from HEW, the program is administered by the states through county and city welfare, public assistance or public health offices. Eligibility and coverage varies by state.

Medicaid is designed to help those with substantial medical bills who are unable to pay. It covers the needy of all ages. Anyone on federal welfare (SSI), for example, is automatically covered under Medicaid. Others *may* be covered, so it is important to check. It is quite possible to have Medicare coverage and then Medicaid as a supplement.

At the minimum, Medicaid provides in-patient and out-patient hospital care, doctor's services, laboratory and x-ray, screening and diagnostic services, corrective treatment for minors, and medically-necessitated nursing home care. Some states provide dental care, prescription drugs, eye glasses, and even annual physical examinations. As with Medicare, you can choose your doctor, but be sure he will accept Medicaid as payment in full.

About thirty states have an extra Medicaid feature for "medically needy." This covers persons who would not ordinarily qualify for Medicaid but, be-

50 THE WIDOW'S GUIDE TO LIFE

cause of excessive medical bills, may receive temporary assistance. If you have unpaid bills piling up, check with the Medicaid office in your area for eligibility.

SUPPLEMENTAL SECURITY INCOME (SSI)

SSI is a federal program to provide a minimum monthly income to persons aged sixty-five or older, and the blind or disabled (disabled is a broad word, so check). Eligibility is based on income and assets. To qualify, you *may* own a home and low-value car, but you *may not* have over a specified amount of cash. Your income, including Social Security, may not exceed an established (quite low) limit.

While the program is administered through the Social Security offices, it is financed from general revenue funds. You and/or your husband have been paying taxes for years, and if you are in financial distress, you should not hesitate to apply. Along with SSI, you become eligible for Medicaid and perhaps additional social services. Many of the states supplement federal benefits for SSI recipients.

ADDITIONAL INFORMATION
Social Security

Books

Teach Your Wife How to Be a Widow. Books by U.S. News and World Report, 1973. For great detail on computing benefits see Chapter 5, Social Security: What Will She Get?

Peter A. Dickinson and the Editors of Consumer Guide. *Getting Your Share.* Publications International, Ltd., 1977. Excellent comprehensive guide to ways of insuring your getting all the benefits you are entitled to.

Pamphlets

Your New Social Security and Medicare Fact Sheet. NRTA/AARP, Department SS 76, 1909 K Street, N.W., Washington, D.C. 20049. An excellent free pamphlet with a benefits chart and other information.

Free publications available from your local Social Security Administration office:
> *A Woman's Guide to Social Security.* HEW Publication # (SSA) 75-10127. Information from the horse's mouth.
> *Your Social Security.* HEW Publication # (SSA) 78-10035.
> *Right to Appeal Under Social Security.* HEW Publication # (SSA)

79–10282. If you feel you are not getting your fair share, this booklet tells you "how to" appeal.

General Information

For a Social Security office in your community, check your local telephone directory under U.S. Government. If there is no listing, check at your local Post Office for the schedule of visits by Social Security representatives, or write: Division of Public Inquiries, Social Security Administration, 6401 Security Blvd., Baltimore, Maryland 21235.

Medicare/Medicaid

Books

Sylvia Porter. *Sylvia Porter's Money Book.* Avon Books, 1976. The High Cost of Good Health, Chapter 8, provides excellent coverage not only of Medicare, but on how to shop for medical insurance, avoid mail-order health frauds, how to slash medical bills, where to register complaints, health hoaxes, etc.

Best's Insurance Reports. Available in your local library. Rating of insurance companies with recommendation to select those rated "Most" or "Very Substantial." Important for help in purchasing supplemental insurance.

Pamphlets

What You Should Know About Health Insurance When You Retire. Health Insurance Institute. 1850 K Street, N.W., Washington, D.C. 20006. From the insurance industry's perspective, an explanation of the gaps in Medicare and how supplementary policies can fill them in.

Shoppers Guide to Supplemental Medical Insurance. National Senior Citizens Law Center, Suite 500, 1200 15th Street, N.W., Washington, D.C. 20005. A two-page guide which provides a checklist for comparing various policies. Send a self-addressed, stamped envelope for a free copy.

Free publications available from your local Social Security Administration office:
    Your Medicare Handbook. HEW Publication # (SSA) 78–10050.
    A Brief Explanation of Medicare. HEW Publication # (SSA) 75–10043.
    How Medicare Helps During a Hospital Stay. HEW Publication # (SSA) 75–10039.
    Home Health Care Under Medicare. HEW Publication # (SSA) 77–10042.
    Right to Appeal Under Social Security and Medicare. HEW Publication # (SSA) 78–10282.

Supplemental Security Income (SSI)

Pamphlets

Free publications available from your local Social Security Administration office:

> *How SSI Can Help.* HEW Publication # (SSA) 78–11051.
>
> *What You Have to Know About SSI.* HEW Publication # (SSA) 77–11011.
>
> *Your Right to Question the Decision Made on Your SSI Claim.* HEW Publication # (SSA) 77–11008.
>
> *Right to Appeal Supplemental Security Income.* HEW Publication # (SSA) 78–10281.

Veterans Administration Benefits

Here's a government agency staffed with nice people who want to help you get everything to which you're entitled. That doesn't mean you can leave it all up to them. You'll need to be aware of possible benefits, then work with a VA counselor on your particular case.

WIDOWS' BENEFITS

We've searched the agency for possible widows' benefits. Your eligibility depends on whether your husband was a war or peacetime veteran, whether his death was directly service connected, or occurred after a service-connected disability. Some benefits are available to practically all veterans' widows.

Our intent is to give you an overview of benefits that may be available to you. If you even suspect that you are eligible, you are well advised to seek out a VA counselor (see additional information at the end of the chapter for how to locate one) and find out for sure.

If your husband was a veteran and discharged under conditions other than dishonorable, he may be buried in a national cemetery having available space, other than Arlington. (This burial benefit is also available to you as the wife of a veteran.) If you wish, a burial flag will be supplied and also a headstone or grave marker.

If your husband served in wartime (Korea and Vietnam included), or had a service-connected disability, you are entitled to reimbursement for burial expenses, not to exceed $300. There is also a plot or interment allowance of $150 for private cemeteries. Millions of Americans are eligible for this benefit and, ordinarily, funeral directors will remind you. If your husband's death was service connected, the allowance is much greater.

If your husband was a wartime veteran and you are experiencing severe financial difficulties, you may be eligible for a VA pension. The amount is small, but if you're in trouble, it could be mighty important. If this sounds as if it might be for you, check with a VA counselor.

For veterans who died of a service-connected cause there are a variety of widows' benefits:

- Home loan benefits under the GI bill are available, though rather limited in today's inflated mortgage market.
- Dependency and Indemnity Compensation (DIC) is available based on your husband's pay grade. There are additional payments for minor children.
- Death gratuity—a compensation payment.
- If you are not covered under Medicare, you can get medical benefits under the Champva program.
- The "Junior GI Bill" provides you with educational benefits for up to forty-five months. Watch—these benefits expire ten years after your husband's death. Your children from ages eighteen to twenty-five are also covered. If you qualify, you'll receive a monthly allowance that covers tuition, subsistence and books.

You'll need a number of documents to apply for VA benefits. These may include:

1. Service papers such as enlistment record, discharge or separation record, reserve status.
2. Certified copy of record of marriage.
3. Certified copy of veteran's birth and death certificates.
4. Certified copies of yours and each child's birth certificates.
5. Statement of dissolution of prior marriages, if any.

Now, here's a nice side benefit: all the records you need will normally be furnished to you free of charge by your state if you advise that they are for VA purposes.

NATIONAL SERVICE LIFE INSURANCE

Most veterans continued to carry their government insurance, typically $10,000. In order to collect, you will need the policy number, death certificate, and statement of claim. In the eastern half of the country file a claim with:

> VA Center
> 5000 Wissahickon Avenue
> Philadelphia, Pennsylvania 19101

In the western half:

> VA Center
> Fort Snelling
> St. Paul, Minnesota 55111

It may be possible that your husband also was insured with one of two other plans—Servicemen's Group Life Insurance or Veterans' Group Life Insurance. If you have doubts, contact:

> Servicemen's Group Life Insurance
> 212 Washington Street
> Newark, New Jersey 07102

Proceeds of National Service Life Insurance may be taken in a lump sum or in some extended payment plan. You don't have to decide at once. Ask to have the proceeds put into an interest-bearing option until you're ready to decide. You can even draw a small amount and leave the balance for a later decision.

VA BENEFIT TIPS

- No claims are paid automatically. It's up to you to know your benefits and apply for them.
- Normally, death claims must be made within two years of death.
- As a widow of a veteran, you may be entitled to special preference when applying for a Civil Service position.
- Many states have their own veterans' benefits. It really pays to check. In California, for example, the educational benefits exceed those of the federal VA; and on other benefits, the eligibility requirements are substantially reduced.

As a widow of a veteran, you are entitled to certain benefits. These benefits are constantly changing, so if you have any doubts, ask. The VA really wants to help you obtain your rights.

ADDITIONAL INFORMATION

Pamphlets

Federal Benefits for Veterans and Dependents. Distributed free of charge by your local VA Office. An excellent guide to all aspects of survivors' benefits.

Need a Lift? American Legion Booklet. Send 50¢ to American Legion, P.O. Box 1055, Department S, Indianapolis, Indiana. Many sources of educational financing and scholarships.

General Information

Check your local telephone directory for a toll-free VA number or call 800–555–1212 for toll-free directory assistance. For problems that can't be handled through local offices, write: Veterans Administration, 810 Vermont Avenue, N.W., Washington, D.C. 20420.

Dealing with the Internal Revenue Service

One of the best ways we know to maximize your money is to *save as much on your taxes as possible*. The odds are high that your accountant and attorney will have substantially less interest in saving your money than you will. Therefore, the information you are about to read is important to your today and tomorrow.

To begin with, you may feel that your government and particularly the Internal Revenue Service bureaucrats have put every obstacle in your way that they can. You will encounter an amazing maze of obfuscating detail, further complicated by incomprehensible terminology, all with one aim—seemingly to encourage you to give up. When you do, they collect more taxes. Those who persevere save money. Now you know why the rich get rich, etc.

If you really work at the business of minimizing your tax obligations, in addition to the money you may save, you will most assuredly contribute positively to your self-image, your sense of personal responsibility and your continuing well-being. It's a good idea not to complete anything beyond a simple individual income tax form without the advice of your carefully selected accountant (see Chapter 8) and perhaps your attorney (see Chapter 3). And, under no circumstances should you let him (them) do the work without your input, concurrence, and double checking.

So, let's get on with it. There are three federal forms that you may be required to file. Practically everyone must file an individual income tax return. Many widows must complete the fiduciary tax return, and a substantial number require the estate tax return. Here is your first important tip to save money: *work on all three forms at once.* There are good reasons for this. You can't claim expenses as deductions on more than one tax return, but, within certain ranges, where you elect to take the deductions can make an appreciable difference in the amount of taxes you pay.

There are certain types of expenses that can legitimately be deducted either on your individual income tax return or on the estate return. Examples are medical and dental expenses, administrative fees, and some charitable contributions.

There are other such possibilities that your accountant can point out. By working all returns simultaneously, you can raise the question, "where does this go?" before an option is closed by completion of one form.

INDIVIDUAL INCOME TAX—FORM 1040

The complexities of federal income tax laws are such that no one person, let alone any one volume, can cover them all. You will never reach perfection, but your knowledge (and self-interest) combined with your accountant's input will produce greater savings than if he did it alone. What follows is a collection of information from the combined experiences of many widows and their tax aides. They are "red flag" items that contain savings for you. There are many others, subtle and involved, that only your tax preparer can point out.

Important Notes for All Widows

- Be a careful recordkeeper. Have receipts and documentation for every transaction that might conceivably have tax implications. Eventually you will know which you can safely discard. Keep track of all income with dates, source, and amount. Where there is a question, the IRS always wants proof.
- Keep records and cancelled checks for at least five years. It is a good idea to retain copies of *all* income tax forms in case you need proof of income for Social Security purposes.
- If there is income still coming in after your husband's death and during the period of probate, it may be possible to channel it into an estate account. (See following section in this chapter on fiduciary taxes.)
- New legislation is constantly changing the amounts that dictate who must file a tax return. The tax form booklet mailed out annually to

taxpayers contains current information. Even though it may appear that you do not need to file, double check with your accountant, as *filing may bring you a refund.*

- In the year your husband died, you can file a joint return. Even if your husband died on the first day of the year, this rule applies. If you have a dependent child, you can continue to file a joint return for two years after your husband's death. This gives you the advantage of a lower tax rate.
- When filing your tax form, write in the signature area "filing as surviving spouse," and show the date of death in the name and address space. Even though you are signing as one person, remember that you are entitled to take two exemptions. If a refund is due, you may need to complete Form 1310, Statement of Person Claiming Refund Due a Deceased Taxpayer.
- Tax forms are due April 15. If you are unable to file on time, you may request an extension. This is granted automatically when you file extension Form 4868 with the District Director of Internal Revenue. It's a good idea to request a receipt so you know you won't be penalized for late filing.
- This one's a bit complex, but worth noting. If your husband had any money *owing him*—for example, commissions from an employer, interest, or dividends—chances are it was accounted for in his estate as a receivable (money due). In this case, federal estate or state inheritance taxes would be paid on the full amount. When the actual money comes in, the tax amount paid is an itemized deduction for the estate or on your personal tax. This is known as "deduction for income in respect of a decedent." Just being aware of this is important, so you can double check with your accountant.
- Assets that belonged to your husband take on a new "tax basis" when they are transferred to you, whether the transfer is from the estate or from the joint ownership of property, stock, or real estate. This has important tax implications when you sell something. It's a good idea to be aware of this and seek tax advice before you sell any assets.
- If you have children under age fifteen that require care by a sitter, day-care center, nursery school, camp, etc., while you work or look for work, a credit is allowed on your taxes.
- If you have an older child (under nineteen, or a full-time student for at least five months of the year) who is working and has to file an income tax return of his own, you can still claim him as a dependent if he received over half of his support from you. This includes food, shelter, clothing, medical and dental care, and education.

Special Notes for Older Persons

Half of the nine million older Americans who normally file income tax returns pay more than they are required to pay by law. Select assistance from someone thoroughly familiar with tax provisions for older persons. These are just a few things to watch for:

- Persons over sixty-five get a double exemption. In the year of your husband's death, *you* qualify for four exemptions.
- Income from these sources is *not* taxable—Social Security benefits, veteran's benefits, life insurance proceeds, railroad retirement funds, and most disability payments. A portion of private or public service pensions may not be taxable—check.
- A 1978 Revenue Act revision excludes the first $100,000 of the sale of your home from taxes provided you are over fifty-five and the home was your principal place of residence. This is a once-in-a-lifetime exemption and applies to property sold after July 26, 1978. This is a really important benefit that is very freeing in your housing considerations. (See additional discussion of this issue in Chapter 16.)
- There are special credits for the "elderly." (That's a term the IRS uses and may have nothing to do with how you look, feel, or act, so don't be ashamed to save money this way.) See Schedule R or RP to file with your return.

General Purpose Notes

- If you made energy-efficient improvements to your home after April 19, 1977, you may qualify for up to $300 in tax credit. This covers items such as insulation and even energy-efficient appliances such as a stove without a continual pilot light.
- After October 31, 1978, 60 percent rather than 50 percent of a net long-term capital gain can be excluded from taxation.
- If your taxable income increases after your husband's death for any reason, you may consider income averaging. This allows you to average out the current year with the preceding four years to lower your taxes.
- If you do anything that qualifies as a business, such as sewing clothes, making specialty items for sale, writing articles for a magazine, or giving music lessons, you can deduct the expenses connected with such an enterprise. If you can set aside one room in your residence exclusively for that purpose, you could be eligible for a "business use of your home" deduction. This is a tricky area and can very easily trigger an audit. However, if the use is legitimate (a business, not a hobby), it is

certainly worth looking into. If you do have a profit-making venture, you will be required to file Schedule C and SE with your Form 1040 tax return and pay self-employment Social Security taxes.
- If you're fortunate enough to get a solid business going, look into a Keogh retirement plan that allows you to defer taxes on a specified amount of income each year.

FIDUCIARY (ESTATE INCOME) TAX—FORM 1041

Most likely, the estate left by your husband cannot be immediately distributed. It is usually held in trust in the name of the estate, most often with you as the executor, until the court orders the assets be distributed. The estate assumes an entity of its own. All entities in our country—individuals, corporations, and estates are fair game for the IRS. So, if the estate has income of $600 or more, you will need to file a Form 1041 U.S. Fiduciary Income Tax Return.

Estate income is taxable at the same rate as individual income, with some differences in deductions and credits. Actually, having the estate pay its own tax may be a saving. Let's say that the estate earns income and dividends of $3,000 during the year or so that it is in probate. The tax rate would be based on total earnings of $3,000. If the $3,000 were added to your personal income, it could be taxed at a much higher rate. Be thankful for small favors.

Here are some informational tidbits on estate taxes:

- Income earned from opening of the estate account until final distribution must be reported annually. You get to choose the filing date, but you would be wise to select April 15 to match with your individual return.
- Since the estate is an entity, it requires an identification number. This number can be obtained by filing a Form SS-4, which is available from any IRS or Social Security office. This number follows the estate until its final distribution, just as your Social Security number follows you to the end of time.
- When reporting income from the estate, it must include dividends, interest, rents, royalties, gain from sale of property, income from businesses, trusts, etc.
- As with individual income tax, you can file for a time extension on Form 2758. You will be required to pay at least one-fourth of the estimated tax at that time.
- Hooray! You don't need to pay the whole tax bite concurrent with the form filing. You may pay in four equal installments on the fifteenth

62   THE WIDOW'S GUIDE TO LIFE

day of the fourth, seventh, tenth, and thirteenth months following the close of the tax year.

- An estate is entitled to exclude up to $100 of its income from dividends. There is only one $600 personal exemption. To deduct contributions to charitable organizations, there must be a provision in the will for such a payment.
- Funeral expenses, and medical and dental expenses may be claimed either on the last personal income tax return or in the estate tax return but *may not* be deducted as estate expenses.
- If any of the income from the estate is distributed to a beneficiary, the estate is allowed a deduction for amounts paid or required to be paid.

It is readily apparent that our admonition at the opening of the chapter regarding the advisability of handling all three tax forms at once becomes increasingly sound. This tends to avoid double deductions and takes advantage of choices, where allowed, in the placement of income and expenses.

One other suggestion: don't be in a hurry to close the estate account. There may be tax advantages in keeping it open. Here's another place you will not want to proceed without competent advice.

ESTATE TAX—FORM 706

Of all the administrative affairs you will be called upon to handle, estate tax work is probably the most difficult. While you will need to deal with a bewildering maze of paperwork, it is clearly the intent of the Federal Government to not put a financial burden on widows with modest estates. The marital deduction of $250,000 or one-half of the adjusted gross estate, whichever is larger, effectively eliminates death taxes on most estates under $500,000.

The paper load requirement, however, does not seem to bear the same intent. From 1981 on, if your estate is valued at over $175,000, you will need to file an estate tax return. Prior to the Tax Reform Act of 1976, the base for filing a return was $60,000. In determining whether or not you must file, you must total all property, real and personal, tangible and intangible, and held in full or partial (joint tenancy) ownership. This means home, auto, furnishings, business, personal effects, jewelry—you name it. In community property states, only one-half of the property considered community is included in the gross estate.

Now, for the hitch. If the inflation rate continues to escalate, an estate can get into substantial figures quite rapidly and, unless Congress raises the dollar amounts, more and more widows will be required both to file and to pay taxes. To combat this possibility, widows' advocacy is required in our federal and state capitols. These and other matters pertaining to widows in the United States are not likely to improve substantially until there is national recognition of the size and commonality of the widowed population. You might want to consider this as a cause worthy of your assistance.

If you don't need to file, you can save your concentration for more pleasant matters and move on to the next chapter. If your initial computation indicates that your estate is large enough to require filing a return, your best bet is to retain an attorney or professional tax preparer who *specializes* in estate matters. No matter the quality of the help you hire, it is still your responsibility to gather all of the information required and to make sure it is accurate. This is a rather formidable task.

An estate tax return must be filed within nine months of your husband's death. You can request, and will be granted, an extension (Form 4768), but if taxes are owed, you will be subject to interest charges. So, it is best to take on this chore early.

A good way to get started is to obtain IRS Form 706 and all of the schedules that go with it. These schedules are listed on page three of the form. Taking each schedule in turn, see if there is property that fits in this category. Then, begin to itemize each one. For example, Schedule B calls for stocks and bonds. You would list each stock or bond with name, number of shares, and value.

For tax purposes, each asset is valued as of the date of your husband's death. Even though he purchased a stock at $10, if it was $28 on the day of his death, $28 is the value you list. Similarly for real estate, jewelry, art, etc. You will probably need to obtain an appraisal. If it is to your advantage, an alternate date six months after your husband's death may be selected for a tax base.

By now, you're getting the idea that this is a rather tricky business and requires some expert advice. However, a bit of time with the forms and some hard concentration on your part will get you through unscathed.

One important note: If it appears that you will not have to pay federal estate taxes, be sure to save any appropriate deductions for your fiduciary tax or personal income tax return.

Obviously, we have just touched on the subject of taxes. Many women, unschooled in such matters, simply throw up their hands and leave it to someone else. We hope that you will look on your involvement as part of the transition process to self-sufficiency. As we have said repeatedly, in various ways, each facet of your life is part of the whole, not separate and distinct. By taking charge of one portion of your life, you benefit your whole person. Besides, overpaying on your taxes is hardly an auspicious beginning to a rewarding new life.

Since federal regulations on taxes are constantly changing, it is advisable to check for the most recent rulings.

ADDITIONAL INFORMATION

These are some of the publications that can be obtained free of charge from an Internal Revenue Service office or by mail from any District Director (check with your local IRS office for the address).

General Information

#17 — Your Federal Income Tax
#552 — Recordkeeping Requirements and a Guide to Tax Publications
#538 — Tax Information and Accounting Periods and Methods
#506 — Computing Your Tax Under the Income Averaging Method

Estate & Survivors Information

#559 — Federal Tax Guide for Survivors, Executors and Administrators
#448 — A Guide to Federal Estate and Gift Taxation
#553 — Highlights of 1976 Changes in the Tax Law
#555 — Community Property and the Federal Income Tax

Special Information for the Older Person

#524 — Tax Credit for the Elderly
#554 — Tax Benefits for Older Americans

Miscellaneous Information

#523 — Tax Information on Selling or Purchasing Your Home
#526 — Income Tax Deduction for Contributions
#587 — Business Use of Home
#508 — Educational Expenses
#503 — Child Care and Disabled Dependent Care
#550 — Tax Information on Investment Income and Expenses
#544 — Sales and Dispositions of Assets
#590 — Tax Information on Individual Retirement Savings Programs

In addition, there are publications on specific issues that are distributed free of charge by other organizations:

Tax Facts and *Your Retirement Income Tax Guide,* AARP/NRTA, 1909 K Street, N.W., Washington, D.C. 20049.

Information on Individual Retirement Accounts and Keogh Plans, Pension Benefit Guaranty Corporation, 2020 K Street, N.W., Washington, D.C. 20006.

Automobile Income Tax Deduction and *Your Driving Costs,* American Automobile Association, 8111 Gatehouse Road, Falls Church, Virginia 22042.

Working with State and Local Agencies

In other chapters, we have been able to give you specific information and reliable references common to all areas of the country. The variation in laws and regulations among the fifty states makes commonality in this chapter impossible. While the information is useful as a guideline, it is general in nature; and you must do some of the digging for specifics on your own. When you need information about procedures to follow in order to comply with state or local regulations, try any of these sources:

- Your telephone book has listings for city (town), county, and state offices and agencies. If you find the correct agency listing but can't find the exact office you want, call the central office and ask to be referred to the source most likely to help.
- The reference librarian at the public library is usually an excellent resource. If the information you seek is not in the library, you will be referred to the proper source.
- Your lawyer or accountant may have the information you need. Remember to keep your conversation with them brief, as many professionals now have automatic timers so they can charge you for phone conversations.

65

- High-school teachers and college or university professors can be excellent sources of information. The civics teacher is usually well versed in local ordinances. For business information, try the professor who teaches courses in small business.
- Most politicians react quickly to their constituents. Call your city council member or state representative.

If all else fails, do whatever seems best to you. Any mistakes you make will be called to your attention by the long arm of the law. Don't worry too much about penalties. Widows who make mistakes are not generally treated as criminals in our society.

TAXES

Whatever the federal government taxes, the states often tax as well. In addition, most states, counties, and municipalities manage to think up some beauties of their own. These are the most common taxes you will need to deal with.

State Income Tax

If you live in Florida, Nevada, South Dakota, Texas, Washington, or Wyoming, move on to the next section. These states get into your pocketbook in other ways. Connecticut taxes capital gains and dividends only. Tennessee and New Hampshire tax dividends and interest, but not earned income. If you're still reading, you will need to file a state income tax return. Some states parallel federal rules on deductions and exemptions. Others have their own system. Some have special treatment provisions for retirement income and the elderly, others do not. Rate schedules vary widely. For specifics, check with your State Tax Board, Department of Finance, Revenue, or Taxation, or whatever else the revenuers are calling themselves these days.

In general, the preparation of a state return is relatively simple once the data has been gathered for a federal return. For tax purposes, in the year your husband died you are considered married for the entire year and, within your state's regulations, you may choose to file a joint return or a married but separate return.

In any case, you will need to indicate deceased after your husband's name, with the date of death. If a refund is due, you may need a special form which will be your statement of claim to the overpaid taxes.

Fiduciary State Income Tax

If you didn't fall asleep reading Chapter 6, you know all about filing a U.S. Fiduciary Income Tax Return. And you know that it is the tax on the earned income of the estate itself during the period it is in probate. Now you also know you may need to file a similar state return. Take heart, as this is primarily transferring information from the federal return. Aside from writing the check, it is practically painless. Unlike federal fiduciary taxes, which can be paid in installments, in some states taxes must be paid in full with the return.

State Inheritance and Estate Taxes

All of the states with the exception of California and Nevada have either an inheritance tax or estate tax, or both. In Chapter 6 we noted that only a small number of widows will pay federal estate taxes. Since the various states' estate taxes are tied into the federal tax, very few will pay these either.

The inheritance tax levied by many states is quite different and has no comparable federal tax. The distinction is that it is levied against the beneficiary receiving proceeds from the estate. Most systems are designed so that the person closest to the deceased (you) pays the smallest percentage of tax, while those further away (for example, a nephew) would pay a higher percentage.

For modest estates, the amount of actual tax is quite low, but the amount of detail and paperwork is quite high. Your state will have a comprehensive booklet covering the tax, and it is a good idea to read it prior to working with your accountant and attorney. As we have said, the selection of your professional aides and the degree to which you are informed and involved will largely determine how you will emerge financially and psychologically from your encounter with taxation.

Property Taxes

If you own your home or any income property, you will be taxed, usually by the county in which the property is located. In some cases, payment of property tax is included in the mortgage. If not, you will be required to pay the tax upon notice, which means planning for this expense in your budget.

In most states, property is reappraised and a new value base is established at the date of your husband's death. In a time of rapidly escalating property values, this has real significance for you. For income property, it establishes a higher base for depreciation, resulting in savings on your income tax. For both your house and income property, the higher valuation decreases the profit when you sell (capital gains), again providing tax savings.

If reassessment is also tied in with reappraisal, that spells trouble. It could mean increased taxes. Most states are alert to this problem and allow the ups without the downs for widows. If you ever feel your tax rate is unfair, you can file an appeal with the local assessor's office.

Property taxes nationwide are high and continue to rise. The passage of Proposition 13 in California, which sharply reduced property taxes, has led the way to similar initiatives and legislative consideration in other states. Since high property taxes impact most harshly those on low and fixed incomes, you may wish to watch this trend as part of your financial planning.

Some states are attempting to provide selective tax relief for the elderly. There are laws referred to as "circuit breakers" that provide help by crediting excessive property taxes against state income tax, or by providing a cash refund when property taxes exceed a certain percentage of personal income. A unique system of full or partial relief for elderly homeowners has been instituted by states such as Washington, Virginia, California, Massachusetts, and Florida that may well provide a model for other states. Those over sixty-two (sixty-five in some states) may enter an agreement whereby the state actually pays the property taxes. A lien is placed on the home for tax monies advanced. At the time of death or sale of the property, the total amount of the note and interest is due and payable to the state from proceeds of the transfer. The only restriction is that participants must live in the home. This plan offsets some effects of inflationary taxation and assures many of continued residence in their own home.

An important tip: if you are considering relocating, carefully investigate the tax advantages of the state you select. Look for help to older persons in the form of retirement income credits and other concessions. Check real property taxes, personal property taxes, sales taxes, and others. Local taxation can make a substantial difference in your lifestyle.

TRANSFERRING TITLES

At some point (see Chapter 2), you will need to transfer title on all real property, bank accounts, stocks and bonds, autos, etc., to your name alone. Property is held in a variety of forms, and how yours is titled will determine the nature of the transfer.

- "Tenants by the Entirety." This is for real estate only when both your name and your husband's name appear on the deed. If your deed(s) is registered this way, you become the sole owner on your husband's death.
- "Tenants in Common" means that each person owns an undivided specified interest in the property. Your husband may have held such property with you or another person, and its disposition will be part of the estate.
- "Joint Tenancy" is property held in both names with right of survivorship. All such property reverts to you on your husband's death.
- "Separate Property" is titled solely in your husband's name and becomes part of the estate.

- "Community Property" is legally recognized in a few states. It covers all property acquired during your marriage and is considered owned fifty-fifty.

Transferring title on real property held in joint tenancy or tenants by the entirety should be relatively simple. Typically, you will need a certified copy of the death certificate, a Certificate of Release of Inheritance Tax Lien (obtained from State Controller's office) and an Affidavit—Death of Joint Tenant (available in most stationery stores). Your Grant Deed will contain the information needed to complete the affidavit. All three documents must be recorded in the office of the County Recorder in the county in which the property is located. There is usually a small fee for this transaction. You can handle this yourself and save attorney's fees.

It is possible that transferring community real property and real property held as tenants in common may also fit the "relatively simple" category. Check to see if this is true in your locale.

All other title transfers become part of complex, often overlapping, rules and confusion on the part of lawyers and bureaucrats dispensing information. If you are wise, you will not rely on any single source of information but will check two or three to make sure you are handling things properly.

Generally, until it has been determined that no inheritance tax is due or until it has been paid, a statutory lien is placed on all real and personal property. To release any property during this period, a Consent to Transfer document is usually required. So that your financial life is not tied in knots, most states provide a blanket consent to banks, savings and loans, and credit unions to release money to you within certain limits.

The best way to obtain information on how to transfer titles is to contact the local office of the controller or revenue officer in your state, or the county treasurer's office.

Try these questions on your friendly state or county agent:

1. How much money can I transfer from a joint savings or checking account without a Consent to Transfer form?
2. How can I close out my joint accounts?
3. What procedure should I follow to transfer a savings or checking account in my husband's name, to my name?
4. My estate is in probate. Do I need a Consent to Transfer form for securities?
5. My estate is not going through probate. Do I need a Consent to Transfer form for securities?
6. What additional forms might I need to affect transfers?

OBTAINING VITAL DOCUMENTS

To process the many forms, file claims, and transfer titles, you will need documents such as a death certificate, birth certificates, marriage certificates or divorce papers. If you're residing in the place where all of these events happened, simply apply at the Hall of Records, Department of Vital Statistics, Department of Health or County Recorder in your county.

If these records are scattered in other areas, your best bet is to send for the U.S. Government pamphlets on where to write for U.S. records. (See additional information at chapter end.) These handy pamphlets tell you where to write and how much money to send for each copy. It's a good idea to order the exact number of copies you'll need of each document as most sources ask for certified copies, and those produced in a copy machine won't do.

Naturalized citizens may need proof of citizenship for Social Security or other benefits. If you're lacking any documents, ask your local Social Security office for help.

Unlike other chapters, this one leaves us with a sense of incompleteness. We would need to write fifty books to cover the requirements of each state. Our hope is that we have alerted you to subjects that need your attention, prepared you for encounters with government bureaucrats, and have further encouraged you to be an active participant in the handling of your affairs.

ADDITIONAL INFORMATION

Taxes

Pamphlet

State Tax Facts. AARP/NRTA, 1909 K Street, N.W., Washington, D.C. 20049. (Free) Provides a broad overview of the differences in taxation and regulations in all of the states. Tax concessions to elderly and low fixed-income people are highlighted.

General Information

Contact the local office of your State Department of Revenue or Taxation for information on specific requirements on income tax, inheritance, and estate tax laws.

Obtaining Vital Documents

Pamphlets

U.S. Government publications, available for 70¢ each by writing: Superintendent of Documents, U.S. Government Printing Office, Washington, D.C. 20402.

Where to Write for Birth and Death Records (S/N 017-022-00618-9).

Where to Write for Marriage Records (S/N 017-022-00619-7).

Where to Write for Divorce Records (S/N 017-022-00617-1).

A Consumer Guide Publication, *Getting Your Share* has reprints of all of the above pamphlets. Look in the reference section of your library.

Vital documents are available through your local county or city office of vital statistics or vital records. Check your phone directory or ask the information operator for assistance.

Working with Specialists

ACCOUNTANT

While few employers are like Scrooge of Dickens' *Christmas Carol,* neither is your friendly accountant like the woebegone Bob Cratchit. The high stool is now a plush leather chair, the green eyeshade a Tiffany chandelier—and instead of trudging home through the snow to a parsimonious Christmas, the accountant of today rides to his residence in the suburbs in his new Mercedes.

Once the domain of the marketing experts, boardrooms of many major corporations are now dominated by financial wizards. These figure fathers manipulate huge sums of money in complex transactions that have only a passing relationship to the product or services of the company.

So, too, many individuals are finding that it is far more difficult to keep money than to earn it. Thus the rise of the accountant, his professionalism, prestige, and affluence.

What to Look for in an Accountant

The accountant of today may be a general practitioner or a specialist in business affairs, personal affairs, tax matters, or estate matters. Many super accountants also hold law degrees, and many lawyers specialize in tax matters.

Practically everyone needs the services of an accountant at one time or another. In choosing, some of the same caveats that apply to attorneys also apply to an accountant. While he may hold one or several of an imposing array of credentials, his ability to perform can vary from terrific to bad. Here is some information that will aid in your selection and utilization of a financial adviser:

- CPA stands for Certified Public Accountant. To reach this exalted and licensed state requires passing a uniform national examination that is prepared, administered, and graded by the American Institute of Certified Public Accountants. The Institute sets technical standards and also maintains a Code of Professional Ethics that requires client confidentially. All states have a certification board, variously listed as State Certification Board, State Licensing Board, etc. They can supply you with the names of accountants' associations, which in turn can be helpful in selection. Personal, informed references are still the best bet. Remember that CPA means that you will Certainly Pay A lot but does not guarantee performance.
- If experience is not a prime factor in your choice, check with a local university for names of outstanding recent graduates.
- Your accountant should be more than a preparer of tax returns. His real role is as a caretaker of finances. He can serve you in the best way if you have confidence in him, can communicate with him easily, and if you keep him informed of your changing financial circumstances.
- The more you understand about your finances, the better service you will get. It is never wise to simply hand yourself over to an accountant. Utilize him as part of your team, but *you* maintain responsibility for everything that occurs.
- Keep careful, accurate records and receipts for all your transactions, particularly those that have tax implications. The reconstruction of records is much more difficult than keeping them as you go along. Throwing everything in a bureau drawer and then taking the drawer to your accountant has definitely gone the way of the Edsel.
- A new field is emerging, the Certified Financial Planner. The CFP provides a sophisticated approach to the handling of your funds. He may help you define your own personal goals, provide recommendations to help you achieve your objectives and assist in the implementation of a plan. If you would like to locate a Certified Financial Planner, consult the information at the end of this chapter.

Alternates to a CPA

If you primarily need help with simple tax filing, and you are able to handle most other financial aspects yourself, consider alternates to a CPA. Services come with varying credentials and fees to match.

- Public Accountant (PA). They have usually studied accounting in school, and many are quite competent. Only seventeen states require licensing of public accountants. In the balance of the states, anyone may call himself an accountant. PA's serve many small businesses, run bookkeeping services, and handle tax returns. They cannot represent you in tax audits or in tax courts. For most routine work, consider PA's. They may save you a great deal of money.
- The Internal Revenue Service will provide unlimited phone advice and personal assistance on tax matters. You can also find tax information in IRS Publication 17. Remember that tax matters can be complex and open to interpretation. Between the pamphlet and the phone, you *may* get adequate help. *Consumer Reports* issues a note of warning on IRS service: error rate on advice given by IRS employees ranges from high to inexcusable. A good way to reduce the error rate is to make several calls, and talk to different people. If you get concurrence, you can feel reasonably safe. The IRS also provides programs of taped instructions available at the public library.
- Volunteer groups offer free help through the Volunteer Income Tax Association Program (VITA). They are trained by the IRS and the state's Tax Board. Information on this service is available through your local IRS office and, in some cases, through notices in public libraries.
- Commercial tax services provide another option, but they are not recommended because of their extremely high error rate. They are staffed by inexperienced people and are not in a position to help you with out-of-routine problems.
- Enrolled Agents have passed an examination held by the U.S. Department of the Treasury, parent of the IRS. Fees vary. Like CPA's, these people can represent you in audits and tax courts.

INSURANCE PERSON

Did you know that the toughest job to recruit for in this country is that of insurance agent? Did you know that the insurance industry has the highest rate of personnel turnover? Imagine all the cold canvassing, telephoning, buttonholing of friends, mailing out of cards, and joining of clubs that is the life of a neophyte insurance agent beginning to build his clientele. Think of the wear and tear on the psyche from rejection after rejection. What kind of a home life for this young person who works evenings and weekends? Yet there are hundreds of thousands of these poor souls, marginally subsisting, trying to sell you a policy. Do something for your country. Take an insurance salesman to lunch! Only don't buy a policy until you read the rest of this chapter.

Notice two more things about insurance people and the companies they represent. The weary young man, if he lasts the first few years, becomes a very wealthy middle-aged professional. The companies he represents are fantastically wealthy and the source of a substantial portion of the capital that feeds our economy. They make all this money on *your* premiums.

While you can't avoid fattening their financial statements somewhat, you can do a lot to hold your costs down and get maximum protection for your money.

In Chapter 2, we spoke about making the proper claims on those policies held by your husband that paid benefits at the time of his death. Now you must think through the coverage you need in your changing life. This involves correcting and updating existing policies, canceling some and perhaps adding new ones.

If you have a professional insurance broker whom you have known for a time and trust, let him take *you* to lunch and give you advice. Just as with your lawyer or accountant, you are not absolved of responsibility in this relationship, so no fair skipping the rest of this chapter.

If you are part of the greater masses, you will need to have one or more insurance brokers to serve you. Note the selection of the word "insurance broker," rather than "insurance agent." An "agent" works for a specific company, and his job is to sell as much of that company's insurance as possible. His interest is primarily in the company, not in you. The insurance broker (sometimes called independent agent) can place your policy with any one of a number of companies to give you the best coverage at the least cost, and he will help you when it is time for a claim. Most brokers specialize in specific types of insurance, (that is, a broker selling life insurance may not work with auto and homeowner's coverage) which is the reason you may need more than one. Use the same selection process you would for accountants and lawyers, but retain the image of the older, polished professional. Remember the high turnover of younger people in the profession.

The recommendations we have just made are sound for the widow beginning a total readjustment. In all fairness, the trained insurance agent may be more expert in his field than the broker. If one were purchasing a group health policy for 10,000 employees, the company agent might be just the person. In certain circumstances, the "medical specialist" is desirable; but right now you need the "family doctor."

Automobile Insurance

At the minimum, you should have public liability and property damage. If you don't and are involved in an accident, you may be required by law to post a substantial cash bond or forfeit your driver's license. Liability protects you against lawsuits should you injure a person or destroy property in an accident. Most drivers do not carry high enough limits in this category. Personal injury cases are being settled at ever higher figures. You will find that you can take high-limit coverage for very little more.

If you have a newer model car, you will want to carry collision insurance. It costs the insurance company just as much to process a small claim as a large one, so the better buys are at a higher deductible. Rates vary by location, age of driver, etc. Check with your broker or agent as to which coverage is best for your circumstances.

Comprehensive coverage is for acts of nature and vandalism. There are savings here, also, if you buy coverage with a deductible. Check this carefully. You may find that the premium is $25 higher for no deductible than it is for $100 deductible. This means you would be paying $25 annually to insure $100, not a very good value.

If you buy medical coverage, make sure that it is over and above all other like coverage you have. Analyze this portion of auto insurance and make sure you are not duplicating coverage from your health insurance policy.

Uninsured motorist coverage takes care of any occurrence where the other party does not carry insurance. This is a part of most policies, and it makes good sense to have it.

Life Insurance

Life insurance is another of those subjects that consumes volumes, and we've made reference to some of them at the end of the chapter. If you have need for life insurance it is usually to protect minor children. The best bet is to purchase term life insurance in amounts you can afford, consistent with the rest of your financial program. Instead of creating a beneficiary for your insurance, have them own the policy. This way the proceeds will not figure in estate taxes. When your children are on their own, the policy can phase out. Many people continue insurance long past the time when it is a critical issue.

Many people choose whole-life insurance because it includes forced savings. A recent report by the Federal Trade Commission shows that whole-life policies yield an average return of only 1.3 percent. Investigate carefully. You may be better off to purchase term insurance along with bank certificates of deposit or other investments.

You may wish to carry an insurance policy that will cover your own burial costs to relieve the burden on your family. However, for this purpose, also consider a savings account that will draw interest.

Annuities

Insurance in this category really belongs with investments and is covered in more detail in Chapter 13. An annuity is designed to pay an income for a period of time or for life. You can put funds into the annuity in a lump sum or at intervals. There are complex tax issues connected with this, and if you are considering such a program, you should consult an expert broker and your accountant or tax attorney.

Health Insurance

If there is one coverage that you need above all else, this is it. Any hospitalization, at today's costs, is enough to throw an individual or family into debt for years. It is not at all uncommon for relatively simple surgical or diagnostic procedures to cost $500 to $1,000 per day.

If you have any way of getting into a group plan through work, a club, church, or other organization, *do it*. Coverage is better, costs are less, and there are usually no restrictions. Individual health insurance is costly, so consider a policy with a high deductible as a possible option. (These are not too readily available, so you may have to shop around.) Such a policy insures for the catastrophe—the type of illness that would wipe out the resources of your entire family. A good example of such a policy would be one with a $2,000 deductible and then 80 percent coverage. This means you would pay the first $2,000 of any medical services, and after that you would continue to pay 20 percent, while the insurer pays 80 percent. Weigh the risk and the economics. Discuss it with experts. Until we have good national health insurance, this could be the best way to cover the unthinkable without becoming "insurance poor."

Another viable option is Health Maintenance Organizations (HMO). These groups provide complete medical services for one set monthly fee. Their emphasis is on preventative medicine. You are limited to the physicians and facilities of the group, but they are usually quite adequate.

Insuring Your Home and Property

For renters, there are all-inclusive policies covering the contents of the dwelling for fire, theft, vandalism, and certain acts of nature or the plumbing system. Compare coverages to be certain the policy you select does the job. You determine the amount of coverage on your possessions, so it is wise to think carefully and not be over or under insured. Certain possessions such as art and jewelry increase in value, particularly during inflationary times. Many policies provide for automatic increases on these items each year. If yours doesn't, remember to reexamine your coverage at renewal time.

Most tenant's policies also provide coverage for your possessions when you are traveling. Make sure yours does, and then don't duplicate coverage by buying travel insurance.

Another tenant's feature is liability coverage. It takes care of your pet, your child, or your clumsiness that destroys someone's antique vase. It also provides medical coverage in case someone working in your apartment is injured. This is coverage you should definitely have.

For homeowners, there is a comprehensive policy that covers the building as well as the contents. It provides all the coverage of the tenant's policy, plus fire and other damage to the structure itself. A good clause to have is provision for temporary shelter while your home is being repaired.

There are a myriad of ways to get the coverage you need, including purchasing separate policies for everything. For ordinary purposes, a good homeowner's or tenant's policy, carefully monitored, should do the job. If you have valuable jewelry or art, you can itemize them as part of the policy, providing additional, specific coverage. If you have a lot of extremely valuable possessions, have a conference with experts in the insurance field.

When you are comparing prices, be sure you are comparing the same coverage. Insurance companies have a way of hiding information in the small print. A reputable major company is a wise choice. Be sure to continually update your policy to cover rapidly escalating property values.

Another good idea is to inventory your belongings, even taking photographs of items and rooms. In case of a heavy loss, your claim will be substantiated and settled rapidly.

Mortgage Insurance

If you had mortgage insurance when your husband died, you already know the value. If you didn't, you also know the value. Mortgage insurance will give you the comforting feeling that if something happens to you, your home will be completely paid off.

Disability Insurance

If you are working, this is designed to protect a portion of your salary should you become disabled. Policies vary widely in percentage of salary covered, date coverage begins, and premium. If you have a group opportunity, take it; otherwise, shop carefully.

Insurance Tips

Following is important information to help you get the most out of your insurance premium:

- Avoid mail-order insurance. You don't get to examine details or ask questions until after you own the policy.
- If you travel a lot and you believe in traveler's insurance, buy an annual policy. It will save you time at the airport and a substantial amount of money.

Working with Specialists **79**

- Protection on casualty or fire insurance starts from the moment you get a memorandum of your purchase. Life insurance goes into effect after a medical exam or when you pay your first premium.
- If you pay for insurance on an annual basis, you are, in effect, waiving your rights to the earning power of that money for a year. If you pay on a monthly or quarterly basis, there is usually a rather high interest charge added to the premium. Many companies help you get around this by arranging with your bank for automatic monthly withdrawals. This allows the insurance company to draw a check on your account on a fixed day each month. They avoid biling and late payment problems. You avoid extra charges.
- If you are driving an old car, consider not carrying collision insurance. You may be paying premiums that are nearly the value of the car.
- Consider joining the fight for no-fault insurance and help lower auto insurance premiums for everyone.
- Even good insurance companies will try to get away with the least payment possible. If you think you're not being treated fairly, learn to complain.
- Whenever you're considering insurance, think catastrophe. Most people can find a way out of a few hundred or even a few thousand dollars loss. It's the big ones—loss of a home, a huge liability lawsuit, or a drawn-out illness that destroys families.
- Shop for price as well as coverage. Many financial institutions offer good deals on insurance for their depositors. So do stockbrokerage firms. You may find it advantageous to join a club in order to obtain group insurance.
- If you're in a minor auto accident and the repairs to your car are only slightly more than the deductible, consider not filing a claim. Your future premiums are affected by experience, and the few dollars you collect could get tacked on three times over when you are rerated. Your agent or broker will give you honest advice.
- Life insurance on outstanding credit card payables and other loans is available but usually costly. Check rates before signing.
- Many credit unions provide free or low-cost life insurance on loans from them. When you are considering large purchases such as a car, life insurance coverage on the loan could tip you toward the credit union.
- If you are a possible target for big liability suits, you can purchase an "umbrella" policy that covers you beyond other insurance you may have. Such policies provide legal defense and may extend to $1,000,000.

STOCKBROKER

Stocks and bonds are common in the estates inherited by many widows. Unfortunately, the knowledge of what to do with them is often not included.

We are *not* going to attempt to tell you how to evaluate stock purchases and sales. This is best left to the experts, although what constitutes an expert and how to recognize one is a highly controversial issue.

One year, at Hialeah Race Track, an elderly woman came daily, proceeded to her seat, and with meticulous detail studied the racing form and the selections of respected handicappers. She always made her selection and purchased her ticket at the last moment, and she won an extraordinary percentage of the time. In vain, others at the track tried to learn her system.

One day, over a gin and tonic, a local reporter was able to obtain her secret. It seemed that she matched the color of the jockey's jersey with her zodiac sign and astrological forecast.

Market experts use tracing systems, computers, economic forecasts, political forecasts, business trends and, probably, at some point in time they check to see if the color on a firm's annual report matches with the color of their jockey shorts. So much for picking stocks.

Whatever system you decide to use, it is well to have some basic understanding of the market itself and the services to be provided by your stockbroker (variously called security salesman, registered representative, account executive, or customer's man).

Choosing a Broker

Big government is always watching out for you in the form of the Securities and Exchange Commission (SEC). It makes sure that your broker is trustworthy, honest, and ethical but does not certify his competence. The latter is left to you. If you deal with a major brokerage firm, you can be certain that your broker is registered with the National Association of Securities Dealers and is SEC controlled.

Ultimately, you are left with the same dilemma in the choice of a stockbroker as with an attorney, accountant, or insurance agent. Whom to trust? The best bet is comparison shopping. A satisfied customer is always a good recommendation. Check with friends and trusted advisers, line up names, and conduct some interviews. Use your intuition to select someone who will be genuinely interested in your welfare. Remember that the only way he profits is through commissions, which he earns only when you buy or sell stocks or bonds. The SEC has particular concern with the process of "churning," building commissions by continual buying and selling of stocks. They are also watchful of high-pressure tactics on widows. If you feel pressured at all, do two things: stop working with this particular broker, and report him to the SEC.

Acquiring Knowledge About Securities

Once you find a caring helper, you may want to simply follow his advice on an investment program. It would be more satisfying, more fun, and contribute in great measure to your new life, if you would become a knowledgeable handler of your own investments. You may find pleasure and profit by pursuing some of these:

- Send for information supplied by the various stock exchanges. See listing at the end of this chapter.
- Ask your broker about one of the free seminars on buying, owning, and selling stocks that are offered by brokerage firms, or watch the financial section of the newspaper for announcements.
- Attend classes on the stock market offered by adult extension, universities, junior colleges, and high schools. Many of them are geared to the needs of single women.
- Begin to read the financial section of your local newspaper.
- Take a trial subscription to *The Wall Street Journal,* and get into the feeling of being an investor.
- Become a researcher. Send for annual reports from the firms whose stock interests you, and learn how to analyze their statements. Make some predictions as to how the stock will do based on information and sound judgment (as contrasted to the color choice). Then, check *Standard and Poor's Stock Summary* or the *Monthly Stock Digest* (available at your broker's) to confirm your notions.
- Spend some time at a stock exchange. The activity is frenetic, complex, and amazing. Ask questions and learn about a whole new world.
- Join an investment club. Make new friends with similar interests—money. There are many such clubs nationwide. If you want to start your own, there is even an organization that supplies help. (See the information at chapter's end.)

Anything you learn is worthwhile. All brokers prefer to work with knowledgeable clients, and you will find added security and power in knowing about your own affairs.

Alternate Forms of Securities Investment

If you have a large sum to invest or a large portfolio to maintain, you might want to work with an investment counselor. Typically, they manage your entire investment program for a percentage fee. Their aim is to provide you with maximum return with minimum risk. Most firms in this business won't work with accounts under $100,000, but some independent counselors will accept smaller accounts. Some financial institutions offer investment assistance similar to that of an investment counselor, usually for large accounts.

Another option is to purchase shares in mutual funds. They are operated by professionals who buy and sell stocks in an effort to provide maximum gain or maximum income. Funds have a variety of goals, from high risk–high gain, to low risk with security. Choose carefully based on the fund's compatibility with your needs and its record of performance.

Transferring Title on Securities

Now that you have an idea of what the market is about, you can explore whether or not you wish to continue investing in this manner. Your first job, in any case, will be to transfer title in the stock to your name.

If only a few securities are involved, you can write directly to the companies for their requirements to transfer title. Requirements vary widely, and you may be requested to supply one or several of these documents: certified copy of the death certificate, Affidavit of Domicile, copy of the will, Affidavit of Survivorship, Inheritance Tax Waiver, court certificate, Consent to Transfer, or Letters Testamentary.

You can make this whole procedure easy on yourself by soliciting the help of your friendly stockbroker. He'll work with you to complete all transfers, usually without charge.

Stocks and bonds are only one avenue of investment. Elsewhere, we discuss a variety of other ways to handle your funds. It's important at this point to go slowly, one step at a time, feeling okay to put things off if you don't feel equal to the task. Do your own version of Scarlett O'Hara and "think about that tomorrow." There'll be a time for consideration of a full-scale investment program once your healing and recuperative process is complete.

ADDITIONAL INFORMATION

Accountant

General Information

For information on Enrolled Agents send a stamped, self-addressed envelope to the National Association of Enrolled Federal Tax Accountants, 6108 North Harding Avenue, Chicago, Illinois 60659.

For information on Public Accountants write to the National Society of Public Accountants, 1717 Pennsylvania Avenue, N.W., Washington, D.C. 20006.

If you feel you can afford or would benefit from the assistance of a Certified Financial Planner, write to the Institute of Certified Financial Planners, 4274 South Huron, Englewood, Colorado 80110, or International Association of Financial Planners (IAFP), 2150 Parklake Drive, N.E., Suite 260, Atlanta, Georgia 30345, for a list of CFP's in your area.

Tax Assistance for low-income people is provided by CPA volunteer organizations such as Community Tax Aid in New York City. Dedicated young CPA's provide free tax help for families who meet their criteria for eligibility. For details on where to locate such an organization, write Community Tax Aid, Box 1040, Cathedral Station, New York, New York 10025.

The American Association of Retired Persons has a Tax-Aide Program manned by volunteers with special expertise on tax issues for the older person. For information write Tax-Aide Program, AARP/NRTA, Department ED, 1909 K Street, N.W., Washington, D.C. 20049.

Insurance Agent

Books

Help: The Useful Almanac. Consumer News, Inc., 813 National Press Building, Washington, D.C. 20045. ($4.95) Information on insurance and how to estimate your insurance needs.

Bests Insurance Guide and *Bests Insurance Reports.* Available in your local library. Ratings of insurance companies with valuable advice and information.

Pamphlet

Life Insurance from the Buyer's Point of View. Edited by Ernest P. Welker. American Institute for Economic Research, Great Barrington, Massachusetts 01230, 1979. ($2.00) Carefully researched information.

General Information

You can obtain information on insurance companies and insurance salesmen by writing:
American Council of Life Insurance, 277 Park Avenue, New York, New York 10017. (Information on life insurance).

Insurance Information Institute, 100 William Street, New York, New York 10038. (Information on automobile and home insurance).

For assistance with insurance problems or complaints, contact the Insurance Commissioner in your state capitol.

Stockbroker

Books

Teach Your Wife How to Be a Widow. Books by U.S. News and World Reports, 1973. Chapter 8, Tell Her About Stocks and Bonds, provides

84 THE WIDOW'S GUIDE TO LIFE

an explanation of the securities market, the different types of securities and basic information on investing.

Louis Engel. *How to Buy Stocks.* Bantam Books, 1972. Comprehensive coverage of the investment process presented in easily understood layman's language.

Sylvia Porter. *Sylvia Porter's Money Book.* Avon Books, 1976. How to Invest in Stocks, Chapter 20, is a practical guide to investing. Information on different kinds of stocks and what causes prices to change.

Pamphlets

Investigate Before You Invest. (#534 G) A Consumer Education Publication by the Securities and Exchange Commission, available free from the Consumers Information Center, Pueblo, Colorado 81009. Information about the federal "truth in securities" laws and useful tips on how to be a "careful" investor.

Understanding the Modern Securities Market. Securities Publishing Division, Commodity Research Publications Company, One Liberty Plaza, New York, New York 10006. ($1.25) An excellent guide to the fundamentals of trading.

An *Investors Information Kit* is available for $2.50 from the New York Stock Exchange, Eleven Wall Street, New York, New York 10005. A packet of useful booklets on "Understanding Bonds and Preferred Stocks," "Understanding Convertible Securities," "Income Leaders on the Big Board," "Understanding Financial Statements," and "Glossary—The Language of Investing."

How to Get Help When You Invest, also published by the New York Stock Exchange, is available free upon request.

Ask any large brokerage firm in your area for their free pamphlets.

General Information

Information about investing can be obtained from:

> The New York Stock Exchange, Eleven Wall Street, New York, New York 10005.
>
> The American Stock Exchange, 86 Trinity Place, New York, New York 10006.
>
> The National Association of Security Dealers (Over-the-Counter Information Bureau), 120 Broadway, New York, New York 10005.

Information about mutual funds can be obtained from:

> The Investment Company Institute, 1775 K Street, N.W., Washington, D.C. 20006.

Information on investment clubs can be obtained from:

The National Association of Investment Clubs, 1515 East Eleven Mile Road, Royal Oak, Michigan 48067.

Information on brokerage firms can be obtained from:
The New York Stock Exchange, P.O. Box 1971, Radio City Station, New York, New York 10019. Ask for their directory which lists member firms that are willing to accept small accounts.

For problems involving securities transactions, contact your regional office of the Security and Exchange Commission or write the Security and Exchange Commission, 500 North Capitol Street, N.W., Washington, D.C. 20549.

Choosing a Financial Institution

Most people see banks or savings and loans as pretty much alike and make a choice of where to put their money in some fairly fuzzy ways—because they like the star who appears in the commercials or the toasters and coffeemakers that are being given away. In fact, there are substantial differences between financial institutions and, despite relatively tight regulations, competition for deposits is fierce.

A good small businessperson or the executive of a large corporation knows that picking the right financial institution may have a great effect on the profitability of his company. He studies interest rates, services, loan characteristics, financial strength, safety, and human attributes. As an informed person anxious to maximize all the potential of your money, you should do no less.

SAFETY

Ninety-eight percent of the banks in the United States are insured by the Federal Deposit Insurance Corporation (FDIC). Most federal and state chartered savings and loan associations are insured by the Federal Savings and Loan Insurance Corporation (FSLIC). Most of the remainder are insured by state funds. Your deposits are insured up to $100,000, and no covered depositor in an insured bank has lost any money.

Note the word "most" in the preceding paragraph. There are a few institutions not covered and, considering the wide choice among those insured, it makes no sense at all to go with one that is not.

INTEREST ON SAVINGS ACCOUNTS

The distinction between banks and savings and loans is federally regulated. At one time, there were substantial differences between the two, but new experiments and new laws are rapidly changing banking in the United States. You can expect to see greater overlap in loan types, interest rates, and services, all leading to increased competition and greater benefits to the consumer.

While it may appear that all bank interest rates are alike and all savings and loan rates alike, this is not true. The way interest is compounded, grace periods (periods during which interest is paid on funds that are not actually on deposit), withdrawal charges, closing charges, etc., affect the actual rate of return. To check the real return, ask various institutions to project dollar return on the same given amount. Try $1,000 as a figure, and note the differences.

The percentage of interest you can earn is determined by the type of account you open. A straight passbook or regular account allows you to deposit and withdraw at any time but bears the lowest rate of interest. The only restrictions on this type of account may be in limitations on the number of withdrawals.

Other types of accounts vary greatly and have as many names as the advertising people can dream up: certificate account, certificate of deposit, growth certificate, time deposit, and many more. They all have in common the element of time. Time frames range from ninety days to four years and more. The longer the time commitment of the deposit, the higher the interest rate. You may withdraw the interest, but if you withdraw principal, you will incur heavy interest penalties. Note that no financial institution can withhold any money you deposit, they can only levy a penalty on the interest payments.

There are some interesting things you can do to stretch and protect earnings in savings accounts:

- On long-term certificates, divide your money into several individual accounts. That way, if you must withdraw funds, you can close out one account without affecting interest on the others.
- Rather than withdrawing funds, consider taking out a loan using the account as collateral. You may find you can pay the loan interest and still come out ahead.

- In order to take advantage of the high rates on accounts that require deposits in very large increments, consider pooling. Join with others and open a joint tenancy account, each contributing and owning a portion. Warning: do this with people you really trust, as any joint tenant may withdraw the entire amount.

OWNERSHIP OF SAVINGS ACCOUNTS

While there are a variety of ways savings accounts may be owned, three are most common:

1. The individual account is in your name only. You may grant power of attorney (allowing someone to sign for you) during your lifetime and, upon your death, the executor of your will or legally appointed administrator will be empowered to act on the account. You are the only one who can make withdrawals during your lifetime.
2. The joint tenancy account is owned by two or more persons. Either can act upon the account and, upon death of one, ownership passes to the survivor(s). You would only want to open such an account with a family member or potential heir.
3. The individual revocable trust account allows you complete control during your lifetime and, upon your death, the person you have named as beneficiary becomes the owner. Only you, as trustee, can make withdrawals, but it makes funds immediately available to your heirs.

For more detailed information, check with the new accounts counselor at your bank or savings and loan. If the amounts are substantial, you may wish to confer with your attorney, as there are some inheritance tax issues connected with the way accounts are set up.

Most people don't read the bank signature cards they sign. Check particularly for conditions such as waiting periods or penalties that might affect your ability to withdraw funds.

CHECKING ACCOUNTS

In a recent publicity stunt, the Bank of America sent a woman to San Francisco for a week with only a VISA credit card. She had trouble with the cable cars and telephone booths until she discovered that her card would allow her to get a small amount of cash at any Bank of America branch.

We're probably not far away from the day when credit cards will take the place of checks, but until then it's a great convenience to have a checking account. Both cards and checks also provide indispensable tax records. Today, you can get practically anything you want in a checking account. Many banks and savings and loans provide free checking if you maintain a minimum balance. New on the scene are interest-bearing checking accounts. For low-balance accounts, you may be charged a fee for each check you write, but nothing else. Then, there are automatic transfer accounts that shuffle funds out of your savings into your checking account either automatically or by a phone call.

If you habitually overdraw your checking account, you can arrange to have overdrafts covered by loans against your credit card.

Just as we have alcoholics, narcotic addicts, groupies, diet faddists, and others who need "fixes," perhaps the new money styles will create "money junkies." Such people will have interest-bearing checking accounts backed up by overdraft credit card transfusions, intermixed with instant transfer savings and automatic bill paying, all connected with a home computer. For a country that is creating a new illness—financial institutionalized psychoneurotics—we offer an amazing cure. It is called "wampum," and works like this: people in each neighborhood create beautiful beaded items that they exchange for the corn and vegetables grown by people in other neighborhoods. . . .

Many socially conscious banks are keeping the elderly out of the mainstream craziness by supplying no minimum balance, no service charge, unlimited checking accounts. If you don't have one in your neighborhood, organize a Gray Panthers group and get in on the goodies.

SERVICES

In case you still think that financial institutions are only places for keeping money, look at what's really going on. Government regulation of interest rates has the same effect on competition as price controls would on the retail business. Without pricing differentials as an attraction, stores would be forced to emphasize services and more subtle things such as image and quality. This is exactly the condition in the financial industry. Today, you can look to your local financial institutions for an amazing array of services. In the list below, most are available in both full service banks and savings and loans. Since regulations are changing so rapidly, we have chosen not to lead you astray by indicating which goes where at the time of writing. If you wish to avail yourself of any of these aids, simply check with your local bank or savings and loan.

Loans
Home mortgage
Home improvement
Mobile homes
Personal
Passbook

Auto
Business and farm
Student
Consumer items

Special Services
Safety deposit boxes
Traveler's checks
Money orders, cashier's checks, certified checks
Notary Public
Travel service
Photocopying
Charge cards/check-cashing cards
Christmas and holiday accounts
Vacation clubs
Income tax preparation
Free books

Investment and Retirement Fund Assistance
Individual Retirement Accounts (IRA)
Keogh plan
Mutual fund service
Sale and redemption of U.S. savings bonds
Trust and estate services
Financial counseling and investment services
Letters of credit and bank drafts
Trust deed and note collection
Miscellaneous financial services

Convenience Features
Bank-by-mail service
Drive-in banking
Robot tellers/night deposits/extended banking hours/Saturday banking
Telephone transfer service (funds transferred from savings to checking).
Transmatic automatic savings program (funds transferred from checking account to savings account on a predetermined basis).

Automatic savings deposits (Social Security checks, retirement checks, civil service checks)

Check-a-month plan (monthly payment to you of earned interest)

Insurance

Insurance programs (homeowners, mortgage life and disability, health and accident, automobile, life, and personal disability, through subsidiary insurance companies or through cooperating agencies).

Term life insurance (at low rates, based on your age and size of account)

It's not unusual for savings and loans to build housing tracts, creating their own loan market. When loans go bad, banks often find themselves owning businesses, farms, autos, and other consumer goods. In the past, these would be sold off. Today, banks may elect to put their own personnel in charge and run businesses or sell merchandise. The next time you see your banker in his neat pin-striped suit, you just may be looking at a chicken and egg farmer.

TRUST DEPARTMENTS

In Chapter 13, we discuss trusts as part of overall financial planning. While you're looking at how to select the right bank as your trustee, try these questions on the trust department.

- What are the fees, and are they negotiable?
- Do you have a say in what is done with your account?
- How do you communicate your desires?
- What is this bank's average rate of return on their investments? How does this performance compare with other trust companies?
- Do you have a choice over the person assigned to your account?
- Who are the people in the department? What are their credentials?
- What outside sources for investment advice do they use?
- If your trust is small, will it be combined with other small trust accounts in a common fund? Are there advantages to you in combining resources?
- Will they work with an attorney of your choice in establishing the terms of the trust?
- Do they have immediate recommendations for improving your existing portfolio?
- Will they advise you of ways to reduce the cost of maintaining the trust?

THE HUMAN SIDE OF FINANCIAL INSTITUTIONS

In our alienated society, most people want a human touch—particularly the widow who is going through a major life transition. So, in addition to high interest, safety, and services, it is important to find financial institutions that make you feel comfortable. Financial executives recognize the commercial importance of a personal approach, particularly since there is so much automation and sameness involved in the handling of their product. Even so, they hire human beings who vary in their ability to make meaningful contact with another.

There are ways you can recognize the "good guys." Begin by not judging your bank or savings and loan by its tellers. For a whole variety of reasons, some caused by the institutions, others by the nature of the job, the teller position is the most unmanageable one in banks and savings and loans. This is an entry level job and has one of the highest turnover rates in industry. Every financial manager wants you to be greeted with a smile and efficiency, but all too often you get gloom and bumbling. Everyone works hard on this problem, so if you catch an occasional off-person in a group of tellers, just ignore it. If you find a whole group of sour tellers, you can bet there's a manager who doesn't care, so find yourself a new connection immediately.

It's a good idea to get to know your branch manager. The smart ones will take pains to introduce you to those who can help in various ways. Having a confidant at the savings and loan or bank to work closely with you on your financial affairs is a valuable part of your transition and relieves you from involving your family and friends.

After you complete your analysis of earnings and services, you will find that the combination of regulations and competition makes a certain kind of sameness throughout the industry. The human factor may well tip the balance. Where you find compassion and caring for you and your individual problems as a person, not just as a possessor of money to deposit, may be the best place to make your financial home.

ADDITIONAL INFORMATION

Books

Sylvia Porter. *Sylvia Porter's Money Book.* Avon Books, 1976. Your Checking and Savings Accounts (Chapter 2) is really a "bible" on everything you ever wanted to know or didn't know you wanted to know about financial institutions. If you need detailed information and specifics on how to write checks, how to guard against forgeries, how to force yourself to save gracefully, it's all here.

Andrew Tobias. *The Only Investment Guide You'll Ever Need.* Bantam Books, 1979. The Case for Cowardice (Chapter 3) is a lighthearted but realistic look at the "minimal risk" aspect of savings accounts.

General Information

Every bank and savings and loan will gladly provide you with all kinds of printed information on their services, accounts, financial condition, and anything else that is at all relevant to selling their services.

Ask the trust department of your full-service bank for brochures on establishing trusts.

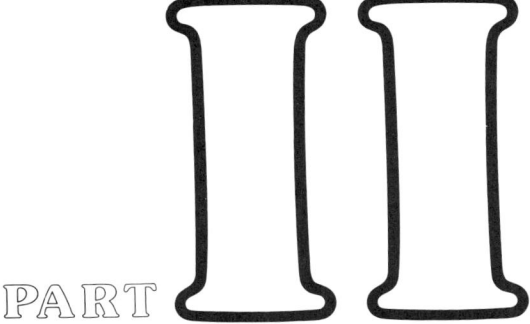

PART II

TRANSITIONING: BEGINNING A NEW LIFE

Establishing Your Identity

In any emergency, the human organism has protective devices. Where there is serious damage to the physical body, as in an accident, shock occurs. The protection for bereavement is more psychological than physical. Perhaps you've felt or heard the expression, "I just went numb." The sense of unreality, the feeling of detachment, helps the human system absorb the impact of the sudden change in life and spread it out over time so it is less destructive. This marvelous ability of the human organism to take care of itself in time of trauma is both lifesaving and healing.

Once the initial impact has passed and the automatic protection is no longer needed, the matter of choice reappears. What to do? How to take care of yourself. How much opening to current reality should you allow?

At this point, it is important to understand one of the major concepts of modern-day psychology, self-responsibility—that everyone has a wide range of choices in the conduct of his or her life. This concept says that each individual is fully responsible for everything that happens to her/him within one's span of control. In your case, as a widow, this means that the loss of your husband was outside your control, but everything else that goes on is your responsibility. You can choose to stay numb completely, stay partially numb, or come out of the numbness altogether. You can make the choice to see your loss as an opportunity to make a new, although different, rewarding life, or to continue protecting against the pain, but also closing down the possibility of joy.

We believe this is the central issue of widowhood, the point at which some women make an extraordinary affirmation of their own existence and go on to a successful new life, while others deny the possibility of any existence without their husbands.

In our work with widows' groups, it is possible in a matter of minutes to tell those who have made the choice to move on from those who have chosen to withdraw. Comments such as, "When my husband died, I died too," and "It's been five years now since my husband died, and I just don't know what to do with my life," indicate withdrawal. Signs of emerging life are contained in, "It took me some months to get over the shock, but I'm making new friends, trying new ways of being, and looking forward to new experiences."

Clearly, the first step on the path to wholeness is a reaffirmation of life, a readiness to leave the numbness behind (after a reasonable period of time) and a willingness to assume self-responsibility in the creation of a new life. Every widow has the potential to make the positive, life-affirming choice. This chapter contains thought starters and resources to speed you on your way.

FREEDOM FROM ROLES

Most of us think of ourselves through the roles we play. Some interesting studies show that male responses to questions about their identity most often are job connected. "I'm president of my company," or "I'm an engineer." Women tend to identify themselves as wife, homemaker, or loving mother.

Wife and mother are *connected* identities, not single identities. They're once removed from the basic, the "me" identity. One of the most important requisites for moving on is the release of role identification, particularly the one of wife. The standards of our society have brainwashed women into thinking that having a man is all-important. What is important is to break free of this and to understand that it's perfectly okay to be a woman alone and not to be classified as an extension of a mate. To do this, it is necessary to find out who you are, apart from others. The exercises in the Life Planning chapter should be helpful, but simply through the process of living your new existence you will begin to discover more of your core identity. When you're further along in the process of self-identification, not role identification, you'll want to consider discarding the role of widow too.

COMING INTO YOUR OWN

Most people are resistant to change and fear the consequence of major moves. Death is the enemy of that resistance, and it always wins. It precipitates the greatest change we know—from connectedness to aloneness. But aloneness need not be loneliness. It can offer an opportunity to begin a new identity, to discover new inner resources, to re-own old pleasures set aside. This *can* be a time of flowering anew, finding new companions, doing things that are not necessarily shared with another.

If you find the transition difficult or the challenge threatening, find others with whom you can share. Try joining or forming a widow's group (see *Support Systems*), or join other types of self-help groups—places where you can explore your emerging person. If it seems comfortable, get psychological counseling. Having a trained person guide your process can be an important temporary aid.

Explore all the things you wanted to do, but didn't, while your husband was alive. This may take a bit of doing, but when you can appreciate what you had while you enjoy what you're having, you're well on your way.

Take some extra time with your personal appearance. Experiment with a new look in clothes and makeup. Do things you enjoy and that help you feel good. Often, how you make yourself look is how you'll feel.

Start a new reading program. Get magazines and books you've never tried before. See what's interesting and try to determine if any of the information suggests a new dimension for your exploration.

Finding the new "you" means discovering your individual likes. If ballet is something you enjoy but didn't attend because of your husband, begin now. Allow yourself to experience all the things you would not do as a couple. Find new people that suit you and the person you are becoming. Discover your survivor's skills, test your inner resources. If you don't drive, learn how. Become a fixer instead of calling a repairman.

> Molly, a member of one of our groups, tells of her growth through a painful learning experience. "It is wonderful to know I have the courage to jump in and try almost anything, and rarely do I find anything impossible that I want to tackle. I now rank myself as a plumber. I installed my own sprinkler system with automatic timers. A carpenter, I designed and installed bookcases and have rebuilt my closets. A stone mason, I have laid tile in my new patio. A mechanic, I do all minor repairs to appliances and my car. In my new neighborhood, I am known as the handywoman. I have many calls for assistance which I happily answer, toolbox in hand. It is wonderful what can be learned with a little faith, a lot of guts, patience, and a sense of humor. I can always stand back and laugh at my failures—like the time I tried to rewire a lamp and blew every fuse in the house. It took me three hours of frantic work to realize what I had done and why the electricity would not work."

Even though the wearing of "widow's weeds" is outmoded and there is substantial acceptance in our society for women coming into their own, a great deal of residual "shouldist" attitudes remain. It is important to watch for this and respond only to your own inner needs, not how someone else dictates you should behave. Possibly the most important thing to watch is the enemy within. Each of us has a behavior pattern that is made up of all the learnings of our lifetime, and often the only thing that keeps us from moving on is the internal voice full of negative warnings. If you hear two voices, listen to the one that leads you in the direction of a new, exciting identity.

> Discovering a new identity can come at any age. Rose was sixty-five when her husband died. She had been married for forty-two years to a powerful, much loved and admired man. Her choice was to remain in his shadow. Most people saw her as a nice but ineffectual person.
>
> For a while after Dave died, she vacillated about where to live, what to do. Then, slowly, a person of great inner strength began to emerge. She took driving lessons and went to classes to learn how to handle her financial affairs. She rented an apartment that was modestly furnished in her own taste, and began to make new friends.
>
> She became an opera fan, went to the theater, and exhibited an intellectual curiosity no one had seen before. With different companions, she traveled extensively. At home she became a volunteer worker for Traveler's Aid and was greatly appreciated by her co-workers and the people she served.
>
> She refused to burden her children and whenever possible learned what she needed to care for herself. Friends and family marveled at the transition and found it difficult to connect this new, dynamic woman with the passive person they had known and loved in another way.

There are many women, now famous, whose individual identities emerged after the death of their husbands. Eleanor Roosevelt, a well-loved first lady, was recognized as one of the finest minds of her time, a leader in human rights and the U.S. Representative to the United Nations. Coretta King has admirably carried on the work started by Martin Luther King, Jr.

Laura Huxley, wife of Aldous, in the years she has been widowed, has written books, created her "Caress" program that brings older women together with children, and is much in demand as a speaker. Muriel Humphrey, housewife, mother, wife of Hubert Humphrey, became a U.S. Senator after the death of her husband.

Catherine Meyer Graham grew up in Washington politics. After working for a year as a reporter, she married Phil Graham, a lawyer, and retired to have four children. When her husband died, she took over management of the *Washington Post* and *Newsweek* and is regarded as one of the most important people in journalism. Margaret Chase Smith became a powerful force in the United States Senate after the death of her husband.

There are many paths to the new, rewarding life, but the widow making a successful transition manages her home life, sex life, and work life to suit who she is, not who she was, and in the process discovers who she can become.

SELFNESS VERSUS SELFISHNESS

If you were a typical child, one of the earliest admonitions you heard was "Don't be selfish." Then it was drummed into you over and over by parents, religious school teachers, and grade school teachers. The result is that the very human need to care for yourself is pushed aside by the more acceptable behavior of caring for others.

The dictionary definition of selfish is a primary concern for one's own interest *without regard for others*. It is probably the overwhelming concern about the "regard for others" that has obliterated all notions in our society of *selfness* as a healthy concept. Yet, being *selfless* is to deny your own self-worth.

This is really a difficult notion to grasp because the "selfish" label is one no one wants. But, the concept of self-responsibility we've been advocating takes the position that you *must* look after your own needs in order to grow into an emotionally sound person.

Let's look at it another way: The old learning about "selfish" would have a mother be self-sacrificing, always thinking of her family's needs, never being concerned about herself. The newer idea is that, as a mother, the greatest gift you can give your children is to be a happy, fulfilled, self-sufficient woman. Think about that.

If you'd like to experiment with taking care of your *selfness*, try concentrating on *your* needs. Instead of shoving them to the background, act them out. Go shopping and buy something you want, just for yourself. Play hooky and take in an afternoon movie. Sign up for a course that does something just for *you*.

We believe that in short order you'll come to understand that by improving *you* and creating greater happiness for *you*, you'll become a more sensitive, happy person who will bring more of the *real you* to others. It's very clear that responsible *selfness* leads not only to self-fulfillment but to improved relationships. Try it—you'll like it.

ALONENESS VERSUS LONELINESS

Although your present state of single existence occurred outside of your control, whether you choose to live the balance of your life in a state of constructive aloneness or in destructive loneliness is quite definitely in your control.

Some people choose aloneness, or solitude, as a means of being with themselves in an enriching way. Many find that solitude can be a high—an exhilarating experience. It can be a time for introspection—getting in touch with yourself and deciding new courses of action. Aloneness can be freedom. You can eat what you want when you want, go where you want, without having to check it out.

Loneliness generally comes with a feeling of helplessness. What can I do? My friends don't call. No one cares. If it goes on long enough, there comes a belief that loneliness is inescapable, leading to a self-fulfilling prophecy, making it truly inescapable. But, you do have a choice to alleviate loneliness by seeking new relationships. And it is terribly important to make new friends, because many old ones will surely drop away.

The way to combat loneliness is to reach out. Join clubs, groups, go to meetings—anything where the type of people you enjoy meet and talk. Start entertaining at home, not elaborately, just a few people, to make new friends. Shore up old friendships by taking the initiative and calling. If you stay home watching TV, the only person you'll ever meet is the TV repairman.

Then, begin to explore all the advantages of aloneness so that you can really enjoy the company of others or simply being by yourself. Living alone can be good. You will soon learn that you have all the resources to survive, and this is splendid self-affirmation.

POWER OF POSITIVE THOUGHT

Strange subject in a chapter on identity, but, more and more, research shows the tremendous power of your outlook on life. The placebo effect in medicine is well known. When people are told they are getting medicine that will get them well, they often do, even though the "medicine" is a harmless sugar pill.

In the chapter on holistic health, we stress the potency of visualizing oneself well as a way of combating illness. In the same way, how you view things may well determine the outcome. Just look at the many people you know. Watch the low accomplishers and the unhappy people. Most often they'll have a sour expression, a "what's the use" attitude. We usually think their attitude is a result of their condition. Wrong! The condition is a result of the attitude.

We are not speaking about the platitudes, the exhortations to "smile, it'll be all right." We are talking about the research-supported knowledge that shows your attitude can control the physical reactions in your body to keep you well and that *knowing* you can make your life a happy one changes the energy flow in your system that brings about the changes you desire.

If the identity you want is that of a competent, successful, lovable, healthy woman, one of the positive steps you can take is to conceive of yourself as such a person. Start the day off feeling okay. Dress okay. Reach out to the world as if you owned it (you do). This may sound over simplistic, but we have watched hundreds of women turn their lives around by turning their attitudes around.

If you want a precise way to accomplish a positive change in yourself, here's how:

- Learn one of the deep relaxation techniques from the chapter on holistic health. Sign up for training if there's a course in your area. Whenever you do your exercise, visualize yourself in glowing health, full of joy and aliveness. In the relaxed state, suggest to yourself that you can do and be whatever you want.
- Every time you catch yourself using the word "can't," substitute the word "won't." This will help you to understand there's no such word as "can't." It's simply a matter of your choice.
- Every time you have a negative thought, say to yourself, "cancel." Then, simply erase that thought and substitute something positive.
- When you look in the mirror, see an alive, vital woman who can have anything she wants.
- Get up, get out, and get moving.

GOAL SETTING

Planning is a vital part of creative living. Having goals makes it a pleasure to get up in the morning, learning new things keeps you mentally alive, and looking forward keeps you young.

There is time to do all you want to do if you plan for it. Using your life planning work (see Chapter 14), make a ten-year plan, a five-year plan, and a two-year plan. Then, make a list of all the things you want to accomplish this year in order to make the long-range plans work. Keep a list in a notebook, and make it a habit to go over it one day each month. Draw a line through those things you have accomplished, add new ones, and rearrange your time schedule as the need arises. The more you work on your list, the more real it will become for you.

On a daily basis, check your newspaper or area magazine to see what events are coming to town, what courses are starting, what books are new, and what organizations might need help. Plan travel. Think of friends you'd like to invite for dinner. If you make plans in detail, then follow through, you will have made another step in establishing your new identity.

So you see, it's all yours—you can choose a "poor widow" identity or an alive, vital woman identity. You can remain sheltered and sink into despair, or you can reach out for new relationships and new pleasures. We've worked with hundreds of women, and we know this is so—the range of human potential is limitless. Don't choose to limit yours.

ADDITIONAL INFORMATION

Roger L. Gould, M.D. *Transformations: Growth and Change in Adult Life.* Simon and Schuster, 1978. Explores the predictable changes in adult life and how to cope with them creatively.

Eda LeShan. *The Wonderful Crisis of Middle Age.* Warner Books, 1973. Pointers on how to start living for yourself, discover and fulfill your ambitions, accept and enjoy the prerogatives you've earned, and enjoy the pleasures that come from the exploration of living fully.

Gay Gaer Luce. *Your Second Life: Vitality and Growth in the Later Years.* Delacorte Press/Lawrence, 1979. A sensitive portrayal of the life issues that must be confronted with aging, and a practical "how to" manual for ways to revitalize life in later years.

Janette Rainwater. *You're in Charge: A Guide to Becoming Your Own Therapist.* Guild of Tutors Press, 1979. A series of exercises to help you find your higher self.

Martha Yates. *Coping: A Survival Manual for Women Alone.* Prentice-Hall, 1976. A practical guide to maintaining a home, caring for children, paying bills, shopping, handling car repairs, and much more. A sensitive sharing by a woman who learned to cope with her radically changed life.

Marie Edwards and Eleanor Hoover. *The Challenge of Being Single.* Signet, 1975. A knowing, honest examination of what being single is all about, with thoughtful suggestions for making it exciting and rewarding.

Stephanie Winston. *Getting Organized: The Easy Way to Put Your Life in Order.* Warner, 1979. A practical guide to time management, organization, and work effectiveness in all aspects of one's living.

Gail Sheehy. *Passages.* Bantam, 1977. A brilliant road map of the changes we go through, viewing each life crisis as an opportunity for growth and renewal.

Lillian B. Rubin. *Women of a Certain Age: The Midlife Search for Self.* Harper and Row, 1979. Learn how to let go of old roles, deal with ambivalent feelings, and explore depression.

Patricia O'Brien. *The Women Alone.* Quadrangle/The New York Times Book Co., 1973. Topics such as youth and age, power, two is even—one is odd, from a historical and contemporary perspective.

Rolland S. Parker, PhD. *Living Single Successfully.* Simon and Schuster, 1980. Stresses the importance of autonomy and how to be your own person. Advice on avoiding destructive and building constructive relationships, handling loneliness and developing emotional self-confidence.

Florence Rhyn Serlin and Angela Provitera-McGlynn. *Living with Yourself, Living with Others: A Woman's Guide.* Prentice-Hall, 1979. Covers everything from reducing everyday stress to juggling the demands of a career and family to handling sexual problems.

Leslie Westoff. *Breaking Out of the Middle-Age Trap.* New American Library, 1980. Concrete guidance on ways to escape the middle-age trap, gain self-confidence and make it through a crucial turning point.

Clark E. Moustakas. *Turning Points.* Prentice-Hall, 1977. Covers scores of inspiring true-life situations and shows how even painful events in life can serve as vital sources of spiritual renewal.

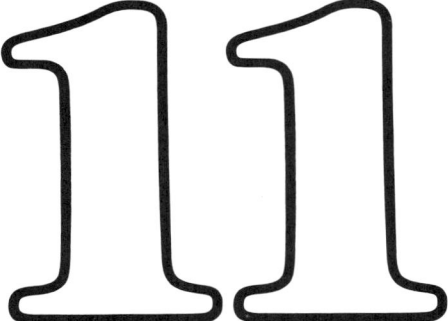

Of Men and Sex

Nothing gets as much attention in the literature as sex and man/woman relationships. Don't you often wonder how a subject this big was kept in the closet for so long? Well it's all out now, and one thing is absolutely clear—there's great confusion about how to be. The advice givers abound, and each claims to know the truth and what's best for you. It's hard to resist doing the same, but we've tried. The truth is—all that really matters is what's good for you, and even that could vary from day to day. Which means that you should go through this chapter the way we wrote it, with tongue in cheek and eyes cast demurely downward, taking any direction that seems best for you—at least for today.

TWENTY SEXUAL POSITIONS

In researching the material on sex, we found that each author has his or her own position on the subject. There are positions by Emily Post, Amy Vanderbilt, Dear Abby, Emily Reed, Morton Hunt, Kinsey, Masters & Johnson and the juicy stuff by A. Nony Mous.

Let's start with some long-held closet views of matters sexual. Before we begin—one warning: judge not—either the other person or yourself. Yesterday's puritan is today's libertarian.

Let's look at one set of ideas:

On Masturbation

1. It is immoral, wrong, harmful to masturbate.
2. If you masturbate too often, you will
   a. Go blind.
   b. Become addicted.
   c. Spoil it for the real thing.
3. Mutual masturbation is obscene.
4. Only men masturbate.
5. If you don't think about it, the need to masturbate will disappear.

On Dating

6. Never call a man for a date.
7. If you sleep with a man before marriage, he won't respect you.
8. Don't have sex on your first date.
9. Never speak to a man first. Wait for his overture.
10. Never pick up a man at a bar (museum, grocery store).
11. Never open your own car door when there's a man around.
12. The man should always pay for dinner, etc.

On Sex

13. The urge will diminish with age.
14. Sex outside of marriage is sinful.
15. People will have less respect for you if you have sex without being married.
16. Men will think you are a loose woman if you have sex outside of marriage.
17. Women should never initiate the sex act.
18. If you have sex with a man, it's disrespectful to the memory of your husband.
19. Casual (recreational) sex is bad.
20. Women need sex less than men.

   Now that you know one kind of "truth," let's look at others.

GOING IT ALONE—MASTURBATION

It's really time that the negatives around masturbation are banned forever. It is an act that is encouraged by professional counselors and endorsed by enlightened people.

You may have already experienced how strong the need is for sexual release. Many women want to put these feelings away, but wanting to have an orgasm, a form of release, is both normal and natural. This is a signal that your body is responsive and alive.

The alternatives to masturbation are walking around grumpy, taking tranquilizers, or jumping into bed with the first available man. Just living with the urge doesn't solve anything, tranquilizers are like taking an elephant gun to a fly, and the man you choose is likely to be a friend or relative who feels he's doing you a favor.

Everyone's sexual needs are different, and some people can suppress these needs. Understanding your needs is part of the recovery process, but don't allow yourself to be governed by old societal inhibitions or by outmoded concepts around guilt over sexual feelings.

There are many ways to masturbate, and there are manuals to describe different techniques, but the important aspect is that it is neither physically nor psychologically wrong, and no one can claim it is immoral. Until (or unless) you establish a satisfying relationship with a man, it is certainly an acceptable way of coping with your sexual needs.

NOT GOING IT ALONE—HOW TO FIND A MAN

For some women, the death of a loved spouse is the end of their male-oriented life. If you are in a place where you would prefer to fill your life with companionship of other women, your children, and family, and not enter into any form of man/woman contact, that is perfectly okay. Just don't reject the idea of moving into new relationships with men out of guilt, or fear of another loss, or fear of being rejected, or any of the other fears that are part of a new venture. Don't be influenced by family or friends. Don't let your children's needs to enshrine the memory of their father stop you from having other men in your life. No matter how well-intentioned the advice, no one can tell you what is good for you. Those who really care for you will be pleased to see you getting what you want out of life.

Hopefully, you will not *need* a man in your life in order to be fulfilled. The reality is that there are many more widows than widowers, many more single women than men. The women who are most attractive to the most desirable men are those who are independent, cope well, and have a life of their own. Being hungry or giving out desperation signals is a surefire way of scaring off an eligible male.

Dating

What a strange sounding word—so part of another time and place. How about "exploring new relationships?" That seems more mature. The reality is that no matter what you call it, you're likely to feel like a forty-seven or sixty-seven (what's your age?) seventeen-year-old. Still, on into the fray.

By this point, you have been working on your identity, your selfness, and your personal appearance. You are an attractive, vital woman and you approach your man quest from a position of self-appreciation. Great! Now where do you go to get started, and how do you do it?

- Let your family and friends know you're ready for male companionship. Accept "blind dates" for openers.
- The expensive (but often effective) ways are cruises, resort areas, computer dating, and country clubs.
- There are singles' bars in most large cities, but they carry the stigma of being just an avenue for a brief sexual contact. (Brief sexual contacts are okay if what you're seeking is a brief sexual contact.)
- Opportunities for not-so-obviously hunting operations occur in the grocery store, or in the laundry room of your apartment building, or the laundromat. A man doing his own shopping or laundry has a high likelihood of being single (well, everyone hasn't heard of sexual equality).
- Choose a counter stool next to an attractive man alone. Try it at breakfast. If he's eating out, he's single or feeling like he is.
- Become an animal lover and walk your dog. Dogs pick up interesting men.
- Throw a party and invite only single women. Have them bring a single man (or men) they know. Pick out a good one for yourself.
- Be imaginative. Take classes, get into politics, become a sports woman, join Parents Without Partners, or the PTA. Try to do something that's really rewarding so the "man thing" becomes incidental. It's interesting how someone comes into your life when you're paying the least attention.
- Don't discount finding a man in the workplace, only avoid the boss as you would the plague.
- Inventive women choose single physicians and dentists. Make your mother happy—hug a doctor.

The best advice (see, we did it after all) is to get out into the world where you can meet people, be open to making contact, reach out to someone who's appealing, take some risks and, if you don't succeed at first, switch perfumes and try again.

Sex Outside of Marriage

Thanks to contemporary morality, you are free to abandon old-time restrictions, reevaluate your notions on sexual activity and proceed in practically any manner you wish. You can say yes without fear of being stoned, say no without destroying some man's psyche. You can make the initial contact, order theater tickets, or invite him over for dinner a deaux. You might start by including him in a small dinner party, as men are known to panic too.

There is nothing wrong with sex for its own sake—it's simply a matter of adjusting your thinking to realize that sex does not have to be accompanied by love to make it work (although most folks report that it is more satisfying when there is real caring). Since there are more single women than men and the choices as you grow older become less, you may not find the ideal man, someone you would like to include in your life on a permanent basis. You *may* find a man (or men) you can go out with, share time with, and with whom you can have a satisfying sexual relationship.

We can learn a lot from the young people of today, who do not make a monumental thing out of the sex act. But, it's not easy to set aside the attitudes you had when you first started dating before you married, and replace them with attitudes that are appropriate for how the world is today. If this all sounds strange, stay with your own convictions, but consider the possibility that by continuing to live with outmoded doctrines you may be cheating yourself of some of the experiences that are available to you and that will make your new life more interesting.

ALTERNATIVES TO MARRIAGE

Before we get into this subject, there's one good rule that we strongly advocate: in the first year after the death of your husband, don't move, quit your job, change your lifestyle—and most important of all, don't remarry. It takes some time to bring your life into a new perspective, and remarriage as a way of finding your new identity has a high chance of failure.

If you are fortunate enough to meet someone you really feel a strong attraction toward, explore the relationship fully, but allow yourself time to find out what your *new* needs are and what you are looking for. Remember that you are very vulnerable at this time, and men who seem appealing can really be wrong for you. For example: one widow's mate was small physically. Now she felt she needed strength in her life and selected a very large man, only to find that his physical size did not bring with it the strength she sought. She was almost trapped by the need for strength, until she was able to see that the "support" she was seeking externally was only to be found within herself.

There is a growing acceptance of more freedom in exploring relationships. You can test your feelings instead of rushing into marriage. Try all of the living together aspects of a relationship. Share all the day-to-day activities—shopping, cooking, cleaning. Most of all, deal with the financial issues. You may find that it is important to have the feeling of taking care of someone. You may also find that you have had enough of that in your lifetime and would rather just take care of yourself. One of the major trade-offs that many women are facing today, as they become more self-sufficient, and as the culture supports that selfness, is the issue of the need for independence versus the need for companionship. There are ways to have both simultaneously, but achieving balance is difficult and it requires highly evolved persons to make it all work out.

The notion that most widows would like to marry again is fast changing. Many have had the experience of nursing a husband through a long illness and do not wish to repeat it. Looking to a marriage as a way of being financially supported is a potential trap. Even a second marriage can end in death, so the choice of economic independence through a career makes for emotional independence as well. All of these new possibilities are creating a group of widows who no longer consider marriage a requisite for survival or even for happiness.

The world is changing. Being a single woman today has many advantages. In the large urban areas there are many choices of social groups and lifestyles. You are free to do with your life as you desire and, as long as you are discreet, there are no areas of life you cannot explore. This is a critical and valuable period in your life. It's important to take the time to find out what is best for you, without regard for family or friends. If you find yourself drawn into a relationship, allow it to develop and value it on its own merits, not by comparison to anything, including your former marriage. Never give up part of yourself just to be connected.

If you allow yourself some time, if you listen to your inner voices, if you do for yourself what really feels right, you can have a second life fully as rewarding as the first.

REMARRIAGE

If you've been planning your new life and career, finding new resources, making new friends, and establishing your new identity, there's no danger of a remarriage just for security or "having someone around." You'll know that the quality of life is more important than any other concern. So, if you're planning a marriage with full awareness, why not? Wanting warmth, companionship, and real intimacy is part of the human condition.

Since you're both mature adults, you might want to consider some prenuptial planning. If there are children involved, it's a good idea to reach an understanding about them. Consider some premarital legal planning. Except by a prior agreement or a specific disinheritance in a will, it is impossible to prevent a spouse, even of short duration, from inheriting a share of their estate.

It's a good idea to make children a part of all your discussions, particularly those concerning the extent of the father role your new husband is willing to accept. It's far better to have an understanding than to build up expectations that are not met.

In widows' groups, when the discussion of a new mate arises, the most important considerations seem to be a sense of humor, intelligence, maturity, responsibility, and integrity. Far different from the first time around when the only word allowed was love. Margaret Mead has said that everyone should have marriages for different purposes and for different stages of life. This is a fascinating idea and one which would allow you to select a new mate very different from the first without deprecation of the life you had.

Society today offers you a great range of freedom in sexual choices, companionship choices, lifestyle choices. It's up to you to select one that matches the real you and that will lead to the most complete fulfillment.

ADDITIONAL INFORMATION

Julia Heiman, Leslie LoPiccolo, and Joseph LoPiccolo. *Becoming Orgasmic: A Sexual Growth Program for Women.* Prentice-Hall, 1976. In an open and sensitive fashion the authors discuss every aspect of sexuality, from being comfortable with your body to intensifying sexual arousal.

Persia Woolley. *Creative Survival for Single Mothers.* Celestial Arts, 1975. Although addressed to divorced women, it has good coverage on developing new male relationships, and the problems children have with the new man.

Helen Singer Kaplan. *Disorders of Sexual Desire.* Brunner-Mazel, 1979. Discusses the stress of bereavement and how it may dampen sexual desire.

Harvey L. Gochros and Joel Fisher. *Treat Yourself to a Better Sex Life.* Prentice-Hall, 1979. A self-help guide to improve and enrich sexual relations. Based on extensive behavioral research.

Janice Wilson. *Sexpression: Improving Your Sexual Communication.* Prentice-Hall, 1980. A revealing look at sexual communication from a professor of speech. In the process of dispelling myths and quieting doubts, it provides insights on being more expressive and open with one another.

Lonnie Garfield Barback. *For Yourself: The Fulfillment of Female Sexuality.* Signet, 1976. Answers all the usually glossed-over questions. An excellent book on sexuality and the female body.

12

The Holistic Way to Health

Note: This chapter requires special reading conditions.

- Sit in a comfortable place, free of distractions.
- Plan on reading the entire chapter at one sitting, rather than in segments.
- Empty your mind of every preconceived notion you have about medicine, doctors, health care, and the nature of illness versus wellness.
- Tell yourself that the information you are about to receive will be extremely valuable and that it has the power to transform you into a glowing, high-energy person, the model of physical and psychic health that you have always wanted.

If you have done as suggested in the preceding sentence, you are taking the first step in a wellness program—utilizing the power of your mind to create a high state of health in your entire being. Does it begin like some new type of voodoo? Not so. Although what you are about to read is certainly different, it is an understanding about life that is the synthesis of ancient Eastern knowledge with the scientific research of the modern Western world. This rapidly growing view of total well-being is spawning new books by the dozen, is reaching into every corner of the country, and promises to dramatically change the nature of health care in the Western world. We call it "holistic health," (dealing with the whole person) and if you follow its precepts your whole life is likely to change for the better.

"The superior physician treats the patient before the illness is manifested. It is only the inferior physician who treats the illness he was unable to prevent." If you couple this ancient Chinese adage with the notion that the essential responsibility for the maintenance of health resides within the individual, not in the physician, you have the essence of the holistic health concept—prevention of illness through personal responsibility.

Translated into practice, it means that you acquire and utilize knowledge about your own body and take the necessary steps to maintain wellness. It also means a new physician/patient relationship. Instead of remaining a passive recipient of the doctor's instructions, you collaborate with him in the healing process.

There is one other important component of the holistic health concept. The current medical view of good health is the absence of disease. The holistic model is one of positive wellness, exceptional vitality, and the utilization of the individual's full potential for the enjoyment of life.

This exciting possibility is already a reality for thousands of Americans of all ages who are utilizing a combination of ancient arts and modern technology to enrich their daily lives.

While there is a vast array of specific techniques and methodologies, the practitioners in the field agree that to achieve a higher level of wellness you must acquire some knowledge of and begin to develop yourself in four areas—exercise, nutrition, deep relaxation, and psychological well-being. Each is important, and all are interdependent.

EXERCISE

A stunning commentary on the increasing national connection with the benefits of exercise may be seen in the elevation of running shoes to first place in sales of foot-gear styles, while James Fixx's book *The Complete Book of Running* hit the top of the best-seller charts. In case you think that running is not for you, consider a California woman, crippled by a variety of afflictions, who changed her life by beginning to jog at the age of eighty and who is now a TV celebrity as she leads the pack in the "senior olympics."

If you can't picture yourself racing through the neighborhood in shorts or a sweat suit, try on a tank suit and head for the swimming pool of the local YWCA. Or, drag out your ten-speed bike and crash helmet for a scenic tour of your hometown or countryside. If leotards are your fancy, you might join the aerobic dancing classes being held in many cities. This exercise combines the fun of dancing with the health benefits of jogging.

Hopefully, one of the outfits will suit you, because jogging, dancing, swimming, and biking are the best of the aerobic exercises. Three times a week is the minimum involvement for the first step toward becoming the healthy person you'd like to be. If you haven't been doing these lung-expanding, heart-rate raising type of exercises for a while, don't just jump in and act like a professional. Start out slowly and easily, increasing bit by bit. Enjoyment is the idea, not competition with the clock or a friend.

If you prefer your exercise the genteel way, brisk walking will do almost as well. Start with a few blocks and work up to several miles a day of arm-swinging, deep-breathing enjoyment of the world around you.

While aerobics are recommended for women of all ages, if you have any doubts, you'll want to check with your doctor before beginning. The first few months are a bit difficult, but once in shape you'll be rewarded with glowing skin and an incomparable inner sense of well-being.

Supplementary to aerobics, and equally as important, are stretching exercises to maintain flexibility and elasticity. A good way is to begin each day with bending, toe touching, sit-ups and other stretches. If your working day includes a lot of bending and twisting of your torso you may fulfill this requirement naturally.

If you'd like to have a supple, flowing body try one of the Eastern disciplines. Yoga can be simply stretching exercises or a whole way of life. Tai Chi Ch'uan is an ancient Chinese exercise that promotes good health through a series of slow, rhythmic movements that require deep concentration. It has been called meditation in motion, as it calms while improving breathing and muscle tone. Through some of the books listed at the end of the chapter you can become familiar with the benefits of various forms of exercise. Select one that appeals to you and find a book or instructor to start you on your way.

NUTRITION

America's growing concern with proper nutrition may best be seen in the proliferation of health food stores throughout our urban areas. Studies of persons in holistic health programs indicate that healthy eating is an essential part of total wellness. In most of our studies, we have found that the transition from poor eating habits to sound ones is gradual, with each person trying new aspects a few at a time, observing results, and then moving on.

There seems to be no one answer to proper diet that fits everyone. Essentially, you must get in touch with the needs of your body by paying attention to the messages you get. The type of diet that is calming, nonfattening, and energizing will be apparent as you monitor your reactions to the varying choices you make. While there are no rigid rules, most physicians and nutritionists working out of the wellness (holistic) model can agree on these issues:

- Whole foods are higher in nutritional value than processed foods. Use whole wheat bread and flour instead of white, whole milk cheeses rather than processed. Whole grain cereals, fresh fruits and vegetables are also preferable.

- There is increasing evidence that preservatives and additives are harmful. It's a good idea to read labels and avoid chemical additions to foods as much as possible.
- Refined sugar is a serious enemy of good health. It is high in calories while providing no food value. In the long run, it is an energy drainer and it increases the risk of diabetes, heart disease, and atherosclerosis. Many knowing people eliminate sugar completely from their diets. Aside from the amount that comes out of your sugar bowl, the worst offenders are ice cream, soft drinks, cakes, candy, cookies, and ketchup. When you become serious on this subject, you'll want to stay away from prepared foods that contain glucose, corn syrup, and other names for sugar.
- Poultry and fish generally are less fatty than red meat, and therefore preferable.
- Caffeine in the amounts contained in coffee tends to be harmful. Cutting down on coffee and tea is advisable, and drinking herb tea in place of both is best.
- The consumption of salt should be greatly reduced. Sodium is just another name for salt.

On the subject of vitamin therapy, there is great disagreement. Some doctors feel vitamin supplements are a waste of money, others prescribe and write books on their value. You might try selected vitamins, using some of the books at the end of the chapter as guides, to see if they help you achieve high energy.

How you approach mealtime, and the state of your body and mind during eating, is also important. If you have children or can be with family members at mealtime, do so, making each a festive occasion. Even alone, you can plan a meal to be a time of enjoyment, treating yourself as your own best friend.

It is destructive to your body to eat at specified times or gulp down a sandwich because you don't enjoy eating alone. Three meals a day is a cultural, not nutritional need. Eat when you're hungry, never excessively, in joyous surroundings, using natural ingredients wherever possible. Within a few weeks, you'll notice the difference in your energy and outlook on life.

DEEP RELAXATION

Daily practice of a deep relaxation technique is one of the most powerful tools in the reduction of excessive stress. After some practice, it can bring inner peace and enable the power of your mind to help in the healing of your body. There are three basic approaches that work well, each slightly different, but all accomplishing the same goals.

Meditation. The Eastern practice of meditation has provided quieting, centering, and healing power for over six million Americans, one million in Transcendental Meditation (TM) alone. It has been called the healing power from within. In many industrial organizations, high-powered executives seek daily refuge in meditative practices. It is an essential adjunct to many forms of Western psychotherapy.

Essentially, meditation is focused attention that allows an expanded awareness of reality, with a quieting of the mind and body. The goals of meditation are to provide relief from stress, get in touch with one's self, with others, and with nature. Meditation begins with quieting the body. This is done by assuming a crosslegged or lotus posture, or simply sitting in a chair with both feet on the floor. The second step is to concentrate, clear the mind and focus on one thing. The effect of this contemplative state has proven physiological results, such as lowered heart rate, improved metabolic state, and reduced muscular tension, as well as deep relaxation and its psychological benefits.

An advanced meditative stage is one of letting go, allowing the mind to accept whatever enters and moving into a state of altered consciousness. Ancient and modern yogas, as well as many Westerners, have found true inner peace and enlightenment in this state.

This is an elementary description of the meditative process. If you think meditation might be for you, try a good book on the subject and join one of the many instruction groups going on throughout the country.

Autogenics. This is a Western way to achieve the results of meditation. The practice of autogenics, in its original form, takes many months to learn. However, there are dozens of adaptations under various names, such as biogenics, that achieve results in just a few weeks.

A primary difference between meditation and autogenics is that the latter uses exercises to induce deep physical relaxation. Once you have learned to enter the deeply relaxed state quickly and easily, you may begin to employ visualization techniques to create a sense of well-being, control pain, aid in dieting, control smoking, or aid in sleep disorders.

There are step-by-step procedures for each phase of autogenics, which appeal to the sense of logical sequence we value so highly. Refer to the additional information section at the end of the chapter for books that contain information on deep relaxation techniques. If you choose the autogenic-type method, you will quickly gain the benefits of a dream-like state that is enjoyable, refreshing, and healing.

Biofeedback. Biofeedback involves electronic instrumentation as an aid to control many autonomic nervous system functions. For example, using electrocardiogram you can watch your heart rate and learn how it reacts to various types of breathing, to pleasant thoughts, stress-inducing situations, etc. As you begin to understand the equipment and procedures, you can learn how thoughts, postures, and various ways of being can affect your heart rate. Through training, parts of the involuntary nervous system can be brought under control.

Biofeedback has the advantage of instant feedback from the monitoring equipment. On the disadvantage side, you must go to the equipment, and training is relatively costly. Science has only begun to tap the potential of biofeedback. In some clinics, patients are learning to control hypertension, flow of gastric acid, and even the formation of white blood cells. Check with your physician for the location of clinics using biofeedback equipment.

Whatever your deep relaxation choice, it is clear that for stress reduction and health maintenance you should learn one method and practice it regularly. As you progress over the months, you will be amazed at the reconnection you will form between your mind and body, and you will have new health options that will improve the quality of your entire life.

PSYCHOLOGICAL WELL-BEING

Many older doctors smile when excited younger people talk about the "new holistic health." The general practitioner of years ago was a holistic health practitioner to some degree. He knew that Mary's headaches and Johnny's asthma were not just physiological. Often his visits would include discussion of family problems, and his prescription for Mary's headaches might have been for her to spend more time doing pleasurable things for herself instead of putting all her energy into the family.

Even the most scientific medical orientation admits that probably half of all illness is psychosomatic. Physicians in holistic health practice say that probably 90 percent or more of all illness has psychological origin. New research in diseases such as cancer indicates the possibility that some self-elected lifestyles may lead to contraction of the disease. Certainly, we can predict with fair accuracy that specific behavior characteristics lead to a higher incidence of heart disease. The evidence continues to pile up, making it quite clear that real wellness is not possible without psychological health.

Most people are willing to run around the block a few times, stop eating junk foods, and take a half-hour a day for centering through meditation or autogenics. But to hear that our emotional health needs attention usually brings resistance and denial. The truth is that most people need as much help in this area as in any other.

It is important to know that seeking out psychological help is not an admission of sickness—it is a search for high-level wellness. Most psychotherapy today is for relatively "normal," functioning people who are interested in the release, the joy, and the good feeling of being deeply in touch with themselves. For many people, attending a "well people's" therapy group is as ordinary as getting a physical checkup.

Therapy goes under many names and forms: Gestalt, Transactional Analysis, Primal, Reality, Analysis, Bioenergetics, Reichian, Rogerian, and many others. If you're interested, sample some sessions in your community. When you find the one, or combination, that looks like it will help you on your journey to high-level wellness, make the treatment a treat and look forward to becoming the radiant, fully alive, fully responsive person you were meant to be.

THE FULLY HUMAN BEING

In our seminars and lectures, we have often been asked to define "wellness" or to give an example. We call such a person a "fully human being" to indicate that she is using all her available faculties and abilities to live life as fully as possible. This is our model:

In a time of dramatic change, there are thousands of people moving into a new age and a new way of being. These people are making their own lives rich and important and, in so doing, they satisfy not only their own needs, they model and point the way to new heights of self-fulfillment for everyone. They are also the leaders of a new order that places the beautification of man above governments, national distinctions, and the goals of organizations. Interestingly, as they pursue their own growth, they improve the quality of governments, nations, and organizations. These are highly developed people. They represent the finest in human potential, and their collective energy is making a profound change in our concept of the limitations on individual achievement.

For most members of our society, being well is simply not being sick, and being happy is just not feeling depressed most of the time. This vast segment of our population functions adequately by ordinary standards. Many have symptoms of chronic, low-grade illness—fatigue, headaches, and repeating colds or flu, but accept them as a part of life. They may be upwardly mobile and experience real spurts of joy at new successes in their careers. But, the joy is short-lived, and underneath it all is a nagging sense of lack of real fulfillment.

Many are happily married or in satisfying relationships. They acquire a better home, take an interesting vacation that gives them material for social interchange, get a better car, feed the children well, and generally take care of the external realities. Eventually they retire, live a few years more, finally get ill and die. They are part of the great masses who were "also here."

Out of this group, a small number experience the need to move past an ordinary existence into one of high-level wellness, exuberant joy, bliss, and even ecstasy. This desire to change may come about through a slowly acquired expanded awareness, or as the result of a traumatic event. Whatever the energizer, the journey, once begun, has no end. It leads to heightened senses and sensitivity, greater appreciation of the essential oneness of all living beings, a deep understanding of the meaning of love, a high state of physical well-being and advanced mental acuity.

While government, science, and academia are based on the assumption that cognitive reasoning is the only important function of man, it is apparent to emerging persons that this is only one part of the whole. Seekers of high-level wellness recognize the essential trilogy of the mind, body, and spirit. They will often refer to them as one word—mindbodyspirit, signifying the totality that is the fully human being. They know that while a teacher may stimulate the mind, the doctor minister to the body, and the connection with a higher power nourish the soul, integration of these pieces into the formation of a whole person is their responsibility alone.

You can recognize persons of high-level wellness by some of these aspects of their beingness.

- Spontaneity is one quality of fully alive persons. They have learned a deep acceptance of everything that is part of their inner being, and they allow themselves to flow freely without worrying about how they will appear to others. Their deep sensitivity allows them to do this in a way that harmonizes with the lives of those with whom they share.
- They understand the power of the mind in relationship to the body and use a positive mental attitude in the process of self-healing.
- No time is wasted on wishing they were someone or someplace they are not. They enjoy everyday living and have an inner contentment and sense of well-being that provides a stable framework for their entire lives.
- They create their lives the way they want, rather than responding to the "oughts" and "shoulds" of their environment. They do not get trapped into believing that the boss can make them happy with a promotion, or that happiness is in a vacation, finding a partner, or in getting a degree. They know that their happiness comes from within.
- Role prescriptions are not for them. They don't fragment themselves into manager, parent, teacher, or any other boxlike description. They prize the flow of their beingness over their labels or expertise.
- Fully human beings accept total responsibility for their lives. They do not blame others as a way of dealing with their mistakes or frustrations. When things go well, they take full credit rather than passing it off as luck.
- They value themselves as unique human beings and enjoy their completeness and high self-esteem. They honor this in others and have no need to turn discussions into contests or become winners while others become losers.

- Change is welcomed rather than avoided. They see new experiences, new challenges, and new ways of being as part of their growth. They know that the only real security is in continued self-development.
- Fully human beings like their fit bodies and live comfortably with themselves. There is a grace in their activities, a radiance in their eyes, and an enjoyment of their physical and sensual dimensions.
- They have an unusual resistance to disease. They know that colds, flu, and many other illnesses are merely signals that they are not being caring enough of themselves, and they are often able to take measures to avoid these common illnesses before they occur.
- Most everyday aches and pains are controllable, and persons with a high level of wellness do not let such annoyances interfere with their enjoyment of life.
- Their relationship with members of the medical profession is one of equality. They don't hesitate to seek assistance when needed, but they are part of the healing process rather than passive recipients of the doctor's ministrations. Their primary interest is in prevention of disease. They are proactive instead of reactive.
- They see the aging process as a continuing transition, not as a reason to suddenly become old.
- They are physically active and have good muscle tone.
- A high level of energy is a sign of high wellness. Extra energy is always available for an extra task. These people undertake huge tasks for extended hours and show relatively few negative effects.
- Fully human beings are deeply in touch with the all-in-all—the connectedness of every living thing. They are attuned to the rhythms and majesty of the universe.
- They recognize a higher power, through Orthodox religion, or as the God in themselves, or as some abstraction of their own creation.
- Privacy is prized, and aloneness is never viewed as loneliness. Being by oneself is an opportunity to commune with other dimensions of the universe.
- They guard their personal freedom and autonomy, allowing others the same. They make no judgment or comparison.
- Fully human beings do not see themselves standing apart from others. They recognize the high value of interbeing—being wholly with another in an intimate, loving relationship.
- They know what it is to experience ongoing unconditional love.

- They have a clear sense about the meaning and purpose of their lives. They value service to others, and identify with all humanity.
- They are in touch with their center—the peaceful place inside themselves where they can contact their senses.
- There is a freshness to each day, a sense of awe and wonder of the world. The child in them is fully nurtured.
- They value in themselves and honor in others the yin and the yang, the strength and the tenderness, the maleness and femaleness, the power and the compassion.
- Faults they see in others are recognized as issues they are working within themselves.
- Fully human beings have a well-developed sense of humor and the ability to laugh freely at themselves.
- Living in the "now" heightens awareness. They know that the past is for reference and that living in the future deadens the pleasures of the moment.
- They display an enthusiasm, vigor, and zest for life that is translated into human energy, igniting themselves and all they contact.
- Fully human beings have a profound inner clarity that allows them to see themselves as they truly are. They know that inner clarity is the pathway to higher consciousness.

Becoming a fully human being is available to everyone. No one ever arrives at the nirvana of *being* a fully human being. Everything is in the journey—all the joys, all the awakenings, all of the discoveries, and, yes, all of the pain and discomfort as well. Once on the way, there is no turning back, for having experienced ecstasy, no other pattern of life will do. The hazards are there, but the rewards far exceed them. All that is required to get started on the journey is to get started.

ADDITIONAL INFORMATION

General Guides

Harold H. Bloomfield, M.D. and Robert B. Kory. *The Holistic Way to Health and Happiness.* Simon and Schuster, 1978. Methods for dealing with insomnia, stress, chronic fatigue, alcoholism, smoking, overweight, high blood pressure, depression, anxiety, tension, etc., based on the premise that to reach your full measure of wellness you must take advantage of your own natural healing abilities.

Elliott M. Goldwag, Editor. *Inner Balance: The Power of Holistic Healing.* Prentice-Hall, 1979. Focuses on stress as the basis of disease and illness.

How to make use of inner resources, rather than drugs, to preserve your health and conquer disease. A guide to achieving inner peace and maintaining good health.

Kenneth R. Pelletier. *Holistic Medicine: From Stress to Optimum Health.* Delacorte Press/Lawrence, 1979. A new definition of medical care with the patient as a responsible participant. The goal is optimum health, beyond the treatment and prevention of disease, through stress-control techniques, good nutrition, and exercise. Research based.

The Holistic Health Handbook: A Tool for Attaining Wholeness of Body, Mind, and Spirit. Compiled by the Berkeley Holistic Health Center. And/Or Press, 1978. A comprehensive and multidimensional view of the entire holistic health field covering topics such as nutrition, naturopathy, healing, herbs, bioenergetics, autogenics, holistic sexuality, massage, reflexology, homeopathy, yoga, health centers, and much more.

Daniel Girdano and George Everly. *Controlling Stress and Tension.* Prentice-Hall, 1979. How to develop your personal "Stress Profile" and how to combine meditation, exercise, and other skills into a Stress Management System. This book will help you feel healthier and better able to cope with daily pressures.

Hans Selye, M.D. *Stress Without Distress.* Signet, 1974. The leading authority on the use of stress as a positive force explains the physiological mechanisms of stress and gives specific advice for avoiding the type of stress that is harmful.

Karl Albrecht. *Stress and the Manager: Making It Work for You.* Prentice-Hall, 1979. Even though this book has a business orientation, its message is important to everyone seeking techniques for designing a life of low stress. Learn how you can avoid self-induced stress and change destructive behavior patterns.

Exercise

Royal Canadian Air Force Exercise Plans for Physical Fitness. Pocket Books, 1962. This old but trusted method is still recommended by many doctors. Particularly valuable for the exercise beginner because it is charted by age and sets realistic goals.

Laurence E. Morehouse and Leonard Gross. *Total Fitness in 30 Minutes a Week.* Simon and Schuster, 1975. How to achieve real fitness at any age. Acquire a reserve of physical well-being to live longer, feel better, and look younger.

Kenneth H. Cooper, M.D. *Aerobics.* M. Evans and Company, 1968. A scientific program of exercise that is geared to provide overall fitness and health. A unique point system for measuring health progress.

James F. Fixx. *The Complete Book of Running.* Random House, 1977. All you need to know about running.

Richard Hittleman. *Richard Hittleman's Yoga: 28 Day Exercise Plan.* Bantam Books, 1969. Yogic secrets of breathing, concentration, nutrition, and muscle control which result in more energy, greater firmness, freedom from stress, and an overall feeling of well-being.

Nutrition

Harry Bieler, M.D. *Food Is Your Best Medicine.* Vintage Books, 1973. Food, rather than drugs, as a curative. Improper food causes disease and proper foods can cure disease. Suggestions about when not to eat, which can be as important as what to eat.

Rudolph M. Ballentine, M.D. *Diet and Nutrition.* Himalayan Institute, 1979. Addresses many of the controversies such as the use and misuse of vitamin and mineral supplements, minimal daily protein requirements, nutritional value of cooked versus raw foods, and comparison of vegetarianism to omnivorism.

The Vitamin Book by the Editors of Consumer Guide. Simon and Schuster, 1979. Separates vitamin fact from fiction. Reviews the merits and hazards (if any) of each vitamin researched.

Earl Mindell. *Earl Mindell's Vitamin Bible.* Rawson Wade, 1979. Contains sections designed for the individual needs of women and the elderly, and gives information on vitamin and nutrient supplement regimens for a variety of illnesses ranging from allergies to shingles.

Deep Relaxation

C. Norman Shealy, M.D. *90 Days to Self-Health.* Bantam Books, 1978. Self-help techniques to achieve new levels of wellness. Ways of achieving total relaxation and control of your body to increase energy and aid in reduction of pain and stress. By one of the pioneers in the holistic health movement.

Herbert Benson. *The Relaxation Response.* William Morrow, 1975. A cardiologist's compilation of various modern and ancient relaxation techniques. A how-to book.

Lawrence LeShan. *How to Meditate: A Guide to Self-Discovery.* Bantam Books, 1974. Describes in clear language the reasons for meditating, how it feels, the psychological and physiological effects, the different types of meditation, and how to go about it.

Harold H. Bloomfield, Michael P. Cain, Dennis T. Jaffee, and Robert B. Kory. *TM: Discovering Inner Energy and Overcoming Stress.* Dell, 1975. Complete documentation on Transcendental Meditation, explanation of what the TM technique is and how it can work for you.

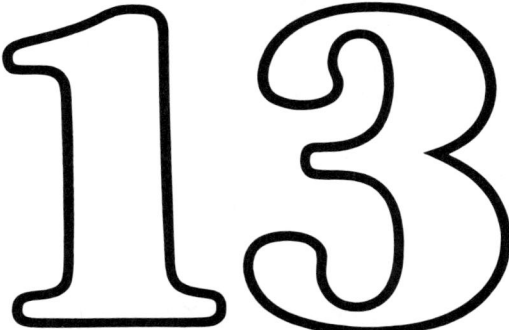

Managing Money

If you have a net worth of over $1,000,000, go back and reread the chapter on identity, or go out and join a game of Mah-Jongg. If you have less than that amount, join the other ten million widows in the United States who have concerns about money, ranging from a nibbling worry to sheer panic. In today's inflationary economy, only substantial wealth qualifies you for financial security. We're all (well, practically all) in the same boat—and it leaks.

So, what to do? You have choices:

1. Panic and run screaming into the street, or hide under the bed.
2. Enter a convent.
3. Join the Army or the Navy (the Marines is a possibility, but a much harder way).
4. Marry for money (but first you've got to find him, and the competition is rough).
5. Hold up a Well's Fargo stagecoach (but first you've got to find one).
6. Learn how to manage your money.

If you've opted for any or many of 1–5, join the rich lady at the Mah-Jongg game. If you're ready for number 6, we're pleased to have you with us.

HOW MUCH ARE YOU WORTH?

In the opening line, we used the words "net worth." That's a business term. It's arrived at through use of a balance sheet. Accountants like to make balance sheets complicated, but they're really simple. You add up all your assets, then subtract all you liabilities, and the result is your net worth—what you own at current market value.

Assets are usually grouped into seven categories:

1. *Cash* in checking accounts, savings accounts, under the mattress, in cans buried in the garden, and in the "mad money" section of your purse.
2. *Notes receivable.* The amount of money still owed you on second mortgages, trust deeds, and the IOU from your kid or baby sister.
3. *Securities.* Stocks, bonds, money market funds, mutual funds. To determine their current value, call your stockbroker, or check them out in the stock market report of your local newspaper. If you don't know how to read stock reports, this is a terrific time to learn. If you ask the right person, you might even make a friend.
4. *Tangible personal property.* Automobiles, art collections, jewelry, collectibles. Don't pay too much attention to household possessions, they're not worth much on resale.
5. *Real estate.* Mortgages, second mortgages, houses, land, apartment buildings, hotels. If you own any of the latter two, you probably belong in the Mah-Jongg game.
6. *Other types of business investments.*
7. *Insurance, pension plans, endowments, annuities.*

If you don't have figures at hand for any of these, just think of all the fun you'll have learning how to obtain them. You may need to get your home evaluated by a real estate person, have your banker bring out his "blue book" to determine the value of your car, and get Aunt Becky's heirloom necklace appraised by your jeweler.

When you are finished, you'll have a clear picture of what you own that will help you in making some investment decisions which will bring in income, which is what this chapter is *really* all about.

Now, for the bad news—what you owe. Some of the debts may not really be bad news because you may have borrowed (used leverage) in order to make money, for example, borrowing business investment capital, borrowing for real estate, etc. Liabilities fall in four categories:

1. *Current bills.* Gas, electricity, rent, doctor, telephone, ice man.
2. *Installment debts.* Credit union, credit cards, student loans, car payments.

3. *Individual debts.* You often must really check around for these. The carbon copy of your husband's scribbled note that says "Ma, I owe you $1,000, Love, Dick," is a real debt in case Ma or her heirs decide to collect.
4. *Mortgages.* The money you owe on your home or hotel. (How did you get out of the Mah-Jongg game?)

Subtract your liabilities from your assets. That's what you're worth—*today*. You can take a deep breath, or a deep sigh. That's the way things are. Bad, huh? Wait a minute! Look at the picture again. See the old house you're living in? You paid only $16,000 for it. It's comfortable, all yours, and it's cheap living. If it's in pretty good shape, it may be worth $60,000 now, or $80,000, or even $180,000. That helps the bad news.

Let's check again. Is it really cheap living? If you want to know what it's costing you to live there, take today's value of your house and multiply it by the interest rate. If the market value of your house is $100,000 and the interest rate is 12 percent, your figure is $12,000. Add that to your maintenance, insurance, taxes, and now you have the *true* cost of living there. Why? Because if you didn't live there, you'd sell the house and invest the money at the current rate of interest. Surprised? Does that mean you should sell the house? No—it's just a measure that will help you in making other decisions about your financial future.

Try another fun project. Over in the corner of the financial picture is the sterling silver tea set that Aunt Mabel gave you for a wedding present. She paid $45 for it. Why don't you check its value at current silver prices? $700, you say. Would you rather have the tea set or a bond that pays high interest? Think about it.

A balance sheet is a picture of what you own at any moment in time. Once you realize its value, you'll want to retake the picture from time to time just to see what turns up.

We're not quite done. Perhaps you're beginning to see the major fallacy in the accountant's approach to a balance sheet. It leaves out one of your most important assets—*you*. What is your earning power for the next umpteen years of your life? How about your ability to juggle your assets so they produce more income? When you add this major factor into the picture, it becomes a lot prettier.

So, before you wear out the carpet pacing the floor, let's consider three ways you can use *you* to improve the picture:

1. Maximize your income through career planning. We discuss this in Chapter 15. Understanding your financial picture may give you incentive to really work on your career plan.
2. Control your present income and outgo through budgeting. We covered this in Chapter 2. If you skipped the budgeting process, go back and

do it *now*. It's essential to your financial plan. If you made a budget some time ago, bring it out for review. The budget gives you a picture of your income and expenses. It tells you where you need to cut or suggests that you may need to beef up income.

3. Reshuffle your present capital so that it is working to bring you maximum income—investing is the word we'll use.

Before we move on, make a note to check and be sure you're getting all the financial benefits that are available to you. It's a good idea to get an update on your Social Security benefits every three years. Send a Request for Social Security Statement of Earnings form or a postcard to Social Security Headquarters, P.O. Box 57, Baltimore, Maryland 21203. Have another look at Chapter 2, and see if you've done everything to maximize your income from your husband's private pension plan. Recheck Chapter 5 on your eligibility for veterans' widow benefits. Finally, see Chapter 4 on Supplemental Security Income to see if you are eligible for any of these benefits.

INVESTMENTS

What follows is not intended to be specific advice on how or where to invest. We hope to point out various investment possibilities that will create thought starters, give you a sense of comfort in dealing with the subject, and pique your curiosity so you will seek out the information you need to make your life more comfortable and your future as secure as it can be in this unpredictable world.

Your best source of help is an "expert" in the field. Unfortunately, recognizing the experts is not easy. Too often, they turn out to be less than real soothsayers. What you can do is to check out potential advisers carefully for honesty, integrity, and results-proven reliability.

Wherever possible, attend seminars, take courses, or read in the investment avenue of your choice. In addition to generally broadening your knowledge, such pursuits will help you recognize those who *really* know. Finally, trust your instinct.

Savings Accounts

Let's begin by agreeing that a passbook savings account is *not* an investment. It's simply a place to put money you may need in an emergency, or for planned purchases or payments. The interest rate is too low to qualify under the investment heading. Other savings accounts *are* investments. Both banks and savings and loans offer a wide variety of accounts under a range of names, some with minimum balances, all with interest predicated on the length of time the institution holds your money.

In Chapter 9 we discussed how to choose a financial institution, provided information on accounts, and outlined the various services they offer. Money with banks or savings and loans is a low-risk, high-peace-of-mind investment and, by selecting the right account, you can realize a high return. Since the only reason for their existence is to serve you, time spent with the knowledgeable financial counselors at your local bank or savings and loan is sure to pay dividends (or interest).

Real Estate

In recent years one of the few investments that has stayed even with inflation is real estate. That's a double-edged sword because rising prices have also forced many people out of the market. Owning your home or condominium appears sound, according to most pundits. It will give you capital appreciation, but it won't do anything for your income.

Income-producing property can provide a tax shelter, since you can take deductions for depreciation, taxes, insurance, interest, and maintenance. With efforts in various parts of the country to introduce rent controls, investment in rental units has lost some of its luster. Condominium office complexes are increasing in number. Ownership of individual condo office units for rental purposes should be checked for potential in your locale.

Undeveloped land is another area of real estate investment. While difficult to evaluate, it holds promise for long-term appreciation. Watch out for questionable practices. The possibility of buying land under water, as happened in the Florida land boom, is unlikely, but there are many offerings of undeveloped areas that will remain so until the end of time, tying your money up in hopes instead of results. Investments in buildings and land build up cash reserves known as equity that you can borrow against for further investment.

You might be interested in Real Estate Investment Trusts (REIT's). This is a form of investing that allows you to participate, with a group, in the ownership of real estate or mortgages. Your liability is limited to the amount of your investment; and you may still benefit from individual tax deductions.

A related real estate investment is second trust deeds. This is a growing field, particularly in real estate boom areas. Interest rates are high, and there are prepayment penalties to the borrower that increase your rate of return. You can share in mortgage funds, spreading the risk on an already relatively safe investment. Interest rates and regulations governing second mortgages vary by state, so check. One way to test this vehicle is to contract for one short-term loan. Be aware that second trust deeds are not always easy to sell, and this investment can become more risky in an unstable economic climate.

There are reference books galore on real estate investing. We've picked out two by people we know to be unusually astute.

Securities

There was a time when the stock market was considered the best hedge against inflation. This has certainly not been true in the past decade. More and more the market is becoming the home of large funds, while the smaller investors seek appreciation and income elsewhere. Still, you can become one of the "experts" if you are willing to take the trouble to learn. All investing needs goal definition, but this becomes most clear in securities. There are speculative stocks with high risk and potential growth. There are low-risk preferred stocks that yield steady returns. Blue Chips have low volatility but pay regular dividends.

Bonds run the same yield/safety gamut. There are everything from AAA corporate and municipal bonds to low grade, small company, and township bonds. Once issued, bonds sell on the exchanges just like stock and other securities. Start by working with Standard & Poor's bond ratings to get an understanding of the bond market.

Annuities

This is an old area taking on new interest. An annuity is really a "life insurance" policy, only instead of paying off to your beneficiary, it pays off to you. For an agreed upon sum of money deposited, you are guaranteed a regular income for a stipulated period of time or for as long as you live. The payment schedule is based on life expectancy and the amount deposited. The main attraction is that it can offer guaranteed lifetime income.

Annuities need some thorough research, but the twist is that the interest earned on your investment is not taxed until you start to take money out. Even then, your entire original capital investment is returned before the payments become taxed. Naturally, the higher your tax bracket, the greater your tax savings using this form of investment. The complexities are great; but, if tax savings is an important goal, it would be worth your time to investigate. Information is available through your brokerage firm or insurance company.

Government Obligations

Treasury bills, bonds, and notes are available on the open market. They can be purchased through your financial institution or at an "auction" conducted weekly at the Federal Reserve Bank. Interest rates vary from week to week, and the length of time varies from a ninety-day minimum on Treasury bills to twenty years or more on government bonds. There's no question about the security on government issues, but you may want to think twice about tying up money in twenty-year bonds at a time of rising interest rates.

Series E Savings Bonds are a tax-deferred savings plan. You can elect to have all interest income reported in a lump sum when you redeem them,

Managing Money

and you can defer cashing them in until such time as your income level is reduced through retirement.

Series H Savings Bonds pay interest every six months. Although they have a ten-year maturity date, they can be redeemed any time after six months. These are not high-interest investments, but they are as solid as Uncle Sam.

Money Market Funds

Relatively new on the scene, these mutual funds have undergone remarkable growth. You can invest as little as $1,000 and receive high interest while retaining complete liquidity. Many funds allow you to write checks, within certain limitations, and still receive interest up to the day the money transfers. If your aim is high interest only, you might investigate these funds through your stockbroker.

Other Money Market Investments

Besides the negotiable securities offered by the federal government, many business and governmental agencies offer bonds, bills, notes, and other certificates that earn high rates of interest. Depending on the type of security, there may be exemption from federal and state income taxes. The investment period can vary from as little as one day to more than twenty years. The risk varies with market conditions and the issuing organization.

Venture Capital Investment

When you make a loan to, or become a partner with, your brother Charlie, or your nephew Jake, in his rocket ship company, you become a venture capitalist. You could get rich or, more likely, you could lose your investment. Eighty percent of all new business ventures fail within three years. No matter how good it looks on paper, or how good it may sound to be the first person on Mars, this is high-risk stuff. This is not to say you shouldn't do it—many people have made their fortunes this way (although no one yet has made it to Mars). Only, don't invest your security money. If you have extra money and you like to gamble, give Jake a whirl.

Precious Metals

A lot of people thought it was pretty ridiculous to buy gold at $150 per ounce. I don't think we need to say more about that. Same for silver and platinum. The next precious metal may be copper. If you like the feel of hard stuff, this may be your forte.

Art, Antiques, and Collectibles

In periods of high inflation, art, coins, stamps, antique automobiles, and such take on a lot more attraction than cash, so the demand and prices soar.

Even old bottle caps become valuable. But you better know what you're doing. Fancies change, and your collection of 1,476 beer cans from all over the world may turn out to be worth just the aluminum.

Others

For some fine esoterica, you can indulge your farmer fantasies by getting into the commodities market. Join a group that leases equipment. Buy some livestock and become a breeder. Buy and lease commercial property. Be part of a combine that drills for oil. But, before you imagine yourself as a sheik, learn what it's all about. These are all tricky areas. Some afford tax shelters, but you'll want real expertise to back up your decisions.

Retirement Investments

One of the best investments you can make is in a tax-free retirement plan. (This is not a purely altruistic move on the part of your elected legislators— if you can pay some of your own way, there won't be as much pressure on Social Security). If you are employed or self-employed, you are entitled to set aside a portion of your pretax income in an investment plan. The money goes directly into the plan, tax-free, to accumulate interest and/or appreciation until you are ready to retire. When you draw money out, then you pay taxes, presumably at a lower rate. The only hitch is that this money is locked in until a specified retirement age, and you can't touch it without severe penalty.

The most common plan is your company's pension program. There are variations galore, but essentially they place some of your money, and perhaps add some of their own, into a fund that is administered for the greatest possible growth. In the past, there has been some mismanagement and even failure of these plans, but recent legislation makes company programs relatively safe. In some cases, you can even move to a new company and have your investment in the program move with you.

If your company does not have a program of its own, or if you would prefer designing your own program, you can open an IRA (Individual Retirement Account). This allows you to select an investment program, put in a specified amount each year (this varies, so check for the current maximum) and build a retirement nest egg.

If you're in business for yourself, the Keogh plan allows you to set aside money for your retirement. For beginners, your friendly banker or savings and loan officer can give you details about IRA and Keogh.

PITFALLS AND PRATFALLS

Since death records are published in the daily papers and probate is open to the public, it is very difficult to retain your privacy. You will certainly receive mail and phone offers from real estate firms and brokerage firms. Some investment firms will offer you immediate cash for your inheritance so you won't have to wait until probate is closed. The catch is, they'll take 20 percent or more of the estate as a fee. Something for nothing continues to be rare.

This may sound like unneeded advice, but when you're feeling lonely, you become a possible mark for all sorts of con artists. It's important to maintain an outgoing, trusting view of the world if you are to grow as a person. But you can be a little protective of yourself as well. Don't make precipitous decisions about money. Don't discuss your financial affairs with strangers. Don't give large sums of cash to anyone, for any reason, without the agreement of a trusted adviser. Be alert to fraud in any money scheme. Very few, if any, deals that require immediate action are legal. If there is no problem, time for investigation will not be denied you.

ESTATE PLANNING

This might be titled "What are you going to do about your assets after you're gone?" Whatever you own is going to go through the same process as whatever you inherited from your husband. If you had a miserable time with lawyers, accountants, and the probate process, you can be sure your heirs will have the same. Well, maybe. You might take all that you learned in the process and juggle things around so your kids or your favorite charity can get your wealth more intact, and with greater ease. That's known as estate planning.

An estate is your total worth—home, insurance, savings accounts, personal property, stocks and bonds, pension plans, etc. Estate planning is for everyone, not just the wealthy. It involves safely maximizing income during your lifetime, and distribution of your assets after your death with the least taxation.

You could do something very simple like making a good will that spells out *exactly* what you want so that a judge doesn't have to guess or use his own initiative. You might go further and consider how to avoid probate on all, or part, of your estate, thereby saving your heirs legal and accounting fees, as well as the distress of dealing with the judicial system. You might go further yet and have someone appointed as trustee so the money gets doled out in stages exactly the way you want.

What you'll want to do depends on your own circumstances and needs:

- If you have a lot of money to worry about passing on, you'll want to surround yourself with a team of experts (attorney, accountant, and insurance person) and become expert yourself, fast.
- If you don't trust your heirs, you'll want to set up a trust fund that will retain your control, from whatever place in the universe that you'll be taking up residence.

- If you've minor children to be concerned about, you'll want to be sure there's proper guardianship.
- If you really don't care about what happens after you're gone, you'll want to make plans to use up all your money while you're here.

Since any of the choices need some kind of knowledge, you'll want to pursue your particular requirements in depth. If you're expecting to find all the answers in the paragraphs that follow, you're in for a big disappointment. As usual, we'll throw out some thought starters, guaranteed to add to your confusion, which we hope will drive you into reading from the experts and finally becoming your own guru. Blessed are the teachers who create in their students a thirst for knowledge that causes them to surpass the teachers.

- For sure, you'll want to create a comprehensive will and put it in a place where it can be readily found.
- If you have specific amounts of money that you want to leave someone, for example, $10,000 for your granddaughter's education, you can set up a savings account "in trust for." You can collect the interest (and pay taxes on it) and the principal will pass to her on your death without going through probate.
- You can consider putting some of your assets in "joint tenancy." When you die, the other person simply takes over without the necessity of probate.
- You can set up a testamentary trust—one that takes effect after you die. You direct a trustee to pass the assets along in a manner you specify. This becomes part of your will and goes through probate.
- A revocable living trust (inter vivos) has some interesting possibilities. You retain control during your lifetime, with specific instructions about disposition of your estate upon your death. In case you are incapacitated, the trustee will see that your bills are paid and your affairs are handled. This eliminates a great concern of many older women—that they will be a burden on their children. Living trusts can also be made irrevocable. There are some tax advantages, but these are far overshadowed by the flexibility of a revocable trust. The living trust does not go through probate.

From here on it get's *really* complex, so you are well advised to consult the trust department of your friendly bank, and your attorney, provided you have selected him with care (see Chapter 3) and have agreed on a fee for his advice. While you can't take it with you, it would be nice if you could leave it in the hands of your loved ones, rather than the legal profession or the government. Only the well-informed avoid the high cost of dying.

INFLATION

It appears that a high rate of inflation will continue to be a reality of life in the United States. Financial planning that does not consider this misses the mark completely. In rough figures, with inflation at 4 percent a year, your living costs will increase about 50 percent in ten years and over 100 percent in twenty years. At an inflation rate of 9 percent, your costs will increase by 50 percent in five years, more than double in ten years, and be five times higher in twenty years. We have had much higher inflation rates, so you can imagine what that does to your planning.

Increasing your income to keep up with inflation is not the whole answer because your tax bite increases with it, leaving you further behind. It is very difficult to get a return on your investment that covers both inflation and increased taxes. What to do? There's no clear answer. Only be mindful that your nest egg won't purchase much downstream.

One possible way out is in continuing to be a part of the work force. Earnings will at least partially keep up with inflation. This gives further credence to our advice that having an active career for as long as you can maintain it promises both inner and outer satisfaction.

Another course of action is to continue to reduce your external needs. Drop off unneeded purchases, join in sharing living expenses with others. Become a part of the voluntary simplicity movement, and take joy in simple pursuits. Learn to repair your own possessions and living quarters. Look inward and to relationships for satisfaction, instead of relying on material goods. True happiness is available at the most simple level. A big order, but if you can make it, you'll have an existence that reaches all the way to the heavens, while your feet are planted firmly on the earth.

ADDITIONAL INFORMATION

Financial Planning

Books

Thomas Porter and Durwood Alkire. *Wealth: How to Achieve It!* Prentice-Hall, 1979. A comprehensive, personal planning book with tips on how to attain the maximum gain from your income, assets and efforts.

J. K. Lasser. *J. K. Lasser's Complete Guide to Financial Planning for Your Family.* Simon and Schuster, 1979. How to get the most for your money with tips on planning a budget, securing a loan, applying for and protecting your credit rating, investing wisely and much more.

Jane Bryant Quinn. *Everyone's Money Book.* Delecorte Press, 1979. Covers budgeting, investing, savings, home buying, life insurance. A total money source book. Well-organized, easy reading.

Donald Moffitt. *Your Money Matters.* Dow Jones, 1979. Solid financial planning advice from the pages of the *Wall Street Journal.*

Gustave and Alice Simons. *Money and Women.* Popular Library, 1979. A how-to book for the financially unsophisticated woman with the aim of helping her become an active participant in her financial affairs. Information on earning, spending, investing, and protecting your money.

Mary Rogers and Nancy Joyce. *Women and Money.* McGraw-Hill, 1978. Basic, no-nonsense, woman-to-woman approach to financial planning. Practical, easy to read coverage of money management with tips and suggestions for women who are taking responsibility for their financial life.

Pamphlets

You and Your Money: A Financial Handbook for Women, available from Merrill Lynch Service Center, P.O. Box 6514, Chicago, Illinois 60680.

AIM's Guide to Financial Security, available free from AIM/AARP 1909 K Street N.W., Washington, D.C. 20049. Also, *Your Retirement Money Guide,* available from the same source, provides helpful information for the older person.

Investments

Books

Andrew Tobias. *The Only Investment Guide You'll Ever Need.* Bantam Books, 1979. An irreverent but rational guide. An easy way to start your learning process—its "light" touch is only a cover for the "heavy" material which is covered well.

Fred E. Case. *Investing in Real Estate.* Prentice-Hall, 1978. Sound facts and helpful tips to lead you through the maze of purchasing income-producing property. Pros and cons of buying new or old buildings, importance of location and condition, tax issues and how to combine leverage and tax savings to maximize earnings are detailed in easy to understand terms.

John Peterson. *Investing for Pleasure and Profit.* Dow Jones, 1979. Information on investment opportunities in art and family heirlooms, jewelry, automobiles, stamps and coins, antique furniture, and many more.

Judith McQuown. *Tax Shelters That Work.* McGraw-Hill, 1979. A wide variety of tax shelters, conservative and high risk, for the middle-income person.

Robert Irwin. *How to Buy and Sell Real Estate for Financial Security.* McGraw-Hill, 1979. Advice on how to choose property, what to fix up, how to handle a buyer, seller, or broker, plus a general overview of real estate finances and market conditions.

Richard Haft. *Investing in Securities.* Prentice-Hall, 1975. How to make it in the market and cope with inflation. Explanation of how the market works, what brokers have to offer, economic indicators, mutual funds, and much more.

General Information

For additional information on securities investments refer back to Chapter 8, the section on the stockbroker and the additional information at the end of that chapter.

Estate Planning

Books

John J. Gargan. *The Complete Guide to Estate Planning.* Prentice-Hall, 1980. For the layperson. Shows you how to establish, document, and value your estate and how to determine specific goals for it. Estate building strategies such as real estate investments and Keogh plans are described.

Arnold D. Kahn. *Family Security Through Estate Planning: The Seven Basic Estate Plans.* McGraw-Hill, 1980. Clearly answers the most frequently asked questions about wills, trusts, estate and gift taxes, and life insurance.

Robert Brosterman. *The Complete Estate Planning Guide.* Mentor Books, 1977. Understandable, nontechnical guide to all aspects of modern estate planning. Excellent coverage on investments, living trusts, and choosing your estate managers with an eye to safeguarding your financial security.

Peter E. Lippett. *Estate Planning: What Anyone Who Owns Anything Must Know.* Prentice-Hall, 1979. Everything you need to know to preserve your estate. Facts about property ownership, wills, probate, trusts, taxes, life insurance, and how to avoid common mistakes and make the right decisions in directing your own estate.

Charles F. Hemphill and Phyliss D. Hemphill. *Wills and Trusts: A Legal and Financial Handbook for Everyone.* Prentice-Hall, 1979. In nonlegal language, explains the need for a will and what it should contain. How to avoid inheritance taxes through trust arrangements, how to build and conserve your property and keep asset erosion to a minimum.

Life Planning

In designing this Life Planning program we have drawn on our own experiences and those of others. But, primarily, we have used the work of Arthur J. Shedlin, organizational consultant, retired professor, and career officer for the Graduate School of Management at UCLA. Dear friend that he is, he gave us his complete **Life Planning Program for Individual Use,** *developed over many years of experience. Most of the material in this chapter is taken directly from Art Shedlin's work.*

Please read these instructions before you proceed. This chapter is designed to assist you in taking a deep look at yourself. Even though at the conscious level you may want to look, your mind has a way of withholding data that may be helpful. To get the most out of the program, we suggest you follow this procedure:

- Read through the entire chapter.
- Do *not* do the exercises at this point.
- Read the balance of the book, then put it aside and allow *at least two weeks* to elapse before you start the exercises.

When you start, turn to page 142, the beginning of the first exercise. Work through all the exercises as directed.

One moment you are half of a team, part of a shared existence, clear about what you will do this day, next week, next month. The years ahead may be planned or not planned, but you have an image of how they will be, and always there are the two of you. In the next moment you are alone, a single existence, wondering what this day will be like, feeling foggy about next week, next month, and totally at sea about the years ahead. The sense of security in your life is gone, and now you must learn how to live and to be in a totally new way.

Throughout the book, we have been suggesting ways to think about the new you that is coming into being. Now it is time to actively become part of the process. What follows is a personal workshop—a journey through your past life and a deep look at where you are now—all designed to chart your path into the future.

Most people just move through life never really understanding who they are or what they want to do. An unknowing, unplanned life can result in being tossed around by whatever wind blows and never really having control of your life, or living a life that was planned for you by someone else and that never fits who *you* really are.

We're not suggesting that you minutely plan the process of your life for, as you know too clearly, changes occur that are outside your control. But, to know the essential you, to understand your strengths and weaknesses, to acknowledge your value and values, all leads to direction in your life and the excitement that comes with facing, even welcoming, change.

There are two ways to approach this life-planning workshop. You can do it with a partner (consultant) or by yourself. If it is at all possible, *we urge you to work with someone else.* Perhaps you have a close friend or family member with whom you can share freely. Another good place to find a consultant is in your support group. (See Chapter 18.) Your partner might like to participate in the workshop by doing the exercises also, and then you can share the data you have produced. Sharing always multiplies the learning process, but your partner needs to be someone with whom you can be completely open or you will find yourself censoring the information.

If it is difficult to find a partner or if you will be inhibited by sharing your work, then do the exercises by yourself and spend additional time going over the results. In order to get the important knowledge you seek, you should plan on spending about fifteen to twenty hours on this project. (It takes longer when you talk things over with a consultant, but it's beneficial. We found in working with many women that they see things more clearly when they share with another.) Work in three- to four-hour stretches. Shorter periods are usually not fruitful. Stop when you feel tired or overloaded with information.

A PERSONAL WORKSHOP OVERVIEW

At some deep level, we are all repeaters of behavior. That is, much of how we act now is learned in early childhood. If we wish to break free and become truly autonomous or at least have some perspective on how we got to where we are, it is important to have some insight into our past. We will dwell briefly on the past, but the major thrust of this experience is on the right-now and the what's-to-come.

Since the workshop evolves in seven stages, or projects, done in sequence, it is necessary to carry through the projects one at a time without looking ahead to those that follow. The idea is to bring out pertinent data about yourself, step by step, slowly, which can then be used in thinking about and working on the succeeding stages. In short, it is an organic whole.

Now, if you assume that your life line looks like this, with X representing the present, _____X_____ then from the standpoint of time, the seven stages of the workshop can be thought of in this way:

1. Self-image—A look at yourself in the formative years   X
2. Selective Life Inventory—A brief review of the past and present in key areas of your life.   _____X
3. Who am I?—Ten statements about who you are—right now, at this moment.   X
4. This is where I am!—An assessment of your present life situation.   X
5. My eulogy—A "do-it-yourself" memorial service.   _____X_____
6. Future Life Inventory—How you would like life to be five or six years from now.   X_____
7. The next two years—What will you have to do in the next two years or so to realize your Future Life Inventory?   X_____

Each stage of the workshop has the same rhythm—individual work first, then, if possible, sharing, discussion, and exploration with another person. Since each stage builds on the previous ones, you'll naturally accumulate more and more organized self-information. It will be apparent that there is no element of being tested or of being right or wrong. The information you bring together is data about yourself and designed to be helpful in bringing about greater self-insight and understanding. You'll get the most from the experience if you are open to all the thoughts, feelings, attitudes, and opinions that come out.

Before you go on to the meat of the program, two things: (1) Remember to carry through the seven stages of the workshop, one at a time, without looking ahead to those that follow. (2) Read the entire instructions for each stage before beginning to work on it. If necessary, think through the instructions so that you know you are following the indicated pathway. This is important because it enlivens the information gathering and enriches the experience.

If you're working with a consultant, try your best to find one whose basic way of being in the world would make it easy for her/him to behave in the ways suggested below. *Here are some guidelines your consultant should read:*

The person you're helping is a seeker, otherwise she would not be doing the program. The central question becomes, how can you best help someone who is reflecting deeply about herself?

Perhaps the best guide is to be fully with her, helping her in every way you can to explore herself as profoundly as possible. As you do this, look inside yourself for your own clues and listen to the music of your responsive feelings. Follow your intuition to produce support when it seems right, and ask questions when you think they will help. If it seems what she needs, confront her when she appears to be wandering in a flower-filled meadow rather than plowing among the thorny juniper bushes of reality.

There are some good hints for doing these things most effectively. Listen with all the equipment you've got—your ears and eyes, your body, and your feelings. This way you can get more fully in tune with her. As you know, sometimes people smile when they're being their most aggressive, appear calm and controlled when they're all torn up inside. If you listen with your whole body, you can respond to much more of what's going on in the other person—her words, feelings, set of body, face and gestures, the contradictions and masks, the directness, the joy, and the unsaid things. This way, you can get nearer to the inside of her, responding with your whole self to whatever is going on. Obviously, this is an intense effort, but it is also intensely rewarding.

How well we all remember the good feeling when someone really listened to us!

This kind of attention is based on love and caring, both for another and for yourself. So, take care of yourself, too.

The key word for a consultant in this project is love. Sometimes tender love—holding tightly someone who is wrestling with the tragic sense of her life. Sometimes tough love—staying away from someone who is wrestling with the tragic sense of her life. Tender—letting her cry it out. Tough—making her stop crying and face what she's crying about. Tender—being with her when she is losing control of her feelings. Tough—pushing her vigorously when she is too tightly controlled. We have great faith that you'll know just when to give tender or tough love, or an alternation of both within minutes.

One final thought: after each exercise and discussion it's a good idea to sit quietly for a few moments in order to make sure there aren't some tag ends of feelings that need to come through. Then take time for a little solitude, thinking through what's been going on, before continuing to the next stage.

Ready now? Let's begin.

PERSONAL WORKSHOP PROCEDURES

1. **Self-image**

    This exercise is a journey into your past—the thoughts, feelings, events, relationships, themes, and dreams that help to form who you are now.

    Begin by finding a comfortable seat in a darkened area, with no distracting sounds. If you do deep relaxation exercises, go into a fully relaxed state. If you've not worked previously on relaxation techniques, simply settle into the chair, or lie down, and let yourself progressively relax each set of muscles in your body. Eyes closed. Just let go, relaxing deeper and deeper.

    Once fully relaxed, imagine in your mind's eye a movie screen or video screen. Inside your head you have a tape or film of your life. Run the tape backwards to your early childhood, the first thing you can remember. Then move the tape forward to your first experience in school. What were you like? See your parents, your family. You can stop the tape anytime you like, for a spot check—to focus in on an event or person in your life. Always notice how the event or person influenced you.

    Then run the tape ahead a bit at a time, watching the major people and events, right on up to age twenty or so. Take your time and get a good picture of your early life.

When you've finished with your tape, open your eyes and slowly return to the present. If you're working with a consultant, discuss your life with her/him. If you're working alone, write down some of the impressions from your journey.

2. **Selective Life Inventory**

So far you've looked at your early life. Stage two focuses on a very brief selective inventory of where you have been in the past and where you are now in respect to some key areas of living.

Using a note pad, respond to each of the seven questions below. Don't write an essay. Just write sufficiently detailed notes to be able to discuss the questions fully with your partner or to review them by yourself. Take your time working on these questions, but don't dwell too long on each. About forty-five minutes to an hour should be time enough.

What have been my peak positive experiences?
These have been the most moving, inspiring, exhilarating, greatest times in your life. They have turned you on, made you feel fully alive, given you a sense of being in touch with things greater than yourself. They may have been momentary kinds of experiences (like a few minutes during a very special ski run) or experiences of some duration which have been very positive (like the first few weeks in the life of your first child). Try to list as many as you can.

What things do I do well?
These refer to *activities* that you engage in, or have in the past. Take things you do well at present as your guide, but include things from the past that you still can do well but which you may have abandoned. These need not be activities which you *must* do, but could just as well be seemingly playful things such as dancing, sailing, skiing. This is a difficult job for many of us because we've been taught to be overly modest, thus often stressing what we do *not* do well. Make your list as comprehensive as possible.

What are my major personal strengths?
These are personal characteristics, abilities, traits of character, states of being and feeling, and aspects of yourself which you value highly. Naturally, these are very personal judgments about your strengths— some people may value aggressiveness, while others might list that same trait as a personal weakness. If you think that being a warm person is a strength, then list it. If you can organize things well and see this as a valued trait, include that. If you're very generous and feel that this is good for you and others around you, list it. You may even find yourself listing that same trait later under personal weaknesses if you feel that you are *so* generous that people take advantage of you because of it.

What have been my key failure experiences?
This list should be a short one—first because we're only talking about *important* failures, and second because we're listing as failures only those things that we have wanted very much, tried hard to achieve, and failed to get. Don't include as failures regret or remorse that you didn't do something which later you felt you should have done.

What are my major personal weaknesses?
This category is in the same vein as the one above on personal strengths, only here it is tuned in to weakness rather than strength.

What have been my major goals in the past?
What goals and objectives have given you motive, power, the energy, the drive to keep going? Goals may include social and personal goals, broad life goals, work goals, achievement goals, and so on.

If I had a magic wand that would let me make two changes in myself at this very moment, what changes would I want?

If you're doing the exercises by yourself, go over your notes, then put them away for a few days before you go back over them again. If you're working with a consultant, it's time for a full discussion. Read aloud from your notes on the first question and expand them as the dialogue goes on. What your consultant says may strike a chord or remind you of something you have left out. If so, add to your list as the talk goes on. Then, go to the second question following the same procedure until you have covered all seven. Since there is really no way to estimate the time necessary for these discussions, just go along at the rate that seems comfortable to you.

3. **Who Am I?**

Stages 3 and 4 are concerned with the present—what's going on with you right now. When the data from these are added to what you have retrieved about yourself in the first two projects, you'll be ready to think about the years ahead from a more solid base. This will make it much easier to define future goals with confidence and direction.

For this project, you need a pen or pencil and ten small slips of paper or 3″ × 5″ cards. What is called for here are ten different answers, one on each sheet, to the question, "Who Am I?" They can be a single word, a phrase—at most, a sentence. They can be aspects of self (I'm gentle), roles (a daughter), attributes of self (a dreamer), traits (weak), characteristics (steady), states of feeling (confused), states of being (secure), or (as is usual) some of each. For best results, when you start, be as spontaneous as possible, write your answers down as fast as you can—a few minutes is all you need. When you have finished, spread the slips before you so that you can see all of them. Put a #10 on the one that seems least important to you. Then look through them again, putting a #9 on the next least central to you. Continue on until you come to #1. This is the core of who you are, the aspect of you that seems most important. Take the slips and arrange them numerically in a pile with #1 on top and #10 at the bottom. Read them through once more, making sure the order you have selected is your final choice.

The way of exploring which works best is for you (using your ten answers and any notes as a memory prod) to go through your answers with your partner. You may come upon some surprises—things you left out, a question or two about the ranking, some revealing deep emotional responses, perhaps an unexpected sense of self-affirmation, a feeling of loss, etc. Go slowly, step by step, and allow plenty of time for good give and take in the discussion. Afterwards, take some time alone to reflect before going ahead to stage four. If you're not using a partner, the reflection time will serve as a review.

4. ***This Is Where I Am!***

After exploring *who* you are, now it's time to make a statement of *where* you are, in the form of a prose poem which expresses where you are in life *right now*.

Naturally, we all have feelings, images, thoughts, symbols, and internal monologues going on, regardless of what we may be doing in our external moment-to-moment world. These internal happenings are often rich and colorful in metaphor, simile, and imagery, but we usually retain this richness for ourselves and speak or write in everyday, all-too-functional language. So don't worry about rhyme or being poetic—just let it flow from inside. This is not a literary exercise, but an expressive one.

Most of us flinch when poetry is brought up, saying it's for creative writers, not for people like us. We've found that most people not only can write poems, but that most of them are beautiful expressions of being. The easiest poem to write is one about yourself, especially if you are expressing where you are and your feelings about where you are. The new poetry (even among the established poets) stresses feelings and emotions, thoughts and images, rather than being concerned with form, meter, or structure.

Find a comfortable spot, think deeply about yourself, your relationships, your joys and sorrows, feelings and emotions, hopes and aspirations—about where you are, right now, as of this day, in life's turnings—and begin writing. Take your time with it. Usually this project takes about an hour or so. When you have finished, make sure it is legible, or write it over legibly so that it will be easy for your partner to read it aloud to you. It's best for someone else to read it aloud so you can receive it coming back to you, rather than being bothered with the mechanics of reading. There is a real advantage in *listening* to what you have said about where you are. The other person should look the poem over first to get the full sense of it so that it can be read aloud smoothly and with feeling. You can do this yourself by using a tape recorder.

After you have heard your poem read back to you, respond to it with a monologue for a few minutes, just saying aloud without interruption the thoughts and feelings which occur to you. Then start a dialogue with your partner, giving him/her plenty of time to respond. It would be helpful if he/she commented not only on the poem but also to its connectedness with all your other previous data. Don't skimp on discussion time—it can be very provocative and powerful.

5. **Your Eulogy and Epitaph**

How long has it been since you've let yourself have a full-winged-spreading fantasy of life, flying out to the very end? If you've done this recently, or ever, you're among the very few. It seems to be too painful, too frightening a venture for most—yet it can be an exciting and freeing experience—leading you on to greater growth and personal productivity. So, take some time to reflect quietly about yourself, dream a bit, start some wishful fantasies going, and write a eulogy. Make it a eulogy which might be said of you at a service by a long-time, close friend who had known you very well. Make it a eulogy that you would like or wish to have and which also has the possibility of being realized by the end of your life.

It's necessary to stretch your imagination to think of a future some years hence so that the eulogy is not one which might be written as of next week or next year. At the end of the eulogy, write an epitaph, a one-liner. One which was written by a life-long hypochondriac read: "See, I *told* you I was sick!"

Your eulogy should cover your whole life—what's happened up to now and what you hope might occur from now on until your inevitable death. Here you can use your creativity to make your own predictions about the future. Why *not* make your own? If your experience has been in any way like most, other people close to you have been doing it *for* you since you've been a kid. "If you keep on the way you're going, you'll be a genius in mathematics," "You'll get shafted if you trust people too much," "If you don't finish school you'll never make it," "You should be a writer (businessman, engineer)," "Finally you've chosen the right career," "You've got such great potential as a _____, why don't you *use* it," and so on and on.

Women in our workshops have found the writing of their eulogy to be an unusual, exciting, and richly rewarding experience. It is a low-key way of making promises to yourself, partly in jest, partly serious, and it brings up all sorts of new ways of thinking about the years ahead.

After you've finished, lie down and have your partner read your eulogy aloud to you, or play back a tape that you have made. With your eyes closed, listen carefully to what you have written about yourself. Reflect aloud for a few minutes about your feelings on hearing your eulogy. Since the pay-off years are the ones ahead, it seems right to spend the bulk of your time discussing what you have written in the eulogy about them, rather than about the past. After the discussion, take a good long solitary break.

6. ***Future Life Inventory***

Before starting on this project, go back over all the data you have brought out up to now. You'll find it stimulating and revealing and truly helpful in your work on the future life inventory. As you review the information you have gathered, you will probably realize there are certain definite themes running throughout all the different parts of the workshop. You can use all this information and your feelings and thoughts about it to good advantage in responding to the inventory.

The idea here is to project yourself five or six years into the future and respond to the questions as if you were already there. Don't write an essay, but make enough notes to be able to explore your responses fully with your consultant. Think deeply about these questions. Take your time responding to them. You should be able to complete the project in an hour or a bit longer.

What areas of my life and circumstances would I like to have changed or improved?

What goals or objectives would I like to have realized?

What particular strengths would I like to have developed more fully?

What personal characteristics that I have had in the past would I like to be rid of?

If I were told that I had twelve months to live and that my vitality would remain as it is now until my death, how would I live those twelve months?

The best way to discuss this inventory is for you to read and verbally expand on your notes on the first question, allowing plenty of time for give and take. After you have explored the first question, go on with the other questions, one by one, using the same procedure for each of them. Without a consultant, you can follow the same procedure, only writing your expanded notes.

7. **The Next Two Years**

During the program thus far, you have ranged all over the time scale of your life by fantasies, inventories, and poems. You've provided your own data and discussed it with someone or reviewed it. The result of all this is that you now have an organized body of material about your life, thoughtfully and creatively produced. For most of you, this has been a first—you've never written it down, pulled as much together, nor discussed or reviewed it as exhaustively.

Now comes the pay-off time. How can you make use of this information in the most realistic way? Think in terms of the next two years.

This last project crisply limits you by posing only a few crucial questions. In the future life inventory, you listed what you would like to see happen in your life within the next five or six years. Re-read this carefully. Now respond to the questions below by making careful and full notes. Take your time about it, because in a way you'll be making promises to yourself about your behavior and actions in the near future.

What particular activities and/or projects will I have to undertake over the next two years or so in order to bring about the changes I want in the next five or six years?

How will I have to change or grow in order to realize these future goals?

Who will I have to take into account in making these changes? And why must I take them into consideration?

Who can help me most in bringing about these changes? (Make this list as comprehensive as you can. You can pare it down later.)

The discussion following this last inventory is a crucial one. Everyone needs help from others in considering the possible steps he can reasonably take. So, even if you haven't been using a consultant up to now, call in a friend or relative. What is needed here is not only encouragement and support, but also critical assessment, new ideas, elaboration of alternatives, suggestions, and potential sources of assistance. The best way to approach this is to go through your whole list of responses to the questions while your consultant listens, responds, questions, assesses possibilities, makes suggestions, shares his or her knowledge of what sources (people, institutions, books, etc.) might be helpful (either directly or as "starters") to you in what you want to do. While the discussion goes on, you should be taking notes, questioning your own assessments, elaborating your ideas, revising estimates, testing limits, and so on.

Now you're at an end and at a beginning. The information-gathering, the soul-searching, the promises to yourself are all behind you for the present. Now, it's time for action in the theater-in-the-round of life. What's the best way for you to continue the momentum you've got? How can you transform your decisions into a realistic program of activities? How can you bring your resources to bear on the next steps you're going to take?

You probably have the best answers within yourself. You know your own ways of doing or not doing, of tackling life head-on or procrastinating. Some people have found that making a contract with themselves has a positive effect on the ordering of their time and activity—but it must be a workable contract for putting one foot in front of the other, first at a walking pace, and only later at a dead run. If you do make such a contract, perhaps it would be more binding if you shared it with your consultant and agreed on some checkpoints. Other people have found that writing a journal for a few months keeps things alive and moving and serves as a place for recording successes and difficulties. You probably know the most effective way, for you, of keeping the cause of change alive.

You've made a long journey into yourself and your world. Appreciate what you've done.

Career Planning

Let's look at some dramatic statistics:

- Eighty-five percent of the women in the U.S. will spend the last years of their lives alone.
- With the average life span for women now at seventy-four and with child-rearing typically over by age thirty-seven, half of a woman's life is free of the tasks usually ascribed to women—homemaking, childbearing and child raising.
- Sixty percent of women with school-age children are working, and the rate is constantly increasing.
- While it's true that 80 percent of the female work force hold traditional jobs, 20 percent are currently breaking the barriers, and that number, too, increases each year.

In our workshops, we've met many women starting their second career (the first is homemaker, wife, mother) at ages forty, fifty, and older. When you consider how important it is not only to provide for yourself but to be part of the life of the community, achieve personal goals and learn new skills, you'll think as we do—a rewarding career outside the home is a key part of every woman's personal growth.

If you're already working, it may be time to reevaluate your career path—to see if there is a real fit between you and the job and if you're getting maximum satisfaction from what you're doing.

If you're going out into the job market for the first time or returning after a long time away, take heart. What was formerly unacceptable is now commonplace. You'll find organizations willing to help and corporations granting you cooperative interviews.

You can do and be anything you want. It takes a modest amount of courage, a reasonable amount of knowledge about the job market, a dollop of inventiveness, and about 480 chewing gum packs of sticktoitiveness.

The first consideration in career planning is how to make your job part of the flow of your life. Many women simply fall into a career by taking an available job and then working their way up in the company. Frequently, this lack of planning leads to the split life we see so often—being one type of person at home and another on the job. Since being two persons in one body is not possible, one of the parts becomes dominant, resulting in an imbalance. Workaholics are an example of imbalance—all work and no play. Women who don't fully enjoy the work they do simply exist on the job and take their pleasures at home—another imbalance.

The trick is to have it all. A fully flowing life is like a mountain stream. As the stream moves on its way, it encounters boulders to go around and over, scarcely disrupting the flow. There are turns to negotiate, movement from dark to sunlight, occasional turbulence. But for the most part, the feeling is calm and the taste is sweet.

Career planning, then, is an extension of life planning. Once you have a general idea about the direction of your life, you can more easily focus on the specific work that fits for you. At the end of the chapter, you'll find exercises that will help you identify your ideal job. But before that, have a look at some current views and new ideas on careers for women.

ENTERING OR REENTERING THE JOB MARKET

For the widow who has never worked, the biggest obstacle in her career path is the undervaluation of her own worth. Typically, homemakers do not see themselves as organizers, administrators, or accountants. Yet the skills needed to operate a home, raise children, and control the family budget are first cousin to many skills required in the world of work.

A good way to begin identifying usable skills is to make a list of everything you do during the day or have done in the past. Then, identify the skills required to do these tasks. For instance, planning a month's meals within a budget for a family requires administrative skills. If you did volunteer fund raising, that requires salesmanship. Designing programs or materials may utilize advertising skills.

Since a traditional résumé with job descriptions and dates won't work for you, try a functional résumé. Check some of the books or resources at the end of the chapter for assistance in preparing a functional résumé. List skills, abilities, and community awards or recognition. Many women have creative abilities such as painting, lettering, or writing that are in demand on the job market. Think positive. Many women are getting and succeeding at their first job late in life.

> Mary W. was the mother of five. At age forty-six, her husband died and left her with three children at home and an estate inadequate to handle her needs. Social Security survivor benefits did not add enough, and she felt that her only choice was to go to work. Among her identifiable skills were a second language, German (part of her family heritage), and typing (learned in her early school days and kept current helping her husband and children).
>
> After a few interviews, Mary accepted a job with a major aerospace manufacturer as secretary to a manager in foreign marketing. One of Mary's other skills that she had not clearly identified was an affinity for people. The company soon recognized this and put her in charge of a typing pool of twenty women.
>
> As a manager, Mary was a natural. The women liked to work for her and she made many innovative changes in departmental procedure. Today, at age fifty, Mary is a respected corporate woman with a substantial salary and many opportunities available to her within the company.

MEN'S JOBS FOR WOMEN

West Point and Annapolis have women cadets. If these last bastions of the macho male are amendable to change, everything is. In every occupation, women are breaking down old barriers, which means that you no longer need to follow traditional callings. That's exciting. If you're willing to go through the learning process and can handle some residual male resistance, you can bring your hidden childhood dream to fruition and even be a fireman (fireperson) if you wish.

One formerly denied area that women are moving into rapidly is repairing equipment. There is good money in plumbing, TV repairs, piano tuning, appliance fixing, telephone repair, furniture repairs, and auto maintenance. There are shortages of skilled people in these fields. Know-how is available in trade schools. This type of work has the advantage of flexible hours and offers real opportunity for self-employment.

The equal employment opportunity laws have forced employers to hire capable women in such fields as engineering, law, business administration, accounting, sales, and many others. Training or retraining in one of these fields can pay off handsomely.

TEMPORARY AGENCY EMPLOYMENT

There are many agencies all over the country that supply employees as vacation or illness replacements to cover overload work or to assist on large projects. It's a type of rescue operation that does not require a long-term commitment on the part of the employer or employee, and is growing in popularity. Depending on your qualifications, you may be able to experience a wide variety of occupations for such diverse organizations as schools, manufacturing companies, banks, accounting firms, law offices, small retail businesses—just about everything.

This is an excellent way to move back into the work force without a commitment to an ongoing job. It is also a good way to test your skills. You can quickly find areas where you need to improve or where your abilities go beyond the scope of the assignment. It is certainly a way of trying a variety of jobs to see which one fits best for you.

Once assigned to a job, you are required to stay on until relieved, but you can make your wishes known in advance as to what you will do and for how long. Usually you can set your own time span between jobs. While temporary agencies offer a great deal of flexibility and accept a wide range of experiences, the pay scale is somewhat low, as the agency takes a percentage of your earnings. Still, this remains a viable reentry option and should be explored.

TIME-SHARING JOBS

This is a new concept that has been tried in major urban centers. It's primary purpose is to provide half-time work for women who have children or who are not willing to take on a full-time commitment. It differs from part-time employment in that two people share one full-time job.

Most often, this type of work is originated by two women who team up. If you are interested in this idea, find someone who has similar skills and with whom you can communicate easily. Then decide on the type of employment you desire and proceed to apply for a single job on a time-sharing basis.

The advantage to you is that you can work out an hourly arrangement with your partner. Since together you are responsible for one job, you must cover the required hours and be able to easily pick up on the flow of each other's work.

The advantage to the employer is that he has people who are working fewer hours so are probably more energetic and creative on the job. When there is an occasional push, both of you could work, so it is like having an experienced relief person on call.

When you consider all the possibilities of time-sharing, it is an exciting concept that could solve many of the problems of working mothers and alleviate the shortage of certain skills. In application, it has met with something less than great enthusiasm, primarily because of computerized payroll procedures and the proliferation of company benefits. What does the company do about hospitalization programs, retirement plans, etc.? How does the computer handle two names for one paycheck? For these reasons, and simply because it's new (which frightens most personnel managers), time-sharing has a long way to go.

If you're excited about the possibilities of time-sharing, one way to get around the negativism is to find a company that will take you on in a consulting capacity. This way, the company has no benefits to pay or tax withholding to consider. You simply set up a partnership with your coworker and have payment made to the partnership. Time-sharing is a really viable consideration for women who have specific skills in short supply and who want to control the hours they work.

Off the subject of time-sharing, but still considering variable hours of work, many companies now offer flex-time. That means, within certain parameters, you may select your work hours as long as they total the required number per week. Flex-time works well where the nature of the work does not require a great deal of interface with other people or attendance at odd-hour meetings. If the selection of hours is important in your job consideration, you might explore companies which have flex-time programs.

CREATE YOUR OWN JOB

Small business ownership is one area of absolute equality. Being your own boss assures you that no one will be assigning you "female work." More women would probably take this direction, but the elusive security of a job is very attractive. We say "elusive" because the reality is that there is no more security in working for a big company than in a business of your own.

A small business can take many forms. It can be in an industry that requires substantial capital investment or one that takes specialized knowledge acquired through long experience or training. There are others, however, that require little or no formal investment and utilize skills many women have acquired through hobbies, volunteer work, or taking care of a home. It is this type of business or "job you create" that is our focus now.

When you set out to create your own job, a number of events occur that are growth producing:

- You have the opportunity to do exactly what you want to do without regard to anyone's input.

Career Planning **155**

- You can select the people with whom you work and interact.
- You have a learning experience, as you design the venture, that is exhilarating and asks you to draw on all your internal and external resources.
- You can make your work self-rewarding so that it exactly fits the person you are.
- You'll experience a sense of accomplishment unlike anything else.

You can decide to have a full-time or part-time venture, set your own hours, even decide how hard you're willing to work, in order to achieve your own goals.

Let's look at some examples of self-created jobs:

- Be a fixit. Repair things around the home, or things that are brought to you—dolls, toys, ceramics, antiques, clocks, furniture, etc.
- Sell things you make—pillows, pottery, rugs, lamps, needlepoint, decorated T-shirts, artificial flowers, jewelry, shell art, candles, greeting cards, food items. You can sell them through friends, house parties, flea markets, swap meets, and even to retail stores. Many big product lines started from an at-home business.
- Try phone services. Wake-up calls, reminder services, dictation service for business persons.
- Become a garage sale expert. Learn how to do it really well. Take things on consignment and sell out of your own garage, or help others to run their sale for a percentage of the profits.
- Start a newsletter. Whatever you're an "expert" in is a good subject for a newsletter. Typewritten copy and quick printing will do. Sell annual subscriptions and watch the list grow.
- Conduct tours through local places of interest. Make contact with the convention bureau and arrange tours for visiting business people and their families.
- Set up a babysitting service. Hire a crew of workers (possibly older people instead of teenagers) and then simply make the arrangements for a percentage of the fees, similar to a nurse's agency.
- Teach classes—dance, yoga, dressmaking, plant arranging, cooking—whatever you do well that others might enjoy learning.

Got the idea? There are possibilities wherever you look—thousands, really, and none require capital or extraordinary expertise.

There are some simple steps you should take to get started:

- Begin by determining exactly what you want to do. Utilize what you've learned in life planning and from the exercises at the end of this chapter to create a job you'd really love doing. Let your friends and relatives be a sounding board. Remember that you're looking for an idea you can develop.

- Contact the U.S. Government Small Business Administration. Ask for SBA Form 115A, Free Management Assistance Publications. Also ask about their free seminars and courses that will help you.

- Create a business plan. Write up the story of your business in a narrative fashion so that anyone reading it will understand exactly what the business is about. Describe a typical day or two in the business. Then outline the equipment and help you'll need. For example, if you chose the babysitting service you would indicate the characteristics of the people you'd employ, how parents would learn about you, pick-up and delivery service, safety precautions, and other elements of your service. Writing about your business will help you to clarify just what it is you're trying to do and the direction you will take.

- Plan how you will market your business. Whatever you do, you need to let others know of the availability of your goods or services. If you belong to clubs or groups, often this is an excellent source of business. Sometimes local classified ads are helpful. Whatever your choice, keep it simple and describe clearly and directly what you have to offer.

- Keep good records. Hopefully, you will need to pay taxes, and having clear records of your income and expenses makes reporting simple. This need not be complicated. The SBA provides forms you can follow.

If you're thinking about starting a really serious small business—a retail store, a manufacturing or service business with employees, there is help available. The Small Business Administration has a congressional mandate to help more women get started as entrepreneurs. In addition to workshops and seminars, they have funds specifically earmarked for helping qualified women start a business. There's also direct managerial assistance and help with securing federal contracts.

Creating your own job is a viable option for every woman. More information about this is covered in another book by Byron Lane, *How to Free Yourself in a Business of Your Own.*

OUT OF THE CLOSET

Even in increasingly egalitarian organizations, women's clothes get more scrutiny than men's. The male engineering genius or the creative art director of a Madison Avenue ad agency may get approval for nonconventional dress, but the woman on the corporate rise will likely not. Women who have made it to the top have some handy clothes hints:

- Don't dress in high fashion. Opt for good quality and timeless styles.
- Watch the woman up the ladder whose clothes look good to you, and then emulate her style.
- Buy less, but buy the best you can afford.
- Select conservative styles—hemlines just below the knee or to midcalf, no matter what the fashion.
- Find a store you like with knowledgeable people, and then ask the fashion adviser to help you find clothes that look dignified, elegant and businesslike.
- The women's "uniform" (like men's suits) is becoming the matched skirt and jacket with a contrasting blouse.
- Avoid sexually alluring clothes. They detract from your credibility.

THE SINGLE WORKING MOTHER

We've worked with single mothers of younger children in many groups. Whether widow or divorcee, the problem is the same—how to be a responsive mother, be effective on the job, and still have some energy left over for one's self.

There are certainly no simple solutions, but many of the women report that they get in the most serious difficulties when they feel guilty about their absence and try to overcompensate with "togetherness" when they're home. Children are amazingly resilient and sharing problems openly and honestly is far preferable to subterfuge and gaming. If you acknowledge your limitations, focus on your strengths, and do what you can, that's the best anyone can expect, including your children. If you tell them they must share in responsibilities while you work, they'll do it and grow in the process. Overprotection is just as destructive to your child as neglect.

It's a good idea to really get in touch with the problems you'll face as a single working mother, and be prepared to behave in ways that will get the results you want. There are good new books (see listing at the end of this chapter), and workshops that focus on this subject. You may find additional help in this area from the chapter *Establishing Your Identity*.

The daytime care of children is the most difficult problem to solve. The need for daycare centers is a growing national issue. Private centers are expensive and many do little more than babysit. Public facilities are confined to the most needy, so the working mother on a modest salary is caught in the middle. During the depression and World War II, getting women into jobs was important, and daycare centers were federally supported. In the absence of a national emergency, attention has been focused away from daycare. NOW (National Organization for Women) is working on this issue and should have your support.

If this is a problem for you, or if you have some energy to put into a good cause, consider starting a collective childcare center—widows banding together, using members as staff. Or, if you're with a large organization, urge them to form a childcare center on company grounds. Where it's been tried, company sponsored daycare has been immensely successful. Children can be visited at lunchbreak and accompany mom to and from work. Mother is available in an emergency, and all of the mothers have a common goal and energy that is supportive of the center. The company gets appreciative, worry-free workers and everybody wins.

JOB FINDING AND GETTING TIPS

In our career planning program we've noted that often the experienced job hunter has little advantage over the novice, because they follow traditional methods of finding a job—answering classified ads and using employment agencies. When they've located an opening, they either fail the interview or take a position at a salary less than they deserve. The professionals at successful job seeking know there are certain innovative methods that, coupled with determination, produce high-paying, rewarding positions.

If you want the perfect job, you'll need to do your homework. Begin by knowing exactly what you're looking for. That's tough. It requires knowing yourself, knowing the type of work that fits your skills, and knowing the companies that can use you. You can get to know yourself better through completing the Life Planning Workshop in the previous chapter, doing the Career Planning exercises at the end of this chapter, and by getting help and feedback through your support system (see Chapter 18). Then, try some of these ideas:

Referrals

Use the referral technique. Everyone knows someone who knows someone. Make a list of friends, family, acquaintances, people who serve you (your beautician, apartment manager), anyone who can help you get an interview. The person you want to reach is a top-level business executive or head of an organization—someone whose name or position commands attention. You'll be surprised how accessible these people are and how many of them want to help.

Have a meeting arranged for you. When you get there, *do not* ask for a job (although before you leave, if you've done well, you might be offered one). Instead, ask for advice. Tell Mr. (Ms.) Big about yourself and the type of work you want. Ask him if he knows of someone who might have a position available, or who might want someone like yourself to create a new position in the company. If he says yes, ask if he would mind calling and recommending you for an interview. If he does call, you're on your way to success.

Notice what's happening. Your next interview is going to be through a referral by Mr. Big. The person you're meeting is predisposed to you and is in a position to make decisions. That's the best anyone can ask for on a job interview. If the second Mr. Big doesn't have anything for you, ask if he knows someone who does—then repeat the process. Enough referrals and you're bound to land *your* job.

Résumés

Try not to use a résumé. That may sound unusual, but the traditional résumé reveals not only helpful information, but information that can hurt you. If you must use one, try a functional résumé without dates, location, etc.

Try a letter campaign on your own. Use reference books in the library (the research librarian can be your best helper) to help you locate companies you might be interested in working for. Prepare a letter telling about the job you're seeking. Enclose a qualifications summary (all the things that make you qualified for the job). Direct your letter to someone high up in the company. You can find their names through published listings. (Your librarian can be a big help here too.) Mail out as many as you can, a few each day. People who have done this well report amazing results. Sometimes they reach a company just as they're about to start a search for someone to fill a new job. Sometimes they start a company thinking about a new position. Always they're out of the rat race of applying for an announced position.

Interviewing

Here are some thoughts on interview conduct that many of our seminar attendees have found helpful:

- Do your homework. Know as much as you can about the company before you go. If it's a listed company, get an annual report through any stockbroker. If it's a private company, get information from suppliers, customers, employees. If possible, get background information on the interviewer.
- Know your objectives in advance.
- Anticipate objections. Be prepared to answer them.
- Get a friend to role-play the interview with you. Let your friend be the interviewer in a simulation of the actual event. Have him ask questions you think might be presented, then work out answers that are effective.

Getting the Right Salary

Never reveal your present salary or salary history. This is a tough one to do but, short of being insolent, withhold this information. Revealing salary rarely can help you, but it provides the interviewer with ways of limiting possibilities. If you've been following our advice, your primary interest is in finding the right job for you, then making the salary fit. You can afford to go through an entire interview without mentioning salary. If you're interested in the job and they're interested in you, salary will come up naturally in the conversation.

Until you're offered the job, never get into a prolonged salary discussion. Just listen to whatever is said and file the information in your head. When the job is offered to you, you're in a position to negotiate salary. Most people don't negotiate. They just say yes to the first offer. That's a big mistake. You can always take the proffered amount, but you'll never know how much more you can get until you try.

One of the most effective ways we've seen to start a salary discussion goes like this:

Interviewee: How much does the job pay?
Interviewer: Mentions a figure usually within a range (for example, $18,000 to $20,000).
Interviewee: Only $20,000? (Or, whatever the *top* figure the interviewer mentioned.) Oh! (Interviewee then casts his eyes downward and does not say another word until the interviewer speaks again.)

The usual response to this ploy is a more complete explanation of the figures. The interviewer has already said he wants you, so he is now understanding from your comment and downcast gaze that you are disappointed, and it's up to him to talk. Often the result of such a beginning is that the interviewer will attempt to up the offer. The very least this will get you is the highest figure for the job category.

WHERE TO FIND HELP

Now that you have some eye-opening tips, you'll want to pursue these and other techniques in greater depth.

- Consult the many good books and periodicals listed at the end of the chapter.
- Check the extension division of local universities or colleges for courses in career planning and job finding.

- Most states have career-planning agencies. Many have specific programs that deal with women entering or reentering the job market. Contact the *Business and Professional Women's Foundation,* 2012 Massachusetts Avenue, N.W., Washington, D.C. 20036 for information about "Displaced Homemaker" services in your community. "Displaced Homemakers" is the new-age term for housewives entering the job market.
- Watch your local newspapers for ads or stories about women's events. In larger urban areas even department stores are offering career-oriented programs for women.
- Check local offices of NOW for career seminars.
- The local YWCA usually offers a variety of women's career programs.
- The U.S. Department of Labor has a source book titled *Occupational Outlook Handbook.* It's available at full-service libraries and is helpful in determining where the job market is headed.
- Each state has an employment agency. Check yours for career-development programs.

If you're over forty, these sources offer specialized assistance. Remember that it's now just as illegal to discriminate because of age as it is for race, religion, or sex.

- Forty Plus Clubs have a unique way of getting employment for their members. Chapters are in most major cities. Call for information.
- Send 30¢ to U.S. Department of Labor, Wage and Labor Standards Administration, Women's Bureau, Washington, D.C. 20210. Ask for *Job-Finding Techniques for the Mature Woman.*
- Many cities have offices of a temporary employment agency called *Mature Temps.* There's no fee to you.

CAREER PLANNING PERSONAL WORKSHOP

In planning a career (life work), the most important considerations are intrinsic satisfaction from the work itself and the attainment of financial goals. Do the exercises that follow in the same manner you did your Life Planning. Tell yourself that your desired goal is to see clearly what type of work is best for you—the work that you will look forward to each day, and that will be an integral part of your personal growth process.

Career Attainments

This is a free-form imaginative exercise. Write ten answers to the question: *What would be your idea of ideal attainments in a career?*

Allow yourself maximum freedom in selecting these ideas. Don't disregard any thought (for example, I want to be president of a dress design firm) even if it seems remote. Don't read ahead—just do this part of the exercise *now*.

When you have finished, go back over your list and assign each a priority value on a four-point scale.

1—Of little importance

2—Of moderate importance

3—Of great importance

4—Of very great importance

This will pinpoint those aspects of a career that are most important to you.

Career Fantasy

You had some experience with fantasizing when you did the Life Planning program. Now, try another, focusing only on your career. You might want to have someone read this exercise to you. Have her read slowly, allowing twenty second pauses where the dots appear.

Find a comfortable place, close your eyes and relax . . . deeply . . . just let go. Imagine you're looking at a video or movie screen. Inside your head is a projector and a tape or film of your *future* life. Turn the projector on . . . watch the years go by. . . . Don't stop the film at any point until you're five years in the future. . . . Now, slow the action down so you can watch it . . . select *one* day and allow the screen to show you all the details of that day. . . . Where are you? . . . Who is with you? . . . Can you see yourself working? . . . What kind of work is it? . . . What is there about the work that is satisfying? . . . How does your body feel as you watch? . . . Allow yourself all the time necessary to catch as much detail as possible. When you're finished, turn off the projector and slowly come back to the present.

If you were able to develop a full fantasy, you have one of the most powerful tools possible to help you in your career plans. Make notes about your journey. Think about what you learned and how it matches with information from other exercises and things you have learned about yourself.

Your career is a vital part of the flow of your life. Except in dire emergency, never just take a job. Select your work with great care, utilizing every planning mechanism you can obtain. If you control your career path, instead of it controlling you, you will have made an enormous step on the pathway to your new life.

ADDITIONAL INFORMATION

Entering or Reentering the Job Market

Books

Caroline Bird. *Everything a Woman Needs to Know to Get Paid What She's Worth.* Bantam Books, 1973. A how-to, tactical book with good resources and bibliography.

Jean Block. *Back in Circulation.* Macmillan, 1969. Helpful information on returning to the world of work, particularly for the divorced or widowed woman.

Sande Freedman and Lois C. Schwartz. *No Experience Necessary, A Guide to Employment for the Liberal Arts Graduate.* Dell, 1971. Especially for women. Analysis of occupations and self-assessment help.

Rochelle Jones. *The Big Switch: New Careers, New Lives After 35.* McGraw-Hill, 1979. Different motivations are revealed through interviews and anecdotes.

Betty Lehan Harrigan. *Games Mother Never Taught You.* Rawson, 1977. A game plan for the woman who is entering the male domain of the business world.

John Holland. *Making Vocational Choices.* Prentice-Hall, 1973. An occupational finder and suggestions for matching occupations and work environments to the type of person you are.

Create Your Own Job

Books

Claudia Jessep and Genie Chipps. *The Woman's Guide to Starting a Business.* Holt, Rinehart and Winston, 1979. A step-by-step guide to turning an idea into a profit-making enterprise.

Maridee Winter. *Mind Your Own Business and Be Your Own Boss.* Prentice-Hall, 1980. Every woman's guide to starting a business. Inspirational stories and practical blueprints.

Charlotte Ann Taylor. *The Entrepreneurial Game: Strategies for Women Who Want to Own Their Own Businesses.* Simon and Schuster, 1979. Sound advice if you are looking to business ownership as a way of achieving economic independence and self fulfillment.

Byron Lane. *How to Free Yourself in a Business of Your Own.* Prentice-Hall, 1980. How to fulfill your life through a small business of your own. Covers everything you need to know. Easy reading.

Out of the Closet

Books

John T. Molloy. *The Woman's Dress for Success Book.* Follett Publishing, 1977. Scientifically researched advice on what to wear for business and why.

Barbara Coffey. *Glamour's Success Book: Effective Dressing on the Job, at Home, in Your Community, Everywhere.* Simon and Schuster, 1979. A definitive guide for every woman who wants to look her very best in the battle for success.

The Single Working Mother

Books

Margaret Albrect. *Complete Guide for the Working Mother.* University Publishers and Distributors, 1970. Excellent coverage of the subject.

Jane Price. *How to Have a Child and Keep Your Job: A Realistic Guide for Working Parents.* St Martin's Press, 1979. Advice on evaluation of daycare facilities, how to plan for emergencies, plus latest research on the kind of care your child should have at different ages.

Job Finding and Getting

Books

John E. McLaughlin and Stephen K. Merman. *Writing a Job-Winning Résumé.* Prentice-Hall, 1979. Step-by-step the authors lead you through the résumé, showing you how to generate a strong, positive self-image and communicate that image to perspective employers.

Richard N. Bolles. *What Color Is Your Parachute? A Practical Manual for Job Hunters and Career Changers.* Tenspeed Press, 1973. Exposé of myths of the "job market," how ads, agencies, etc., help or don't, with a suggested do-it-yourself approach.

Ross Figgins. *The Job Game: Winning the Job That's Right for You.* Prentice-Hall, 1980. Handy worksheets assist you in defining marketable skills, calculating salary needs, and building an effective network of job leads.

Barbara Prentice and P. Sandeman. *Back-to-Work Ideas for Housewives.* Macmillan, 1971. A practical book listing possible jobs with descriptions and listings of further sources for personal investigation.

Eric Kocher. *International Jobs—Where They Are, How to Get Them.* Addison-Wesley, 1979. A handbook on specific international job opportunities, with data on background and experience needed and how to apply.

General Information

Employment projections, statistics, and job advice may be obtained from the Women's Bureau, Employment Standards Administration, U.S. Department of Labor, Washington, D.C. 20210. You may also request a listing of their free publications covering issues such as child care, nontraditional employment, facts about women workers, as well as information about the bureau itself.

16

Housing Options

If you're like most people, your home is your personal haven, so the choice of housing is one of the most important decisions you will make. A complex choice it is, too. Major considerations include financial aspects, geographical location, the neighborhood and its future, type of dwelling, provision for children and pets, to go it alone or with others, rent or buy, and the choice of an ethnic or mixed community. There are many additional, less critical, conditions, to weigh—the type of furniture you own or prefer, noise levels, interior light, and so on.

With all the possibilities, how do you make a wise choice? The first decision should be *not* to make a decision for at least six months (preferably a year) after the death of your husband. It's just too difficult to get a clear perspective of what's best for you in this all-important move until you have become fully adjusted to your new situation. When you have worked on all the other aspects of your new life, then it's time to consider the possibility of moving. In the meantime, sit tight in the residence that's familiar to you.

Okay, you're ready to consider housing alternatives. In the pages that follow, we'll be giving you a lot of data and ideas to help you in your choice. But, ultimately, you alone must decide what's best for you. One of the things you may discover is that your present residence is just fine for your future. But if a move is in order, you'll want to weigh everything. It's important that you make this decision not only with your head, but with your heart, and by paying careful attention to your feelings. Pure, rational choice does not always lead to the best result. Don't be influenced by the well-intentioned advice of family and friends. If they're not going to live with you, take their offering as just another piece of information.

As you go through the decision-making process, do it with a light heart. This is not a banishment to Siberia—it's an opportunity to create an environment that is suited to you, one that will make your days pleasurable and your home life rich.

CHOOSING A LOCATION

If you're working and plan to continue on with your job, that's a limiting factor in your choice of location. If such is not the case, the limiters are more amenable to change. Being near family or friends may be important, but perhaps you have family in other locales who would be the nucleus for a support group. Or, perhaps you're venturesome and would like to seek out an area with greater opportunity and better weather. Vast numbers of retirees have moved into Southern California or Florida and find the climate and people hospitable.

Whether you're young or older, moving to a new state usually has long-term implications, so you'll want a good deal of future-oriented information.

- Are the tax laws favorable?
- What's the cost of living relative to other areas?
- What's the state's attitude toward senior citizens? Is there adequate, protective legislation in existence and contemplated?

A good way to get in touch with what's happening in a community is through the local newspaper, so order a subscription and read about your possible new home. It's a good idea to live in the town of your choice for at least two seasons before making up your mind to live there permanently. This is difficult if you're holding a job; but if you consider the importance of the choice, perhaps you can at least work out some prolonged visits. While you're there, explore the telephone book Yellow Pages. This directory will tell you a lot about the types of goods and services offered.

If your location quest is limited to your present town or city, you'll want to focus on a particular neighborhood. There are all the obvious things to watch for such as convenience to transportation, shopping, recreational facilities, and schools. There are also less obvious things you'll want to look into—crime rate, population density, air pollution, and, particularly if you're buying, the desirability of the area some years in the future.

THE INTERIOR ENVIRONMENT

It's a bit of a tightrope act, this business of breaking free and creating your own life, while still retaining the memories of the past and their inspiration for the present. You'll find this particularly true when you consider the furnishings of your new environment or the rearrangement of your old one. At the proper time, changing or creating the scene to fit your own special needs and ideas is an important adjustment to your new reality.

A beautiful place to live and high cost do not necessarily go together. There are many magazines and books that can point the way to imaginative interior design for a modest amount. If you explore this idea thoroughly, it gives you other options—including selling or giving away some of the furnishings you presently own. It won't interfere with your memories if you give your children (or worthy causes) some furniture and accessories that may be adding clutter to your life. Some of the things you've stashed away may have real value as collectibles and can be turned into cash.

When you're moving to a new environment, consider different interior design possibilities. A one-bedroom apartment can be arranged to give you a den, sewing room, or reading room, using a portion of the living room for a sleeping area. While you can't create an external view if it's not there, you can make the interior warm and satisfying with paint, plants, throw rugs, wall hangings, and other inexpensive decorative accessories.

If you're able to work it out without sacrificing other amenities, give special thought to your bedroom. Make it a place where you can indulge all forms of your passions—reading in bed, watching the late show, and taking a lover. Consider another place for the photos of your husband, so there won't be constraints on you or your friend. This is not a denial of your former life, it's simply dealing with the realities of creating a new one.

LIVING ALONE

When you consider this option, do it from the viewpoint of utilizing your *aloneness* as a part of your growth process. If being *alone* appears that it might serve your *loneliness,* consider other possibilities.

Living alone offers many rewards:

- You can design your living space to reflect who you are and how you want to live, without regard for others.
- You can come and go as you please.
- You can have that greatest luxury in this crowded world—privacy.
- You can be intimate with one person at a time. You don't have to share friends.

- You can run around in dirty clothes, without makeup, eat crackers in bed, watch the late, late show, play mayhem with the leftovers, and get nary a hassle.

If you have the finances that allow the single life-style with ownership of your own residence, you will be joining huge numbers of others who are making single-owner homes and condominiums a growing national phenomenon.

LIVING WITH OTHERS

Another growing national trend is toward some form of shared living space. For many this is simply a way of beating the high cost of living. For others, the central issue is sharing and companionship. No longer confined to an unwashed few, being in community is providing an inspirational living style for women of all ages.

> Recently, a Los Angeles widower with a ten-year-old son placed a newspaper ad, hoping to find someone to split the rent on his large, expensive apartment. Within a few days, he received thirty calls from women and men with similar problems.
>
> Like many other urban areas, the Los Angeles rental market freezes out children. Combined with high costs, this creates an extremely difficult situation for renters.
>
> Out of the initial contacts, he began a service for single parents. For a modest fee, he matches people on the basis of overall compatibility and mutual needs, and they search for a living space together. His clients find that at lower rents there is little available, but at higher figures two mothers can afford a nice-sized house. While economics is the major consideration, they soon find that getting emotional support and having someone to talk to makes the arrangement doubly attractive.

If you're living in a large house now, consider renting a room. If you can deal with the change in privacy, there are all kinds of possibilities. A young college man can be helpful around the house and provide a measure of security. Think about trading services—babysitting, light housework, yard work, or transportation for whole or partial rent.

It's a good idea to have written agreement about the house rules in advance: kitchen privileges, smoking, stereo sound, entertaining friends, use of the telephone, use of the bathroom, and any other issue that might cause conflict. With strangers, carefully checked references are a must.

Beyond room rental, you can share your complete dwelling with another person, perhaps a good friend. You'll need to be prepared to deal with interpersonal issues, but the trade-off will bring you warmth and comfort. Even the sharing of cooking, shopping, and housework responsibility can be fun.

If the consideration of one roommate is palatable, you may be ready for the real thing—communal living. That's three of you or more (possibly dozens) in the same residence or complex. Living in community is as old as man, but in modern times the concept has grown in importance far beyond protection from the elements and enemies. Being in community with others is a way to combat the alienation, disconnectedness, and superficiality of modern life. Highly developed living communities work toward satisfaction of the utopian hopes that life be more caring, that life be more intimate, that life have greater depth.

Any group of people willing to come together to share the responsibilities and enhance the joys of daily living can form a community. Congenial people with similar life interests sharing a residence can be an adventure. Children can benefit, particularly, by having a variety of adults as role models and other children to share with.

Any number of community projects have been tried—older people forming a cooperative as an alternative to a retirement home, older people mixed with very young children (who enjoy all the surrogate grandparents), widows banding together, young marrieds, and cross sections of people of all kinds. Being in community (as opposed to simply living together) is a viable concept for modern Americans.

Last, but far from least, live with one man. In our enlightened society, there is a growing acceptance of nonmarrieds living together. Even the government conspires against wedlock. Though new Social Security regulations are somewhat helpful to those over sixty who remarry, those under sixty lose some benefits. The IRS continues to reward single bliss. Besides, it's fun to be a "dirty-old-unconventional woman."

Other forms of sharing you might consider: bring a grandmother home. Find an older widow alone who can live in, take care of children, and housesit while you work. Or, if you're the older widow alone, adopt a family.

RENTING AN APARTMENT

The living arrangement with the least responsibility and the highest mobility is an apartment rental. Repairs, maintenance, taxes, and insurance are all someone else's concern. There are a variety of rental unit types. Some cater to singles, some to the elderly, some to young marrieds, some allow children. There are deluxe facilities that include saunas, tennis courts, recreation centers, swimming pools, and other special features. In times of plentiful housing, you are likely to find whatever you want. In times of high interest rates or restrictive legislation, the range of choice may narrow temporarily. When thinking of an apartment, consider these advantages:

- Usually, you will be able to find a convenient location. Apartment complexes make more efficient use of land than homes, making close-in living affordable.
- There's a maintenance person on tap through the landlord.
- Apartments are generally designed to make maximum use of space. This results in easier cleaning chores.
- You may find recreational facilities as part of an apartment complex.
- If you want it, there's companionship close at hand. Many apartment buildings have an air of communal living around poolside or lobby.
- You can select an above-ground unit that provides good security.
- You can go off on a vacation, close the door and forget about it.
- You can select from a wide range of prices and styles to suit your taste and budget.
- In most cities, it is customary to have carpets, drapes, and major appliances furnished with the apartment.
- There's no heavy initial investment. Ordinarily, the first and last month's rent will get you started.
- In the *short haul,* apartment renting is less costly than homeowning.

There are disadvantages to apartment living too:

- In inflationary times, you can expect annual rent increases, which is hard on budgeting.
- Apartment units that accept children are becoming increasingly rare.
- You can forget about having a garden and other open space around you. Living in a concrete jungle requires some compromises.
- Noise is a problem. It's a good idea to check the unit at different times of day and night to see how the strange sounds of your neighbor's stereo system affect you.
- Space is always at a premium. If you've been conditioned to over-sized furnishings in a home, you'll discover they won't fit modern apartments.
- You're not building equity. In times of rapidly escalating real estate prices, renters suffer most.
- Your pets may need to find a new momma.

HOME OWNERSHIP

If you're living in your own home now, you may be weighing whether to stay or move. There are worldly considerations that need analysis in your head and emotional considerations that need to be contacted through your feelings.

As always, financial matters are very important. For most widows, retention of their home usually flunks the money test. With one member of the family gone, the house is oversized. If you were a two-income family, there's one less. If you are over fifty-five and sell, you are exempt from capital gains tax up to $100,000, which means you could have a bundle of cash. It's easy to line up a host of financial reasons for selling.

Add some other negatives: routine maintenance may be a problem. A house is a responsibility requiring steady attention. You can't walk away for extended periods of time without arranging for someone to look in.

The other side looks like this: if you can afford to stay, owning real estate represents an excellent investment and tax shelter. If you sell now and move into a rental unit, because of the rapidly escalating price of homes, you may not be able to get back into the homeowning market.

You may reason that your home has the room you want, it is close to friends and relatives, it is easy to get a young man in the neighborhood for light maintenance. You can probably find many logical reasons for staying.

So much for the head things. What about the less tangible heart things? There may be a feeling of real security for you in your present home. With a few changes, it can retain the old memories and make way for new ones. Perhaps there's a feeling about the neighborhood and a particular style of life that's important to you. If deep down you get the *feeling* that it's right to stay, all the other logical negatives are worth canceling out. It's been our experience that no amount of conscious effort is great enough to offset the flow (the direction) of your life. If you go against your own natural flow, it can result in real trauma or even physical illness. It's healthy and it's enriching to follow the dictates of your own inner person.

If you're an older woman and want to stay in your present home, there is financial help available. Some states have laws that allow you to postpone tax payments until you sell your home, or until you die, when they are paid out of proceeds of your estate.

Another motivation to stay, the "reverse mortgage" was introduced by the Federal Home Loan Bank Board. Called the RAM (Reverse Annuity Mortgage), it allows certain savings and loan institutions to purchase your home over a long period of time, making monthly payments to you and taking over the property only when you die. This assures you both an income and a place to live for the balance of your life. There are various forms of the RAM. If you're interested, check at your federally-chartered savings and loan. Be prepared for some searching, as this is a new concept that needs a little time before it becomes commonplace.

Everything we've been saying about staying in your own home goes for buying a new home. There may be just the right one for you, and you'll know it. If you want to move, there are options other than selling you house.

Consider renting it and using the income to apply against the new place. You can even borrow on the equity, buy a new home, and still retain the original one.

CONDOMINIUMS AND CO-OPS

The most common form of ownership in a multiunit dwelling is the condominium. It parallels in many ways the advantages of home ownership. You are the sole owner of the residence, are taxed on your unit, you can borrow on your equity and, technically, you are not responsible for the other owners. You have the advantage of carefree maintenance and security, but you share in the cost of maintaining all common areas.

The co-operative form of ownership is different. You do not actually own your unit. You own shares in the co-operative. Typically, you have one vote in the governing body and must work through this group in every matter, including sale of your shares. If one member defaults, the co-operative is responsible. As in the condominium, you can deduct taxes and interest on your mortgage. You accumulate equity, but you may not be able to use that equity as collateral for a loan. There are far fewer co-operatives than condominiums, but changing legislation may increase popularity of this type of ownership.

Both condos and co-ops offer a form of living that is rapidly increasing in popularity. While there are communal restrictions on what you can do with your property, particularly the exterior, if you can give up a little autonomy, there are many advantages; you may find certain physical amenities—swimming pool, tennis courts, etc. There may be a resident manager, which means you can leave for extended periods of time with no worry.

Before buying a co-op or condo, check the house rules to see how they affect you. Then, you might want to take one of the extension courses offered by colleges and universities on condo purchasing. Read the contracts of several units and compare. In a short time, you'll become an expert and can make an enlightened choice as to whether this living style is for you.

LEISURE (RETIREMENT) COMMUNITIES

If you're of an age (meaning fifty or older), or of a mind to live in a more sheltered environment, one of the new retirement communities may be for you. They come in all types: mobile homes, houses, apartments, townhouses, and can be rented or purchased. They may incorporate many of the features of a small city, including transportation, shopping, and extensive recreational facilities.

It is a way for a person alone to maintain a greater measure of independence than in a retirement home and yet avoid some of the perils and problems of living in a conventional community. You can have all the social activity you want and can often select from a great variety of courses and programs. Bus service and security service add to the comfort.

Retirement communities have entrance age limits and impose restrictions on children (some even restrict visitation rights). This means that your companionship will be with older persons only. This is a heavily loaded trade-off for other amenities, so consider carefully.

Costs vary tremendously. Check with your local realtor's exchange, senior citizen centers, and Chamber of Commerce for such communities in your area.

RETIREMENT HOMES

If you're weary of cooking and cleaning, you may wish to consider a retirement home or hotel. They vary from subsidized low-cost units to deluxe, hotel-like facilities with choice of dining rooms, beauty shops, and recreation. Some even supply residential or nearby medical care.

There are some light-care facilities which charge entrance fees and can require that you turn over all of your assets to them in exchange for care for the rest of your life. There have been instances of such facilities going out of business, leaving older people destitute. You're probably best advised to select a home that provides services on a straight fee basis, retaining control over your assets and income.

There are goods and bads about retirement home living. The companionship, security, and freedom from the responsibility of shopping, cooking, and cleaning is offset by the institutional setting and the confinement of living in one room.

Before making this choice irrevocably, do a trial run. Store you furniture or sublet your present dwelling and commit yourself to a specified time period of experiencing this lifestyle. A good way to choose a place is to visit, talk to residents, have a guest meal, observe the service people, check the rules and regulations. Comparison shop several. After all, this is your life.

MOBILE HOMES

Not all mobile homes are mobile. Some are located permanently in special parks, often in very desirable beachfront or resort locations. Many have recreational facilities and a common area. You own your unit but usually rent the parking area.

Many of the newer mobiles have deluxe features such as well-equipped kitchens and modern furnishings. They're compact, but considerably less costly than conventional dwellings. Until recently, financing was somewhat restricted, but new regulations have eased this, and you can own a mobile home on favorable terms.

As you would for any other facility, check the area, speak with residents, compare features and prices. Many cities hold mobile home shows so you can learn about the units themselves.

You might be interested in a mobile home that goes.

[1]"Hello out there, all you big 18-wheelers, this is Gadabout Granny." That greeting crackles over citizens band radios dozens of times each day on America's highways. "Gadabout Granny" is Mrs. Peggy Hoskins, who has been traveling in a motor home since 1974. So far she has logged more than 60,000 miles in the United States, Canada, and Mexico. A widow, she raised the last of her six children and then decided to "hit the road." She sold her house and purchased a recreational vehicle that has "just about all the comforts of home," she said.

She has visited Key West, Fla., toured Mexico, and traveled through the Rocky Mountains to Calgary, Canada, before moving on to Portland, Ore. and Phoenix. The next leg of her itinerary included the 1400 miles of the Alcan Highway to Fairbanks, Alaska.

Mrs. Hoskins has been a "loner," though her handle is widely known by America's CBers. She has been to the most distant points south, north, and west in the continental United States, as well as the lowest point in Death Valley.

Does "Gadabout Granny" ever regret her life on the road? "I've driven through floods, snow, rain, wind, sleet, fog, droughts, and heat," she said, "but no matter how tough it sometimes gets, it's better than sitting at home twiddling your thumbs."

Remember, what's done can always be undone, so if you find that your best-intentioned choice doesn't work out, shrug it off and move again.

ADDITIONAL INFORMATION
Books
Fred E. Case. *The Investment Guide to Home and Land Purchase*. Prentice-Hall, 1977. All the practical advice and information needed when buying a house or property. How to shop for and finance a loan, secrets of assessing the condition of a house, rating a neighborhood, plus many more helpful tips.

Michael Sumichrast and Ronald G. Shafer. *The Complete Book of Home Buying*. Dow Jones Publishing, 1979. The facts you need to be a wise investor and tough buyer. What to look for in a single-family home or condominium, how to shop for the best financing, and how to get the most for a home when you decide to sell.

---

[1] Gadabout Granny, AARP News Bulletin, November, 1979, page 6.

Lee Butcher. *The Condominium Book: A Guide to Getting the Most for Your Money.* Dow Jones Publishing, 1979. The difference between a rewarding way of life or a nightmare can depend on how well you know the condominium facts of life.

Helene Levenson. *Creating an Interior.* Prentice-Hall, 1980. A step-by-step guide to planning and creating interiors that are both comfortable and eye-pleasing. Packed with professional tips and suggestions on how to achieve an attractive house or apartment without spending a lot of money.

Sarah Faulkner. *Planning a Home: A Practical Guide to Interior Design.* Holt, Rinehart and Winston, 1979. A practical problem-solving manual for creating an environment that meets your needs, desires, and tastes with a realistic concern for your budget.

Pamphlets

Home Buyer's Checklist, National Homebuyers and Homeowners Association, Dept PW, 1225 19th Street, N.W., Suite 602, Washington, D.C. 20036. ($1.00) Information on closing costs, mortgage arrangements, rent with option-to-buy contracts.

AIM's Guide to Housing Choices and *Your Retirement Housing Guide,* both available free from the AARP/AIM, 1909 K Street, N.W., Washington, D.C. 20049.

How to Save Tax Dollars When You Sell Your House, available free from your real estate professional.

Fair Housing USA, (#150B) Public Documents Distribution Center, Pueblo, Colorado 81009. Free government booklet provides information on Fair Housing Assistance offices throughout the country. Helpful information if you have problems with discrimination in either rental or purchase.

General Information

HUD, U.S. Department of Housing and Urban Development, 451 Seventh Street, Washington, D.C. 20410. Another source of help if you feel you are being discriminated against. Explain in detail to HUD what the problems are and they will investigate and provide assistance if possible.

Information on cost of living in various communities can be obtained from the U.S. Bureau of Labor Statistics, 441 G. Street, N.W., Washington, D.C. 20212.

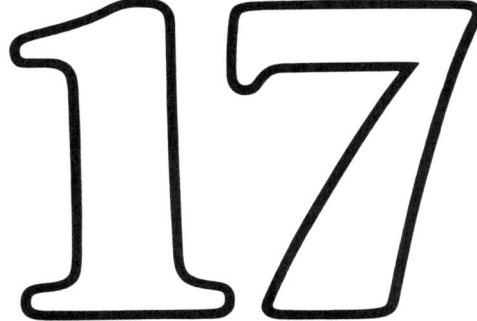

New Vistas

There are many ways to put new zip in your life. Some of the best are recreation, travel, education, and service to others.

RECREATION AND TRAVEL

When you've spent a good portion of your life as one-half of a couple, venturing out as a single person may seem like being half there. Even going shopping alone and observing couples doing things together can be incredibly painful. What we're about to suggest is that you'll have to overcome the national propensity for pairing, that you need to put aside your embarrassment or shyness as a single. It's relatively *easy* to put this into words, but most difficult to accomplish, because it requires a substantial life reorientation.

Yet, unless you take those first hard steps, you'll find yourself turning your energy primarily into inventing excuses for *not* moving out. It's easier to be too tired at the end of the day, feel unsafe going out at night, feel you shouldn't leave your children, have nothing to wear, or plan on watching a TV show. Staying closed down takes a lot of energy. Diverting the same energy into new adventures can open up your life.

One possibility is to stay paired in new ways. Take your child along for companionship. Go out with a woman friend. Go to parties or gatherings where you know most of the people. There's nothing wrong with this, and we're certainly not suggesting you become a loner. But there's a lot of excitement, opening of new vistas, and possibility of making new friends when you engage in activities as a single. Going it alone has some real advantages:

- It's much easier to meet new people when you're not involved with a companion. People are more apt to engage a single person in conversation than to interrupt a couple.
- You can decide at the last minute about a play or concert. Single tickets are almost always available. Talking to the stranger next to you is a way to experiment with new behavior.
- At a party or gathering, you need not be concerned about how your companion is faring. You can talk to whom you want, avoid those you'd rather, and leave when you please.
- You're free to engage in any activity you like, night or day, without checking it out.

If you're interested in trying, here are some ideas:

- Don't go out with the idea of meeting men or of looking for that one "special man."
- Don't think of the things you want to do as requiring a companion. (Even things that take two, such as tennis, can be attempted alone, with the idea that there might be another brave single you can pair up with.)
- Don't depend on your couple friends, and don't go only to couple events.
- Don't concentrate on activities that require a companion such as a dinner place with dancing.
- Do go out with the idea that you might meet some interesting people and make new friends.
- Do go to events that really interest you and will bring you pleasure out of the experience itself.
- Do look for activities that are communal in concept, such as folk dancing.

There are a few problems in single adventuring, particularly in eating out or when traveling. Even in the age of the traveling woman executive, many maitre d's try to hide single women or discourage them with a table next to the noisy kitchen door. Single rooms are a norm on the business circuit, but in resort areas you may be offered the former servant's quarters or the room next to the elevator. For these minor annoyances there are also answers:

- March into a fine restaurant carrying an attache case, acting the executive role.
- Make a table or hotel reservation for two, then after you are seated or roomed, announce that your associate will not be joining you.
- Some restaurants cater to singles, occasionally with large tables that seat ten or twelve, for sharing. Learn about these, and have a meal with potential new friends.
- If you feel overwhelmed with it all, take a course in assertiveness. This helpful training will allow you to outmaneuver even the most domineering maitre d' or concierge.
- Before you try a fancy restaurant, do your basic training in a coffee shop. Start with breakfast. There are always single diners. Move up to lunch, striking up conversations as you go. Make dinner at a fine restaurant your graduation present.

Travel

Until you try it, traveling alone can seem scary. Yet, the reports from globe-traveling women are that the excitement and adventure are well worth the initial anxiety. Imagine the low-risk experience of flirting or making contact with a man far away from your home base. How about experiencing a new culture, with the only restrictions being those you impose? Spontaneity and inventiveness can open all kinds of new doors.

Ready? It's timely tip time again:

- If you're headed for a foreign country, pretend you're going to open an import shop in your hometown. Plan to visit the country's cultural headquarters and get an idea of the articles available for export. See if you can get contact names. When you arrive, you'll have interesting experiences waiting.
- Read up on the art of the locale you plan to visit. Make a commitment to exploration. Nothing invites communication more quickly than an open guide book as you wander through a museum or gallery.
- If you're going to a country where the language is unfamiliar, make essential reservations in advance. It will cut down some of the spontaneity, but the trade-off is peace of mind for a first timer.
- Whatever you do, don't load yourself down with heavy luggage. A good rule is not to take more than you can carry yourself. Remember that it's not like home. You won't be seeing the same people each day, so less changes of clothes are required.
- Don't carry a lot of cash. Use traveler's checks and credit cards. If you leave valuable jewelry at home, you can move freely and without concern.

- Do a lot of planning for the first trip—taking care of home events while you're away, clothes, travel documents, guide books. If you make the first trip a success, you'll set yourself up for many more travel pleasures.
- Ask friends, relatives, acquaintances, for letters of introduction to people they may know in places where you are traveling. Getting behind the walls is a sure way to enhance your fun.

Don't let the first glance at cost be a deterrent. If you're interested in going someplace, there are all kinds of possibilities in group travel with individual freedom, swap clubs (you trade your home and, possibly, car for the same in another country), bus tour specials and many others. Try these money-saver ideas:

- Travel in off-season as much as possible.
- Excursion fares and reserve-in-advance packages save money.
- Many airlines have stop-over privileges with no extra cost.
- Some package tours include meals. While this takes away some of the adventure, it's cheaper.
- Use a travel agent. They make the calls and write the letters, without charge. If you want to make your own reservations, use toll-free numbers.
- Some travel books have coupons which offer discounts.
- Try the Arthur Frommer guide series. They're based on budget travel.
- If you're an AAA member, they have free maps and guide books.
- Hosteling is the least expensive mode of travel. Though most of the users are young people, there's no upper age limit.
- Check your alumni association, credit union, and other memberships you hold for travel specials.

If going it alone is just not your thing, there are options galore. There is a widows' travel club with over 10,000 members. For a fee of $25, you can be matched with someone of your age, profession, and travel preferences. Widowers are in the group now, too. There are many other single persons' travel clubs with an endless list of destinations and arrangements. If you like even more specialized groups, there are travel agencies for the handicapped, the traveler over fifty, the senior citizen, or whatever you seek. Some groups are arranged for specific interests—opera tours, museum tours, archeological tours, etc.

Of course, you can simply arrange to go with a friend or get into the matching game yourself, using your widows' support group (see Chapter 18) as a base. The main idea is to get going.

Entertaining

One of the ways to make contact with people, and a good way to repay neighbors, family, and friends for their care and concern in the early days of your widowhood, is by having a party. It can take one of many forms: cocktail party, buffet dinner, open house, brunch, picnic, beach party, or a series of small dinner parties.

No matter which you choose, plan on enjoying the people you invite. No one cares that much about what is served. There are all kinds of shortcuts and innovative ways to handle the food at a party. It's more important for you to concentrate on being with people.

Consider some other interesting party ideas: invite only your women friends (both married and single) to a dinner. You may be surprised to find how stimulating and interesting your women friends are when they are contacted as women, not as wives, widows, or divorcees.

Want to make your home a center of people gatherings? Try bringing home some members of the local senior center. Contact the foreign student's center at your university and arrange a mixed or single country dinner. Share your cultural heritage with them.

If you have a special joy such as music, art, literature, or drama, arrange an evening around that interest. Make music with a group of musical friends. Visit an art gallery or museum with other friends and then have them to your home for a light supper and discussion. Do the same with a play, concert, or sports event. You may even need to cultivate an interest in order to cultivate people, but it's okay to open up new horizons at any period in life.

Face the reality that you'll be concerned about being both host and hostess for your gatherings. But don't avoid entertaining because of your fears. Share them with your guests and let them help you through the initial experiences. Entertaining by yourself is a reinforcement of your personhood and your ability to function as a single person. Experiment with a variety of forms of entertaining until you find the way that suits you best.

Recreational Activities

Check the calendar section of your local newspaper or city magazine. You will find the choice of activities incredibly varied. Many are free, others have very minimal costs. Venture out and try something new—a square dance, a lecture on self-hypnosis, a bicycle excursion, a new dining club. Stretch beyond your imagined limitations, and see what will happen. Try not to discount any activity. You'll be surprised at what might work for you.

In most large cities, there are singles' bars. And in most small towns, there are neighborhood meeting-place bars. If this seems outrageous, why can't you enjoy a drink and some camaraderie just like the men?

Even if you do not have a religious affiliation, local churches have activities that are open to participation by all. Don't discount this way of getting into special activities, but watch that it doesn't become an all-pervasive crutch.

Join a cause. Help your local political candidate. Work at party headquarters. Work in community organizations. These may not sound like recreation, but anything that gets you out of the house and into contact with others is a part of the re-creating process.

Universities, colleges, and high schools have adult events. Check the local Tourist Bureau, Recreation Department, or Chamber of Commerce for information about special events and recreational facilities. Community centers and Y's often have events for nonmembers. Even joining might suit you.

If you're stuck for choices, try working through this list:

- If your interests are musical, join a local choir or orchestra.
- If you suspect that you have acting, directing, or writing talent, join a little theater or community theater group.
- If you like cards, chess, or backgammon, join a club or pull together a group of your own.
- If you are interested in public speaking or want to learn more about communicating, join a Toastmaster's club.
- If you like reading, join a Great Books club. If taking pictures is your pleasure, join a photography club.
- If the thought of dancing gets you moving, take a class in disco, swing, ballroom, or folk dancing. Parks and recreation programs in your community usually have dancing events.
- If you want to explore your cultural heritage, try an ethnic club.
- If you have concerns about the environment, do something about it through an environmental protection organization.
- If you love kids, scout leaders and youth organization leaders are always in demand.
- If art is your thing, join the local art museum and attend their special events.
- If you love the outdoors, get a backpack and hit the trail. Many activities are available through organizations such as the Sierra Club.
- If you were a skating whiz in your youth, get back to it at an ice rink or on rollers, the newest craze.
- If you want pleasure with practicality, get on your bike. Fitness fever has created bike clubs by the dozen. In addition to socializing, you can get healthy and save fossil fuel energy.
- If you feel competitive, take up tennis, racquetball, or golf.

- If you really want to get fit, take up jogging. The streets and trails are filled with people of all ages puffing away.
- If you're not a sinker, swimming at public or private pools can be fun and healthy.
- If money is no object, try boating, horseback riding, flying.
- If you want some really different activities, be a hangglider, skydiver, white-water kayaker, or free ballooner. Somewhat less energy and risk is involved in whale watching.

Forget about your feelings of inadequacy, fear of looking foolish, fear that you're too old (or too young). America is full of people treating themselves to satisfying recreational experiences. Once on your way, you'll wonder what took you so long.

BACK TO SCHOOL

Put yourself in this scenario:

> Jacqueline's husband died when she was fifty-two. Her three children had all been to college and were married. She had one granddaughter, age four, who came to visit her occasionally, one aging Schnauzer with the incredible name of Fido, a houseful of floral prints and numerous memories, and fifteen extra pounds that were unequally distributed on her frame.
>
> So, she took a job, only to find that grandmothers with fifteen extra pounds, a dog named Fido, two years of college, and no experience were not in extra special demand. But she got started with a good company, which made weapons of destruction for the U.S. Government, which means that they were very careful not to discriminate because of age or sex. They even offered to pay for her education, if she'd get one, and held out the promise of a better job, commensurate with her degree.
>
> One evening, there she was in this classroom full of working adults, beginning on a Bachelor's Degree in Management. At a private university, yet, paid for by her employer, whee! There were a few students in their twenties, many in their thirties, several in their forties, Jacky, and a terrific executive, age sixty, who had made it to the top and was back in school to find out how he did it.
>
> The first semester was awesome. The human relations course pushed her into looking at herself, finding new ways of being, and examining her career and future. In a matter of a few months, the class became a complete new support group, including the terrific executive, she had

read a dozen new books and was as excited with life as she had ever been before.

The rest of this story you may have guessed. Jacky ditched the extra fifteen pounds, redistributed what was left, redid the house, gave Fido to the little boy next door, and took in the terrific executive as a new pet.

Every woman going back to school may not find her story ending exactly the same way, but the rejuvenating effect of the educational process is well known and shared by all who make the effort. As the youth population declines, colleges and universities are putting extra effort into their adult programs. With a little checking, you'll find many alternatives to the traditional campus scene. This activity is not confined to private institutions. Public schools are becoming more oriented to the working adult, so the range of programs and tuitions keeps widening.

You will also be welcomed into the regular daytime, on-campus classes. While you may not be interested in the panty raid at the local sorority house, it can be fun to match wits and experience with the bubble gum crowd. Do expect that your stimulation will come mainly from the professor, however. One offshoot of this is the possibility of engaging in a reverse June–December romance. "Hey, Mrs. Robinson, join me on my surfboard."

If you're contemplating becoming a student in residence, pay a call on the women's center and ask questions. You'll be able to tell from their welcome how it will be in class. You may also find career counseling here. If not, ask for the school counselor. They're usually able to give you guidance in many areas.

You can expect universities, vocational schools, and special training schools to have placement offices. Check out the one in the school of your choice, and let them tell you what your job chances are when you complete your program. This may influence your course of study.

Degree Programs

Unlike the youngster who chooses the wrong major in school and has plenty of time to correct his mistake, your allowable margin of error is slim. It's important that you choose a school and a curriculum that will get you where you want to go. This takes us back to planning, so if you haven't worked through the Life Planning and Career Planning chapters, you may want to do so before you sign on for school.

Even after you're sure about your direction, deciding on the best program means work on your part. If you're starting with just a high school background, you can consider the community or junior colleges. They cover the first two years only and may give a certificate or Associate in Arts degree. The professional undergraduate degrees for working adults, such as business, psychology, and education usually pick up from there. If you're interested in other than liberal arts studies—sociology, nursing, or any other specialty, check carefully at the very beginning to make sure the courses you are taking will help you get where you're going.

Unless you've decided on some specialty where the number of applicants is restricted, the choices will continue to be extensive. Finances may start the narrowing process. Public schools are less expensive. Consider the reputation of the schools within your budget, and find out what happens to their graduates. You'll find ample ways to do this if you ask questions of current students.

Most incoming students select their school based on convenience of hours and class location. A much better idea is to check out the faculty. The better schools who serve adult populations choose professors with real-world experience as well as academic degrees. You'll surely find yourself bored by a brand new doctorate attached to a kid the age of your son.

One last caveat: check your school out carefully. Accreditation assures you of recognition of your degree. There are many degree-granting institutions that pass out paper rather than learning. The importance of an education is in the meaning it adds to your life.

If a degree is what you have in mind, don't be stopped by high cost. For the really persistent woman, there are enumerable ways to get money. Start by obtaining the HEW Student Consumers' Guide (see details at chapter's end). There are grants available, low-interest, long-term loans, and specialized programs for adults. Go to the financial aid office of the school of your choice and ask for information about loans and scholarships. You'll be amazed at the partial or full scholarships available (this is a good reason not to pass up a qualified private institution before you check out scholarship availability). If nothing else works, check the local office of NOW, and see if they have anything on tap. Also, remember that many good employers will be happy to pay for a business education. It benefits them too. Ask before you sign on for a new job.

Vocational Courses

A degree is not the "open sesame" to more money that it once was. In today's service-oriented, technological society, the skilled worker often makes more money than his degreed counterpart in the office. In San Francisco, the street cleaners make more money than many of the professors at San Francisco State University who hold doctorates. Now that many of the high-paying trades are not sacrosanct male domains, you may want to consider learning how to be a plumber, for example, and earn over $30 per hour. One important advantage of specialized training is that it may lead you into a job with as little as six weeks of schooling. Most, however, take upwards of a year.

There are certificate programs for licensed vocational nurses (in high demand), dieticians, medical and dental assistants, computer programers, bookkeepers, secretaries, and a host of others. Begin by checking free and minimal-cost programs in high schools, city, community, or junior colleges. Most have night programs for adults. Private schools also offer certificate training, particularly in careers such as real estate, travel, restaurant management, hotel management, and other specialized fields. Some are reputable, others are not. The best way to check on them is to get a list of graduates and make some phone calls. The Better Business Bureau in your area will be able to tell you if they've received complaints.

New opportunities have opened up for paraprofessionals in the legal and medical fields. With some rigorous special training, you may find yourself being a respected member of these important professions.

Schooling for Fun and Fantasy

Nothing says that you must go to school to advance your career. You could go just to enhance the quality of your life. If you live in a large city, the array of courses is staggering. Even in small communities, the opportunities are extensive. You might wish to pick up on the musical talent you set aside. In addition to specific instrumental instruction, try a class in music appreciation, history of jazz, pop, or rock. Study Beethoven and other great masters. Many courses are experiential, including attendance at concerts.

You can get involved in cooking styles, utilizing new kitchen technology such as food processors and microwave ovens. Become a photographer, ceramist, sailor, or beachcomber. Take bicycle journeys with other enthusiasts. Learn a new language, become a writer. Consider the many specialized courses for women—assertiveness training, women in management, women as entrepreneurs. Whatever you can think of, someone is teaching. Whether you want to improve your intellect, psyche, or body, there's a course. If you have a special skill, reverse the process and teach.

There's another legitimate reason for going to school—to meet and be with people. If you're looking for someone to share your joy in dining, you're sure to find someone in a gourmet cooking class. If you want a sports partner, try a class in your favorite activity. The same goes for dancing. Psychologically-oriented courses are a good place to meet people looking for intimacy.

There are other nonformalized educational pursuits. Go to the library, make friends with the librarian, and become an expert through reading. Go to lectures and discussion groups.

Only if you're housebound physically, take a homestudy course or one of the early morning TV courses that have been recently introduced. If at all possible, however, do your learning with others. The power of a group in multiplying the learning process is most surprising.

Don't let age hold you back. People in their seventies and eighties are finding they can meet and enjoy the challenge of college classes. One large university started a degree program for persons over the age of sixty. They hired a faculty of retired professors and expected thirty or forty people to register. On the first morning, over 200 senior citizens showed up. Education for seniors is gaining national attention. Consideration is currently being given to improving Title I of the Federal Higher Education Act, which would create greater gray matter stimulation for graying heads.

This is a great time in history for women. If you're willing to pound at barriers, you'll be in the company of hundreds of thousands of your sisters. So let go, feel free, and have a ball with your education.

VOLUNTEER WORK

Among the sizeable group of psychologically-aware, humanistically-oriented American leaders, there is a growing spirituality. Individually, they may operationalize this concept through attachment to an organized religion, by recognition of the God within, or simply by understanding that ultimately they will answer to a higher power. The most important tenet of this spiritual movement is the belief that the highest form of human endeavor is service to others. In America, we lump this under the simple rubric "volunteer service."

It's usually true that the giver gets more than the receiver. Even if you don't believe this at the beginning, if you focus on it as a possibility, you may just create a self-fulfilling prophecy. You don't need to get your reward in the hereafter—volunteer work can greatly benefit your life in the here and now.

Some personal benefits you can expect: feeling needed, active involvement with others, aiding causes you believe in, and getting hugs from children. You can also use volunteering as a way to polish your skills prior to reentry into the paid job market. The real reward of volunteer work is in the intrinsic satisfaction of doing something worthwhile. Nothing in life matches up to that.

There is volunteer work in all categories and in chunks of time to suit you. If you are okay financially, you may want to support an organization on a full-time basis. Usually, you'll be welcome with any degree of time commitment. Even if you're working full time, you may want to consider volunteering during your leisure hours.

Volunteer work comes in as many forms, requires as much effort, and takes as many diverse skills as paid employment. Here are a few opportunities among the many you can consider:

- Two of the best-known areas for volunteer work are traveler's aid and hospital service. Both deal with people who are feeling frightened and alone. If you feel able to reach out to others, your help is sorely needed. There are never enough hospital volunteers. More than just a deliverer of papers, juice, and library books, the sensitive hospital volunteer can help patients through severe trauma, bridge the gap between the sterile hospital and the waiting family, be a bearer of good cheer, and ease pain of all types.

People rarely think of traveler's aid as helping the seriously needy, yet there is nothing so bottomless as the feeling of being alone in a strange place. And, there's nothing like caring, supportive help to get one acclimated and integrated.

- Nursery schools and day care centers frequently need volunteer assistance. You can be a foster parent or grandparent, enjoy the contagious joy of little children, minister to runny noses and scraped knees, and receive your reward in hugs and juicy kisses.

  There's a wonderful program, started on the West Coast by Laura Huxley, called *Caress*. It is based on the premise that life-giving nutrition for children is contained in holding and caressing and that the need is not usually met in sufficient quantity or quality. Laura matches huggers (older women) with hugees (children) to the mutual benefit of all.

- School districts are always short of money, and volunteer workers are utilized in libraries, doing clerical work, and directly in the classroom. School help comes in many forms and under various titles. *School Volunteer Grandparents* is one organization. *Doves* (Dedicated Older Volunteers in Educational Service) began with the Los Angeles Unified School District and now has similar programs in New York and Washington, D.C. All types of backgrounds and experiences are utilized to provide tutorial help, be game leaders, teaching assistants, storytellers, and just spread around a little caring.

- If you want to really do it up right, consider Vista and the Peace Corps. Applicants are screened for specific abilities to handle various federal projects. Once accepted, you may receive a domestic assignment or one overseas. You could spend several years in another country, all expenses (but no salary) paid by the government. One of the better-known Peace Corps members is Lillian Carter, mother of former President Jimmy Carter, who was in her sixties when she went to India as a volunteer.

- If you like books, see if the local library can use some help. Conducting a story hour for small children or a "great books" club for adults can be stimulating.

- Give some time to your favorite political candidate, it's an activist way of making yourself heard.

- *Meals on Wheels* is a national program, completely self-supporting, that provides nourishing food to the disabled, aged, or ill. This allows people to remain in their homes instead of going to institutions. When you think of all the important benefits this brings to lives in real trouble, you'll want to hurry on down and join the helpers. Check with your local Chamber of Commerce, senior citizens' centers, or social service agencies for information on your local program.

We touched on just a few available volunteer jobs. There are countless other programs in operation or that need to be started. If giving to others is a possibility for you, this is a surefire way to put new vigor and meaning into your life.

ADDITIONAL INFORMATION
Recreation and Travel
Books

Marie Edwards and Eleanor Hoover. *The Challenge of Being Single.* Signet, 1975. An excellent examination of what being single in our culture is all about and, more importantly, how to make it work for you.

Emily Collins. *The Whole Single Person's Catalog.* Peebles Press, 1979. A catalog of activities, interests, preferences, problems, and solutions. It suggests guidelines for becoming a successful single.

The Leisure Alternatives Catalog: Food for Mind and Body. Dell, 1979. How-to information on a varied range of novel leisure-time experiences for your body and mind.

Donna Goldfein. *Everywoman's Guide to Travel.* Celestial Arts/Les Femmes, 1977. Packed with valuable tips to take the stress out of traveling alone, and to help you enjoy the special sense of freedom travel can offer.

Burt W. Lief. *EURoad: The Complete Guide to Motoring in Europe.* Prentice-Hall, 1979. Contains thirty-seven suggested tours from three days to three months, with motoring maps for eighteen Western European Countries.

Travel Agencies

Widow's Travel Club, 10 Rockefeller Plaza, Room 522, New York, New York 10020. Contact Beatrice Green (a former widow) for information about her "matching" service. With a membership of 10,000 widows, its sole purpose is to provide travel companions for its members.

Singleworld, 444 Madison Avenue, New York, New York 10022. Richard Lowenstein has been sending singles off to see the world for twenty-two years. Ask for his catalog that is packed with tour offerings. He makes one promise—no one will be lonely on one of his tours.

Check your local tour agent for information on other travel agencies that cater to the person alone and the older traveler.

Grand Circle Travel, Inc., P.O. Box 1510 FDR Station or 555 Madison Avenue, New York, New York 10022, provides travel service and escorted tours for the over-fifty traveler.

Society for the Advancement of Travel for the Handicapped (SATH), 26 Court Street, New York, New York 11242, will provide information on travel agencies that work with the handicapped. Don't let a physical infirmity keep you homebound.

Air Travel

How to Fly for Less and *1001 Sources for Free Travel Information,* are available from the Travel Information Bureau, P.O. Box 105, Department C., Kings Park, New York 11754.

Group Inclusive Tours (GITS) include air fare, car rental, and hotels in various combinations.

All of the major airlines have special tours. Pick up their catalogs and compare prices and offerings.

Rail Travel

Contact Amtrak for U.S. rail information. Call 800-648-3850.

Contact Canadian National Railways, 630 Fifth Avenue, New York, New York 10020 or Canadian Pacific Railway, 581 Fifth Avenue, New York, New York 10017, for information on Canadian rail travel.

Eurailpass gives unlimited rail travel in thirteen continental countries. Ask your travel agent for information or write Eurailpass, c/o French National Railroad, 610 Fifth Avenue, New York, New York 10020. Also, the Austrian, German, Italian, Scandinavian, and Swiss railroad offices in the U.S. will provide information.

Mexican Government Railway System, 500 Fifth Avenue, Room 2623, New York, New York 10036, will provide information about rail travel south of the border.

Auto Travel

Car Tours in Europe, 555 Fifth Avenue, New York, New York 10017 or Auto Europe, 1270 Second Avenue, New York, New York 10022, will provide information on car rental and purchase plans.

International drivers licenses and auto registration information can be obtained from the American Automobile Association, 28 East 78th Street, New York, New York 10021, or your local AAA office.

Vacation Home Exchange Services

The Travelers Directory, 51-02 39th Avenue, Woodside, New York 11377, is a listing of hundreds of people and places that will offer free housing. You must be willing to reciprocate to get the directory. A modest contribution is requested to cover printing costs.

Home Exchange Service (HES), 119 Fifth Avenue, New York, New York 10003, publishes an annual directory of home exchange members. Members work out their own arrangements. Dues are moderate.

Vacation Exchange Club, 350 Broadway, New York, New York 10013; Adventures in Living, P.O. Box 278, Winnetka, Illinois; Holiday Home Exchange Bureau, Inc., P.O. Box 555 Grants, New Mexico 87020; Interchange, 888 7th Avenue, Suite 400, New York, New York 10019, all operate worldwide.

General Information

American Youth Hostels, 20 West 17th Street, New York, New York 10011, for the young or the young at heart.

Contact the National Park Service, Room 1013, 18th and C Streets, Washington, D.C. 20240. Ask for a copy of the booklet *Visit a Lesser-Used Park* as well as for other free information and listings of parks in any region.

Customs Information can be obtained from the Bureau of Customs, Treasury Department, Washington, D.C. 20226. Ask for *Customs Hints for Returning U.S. Residents* and *Know Before You Go*.

To check on qualifications of travel agents or agencies, contact the Consumer Affairs Department of the American Society of Travel Agents (ASTA), 711 Fifth Avenue, New York, New York 10022, or the Better Business Bureau in your community or the city consumer affairs agency.

Passports can be obtained from Passport Agency listed under U.S. Government Department of State in your telephone book or from a clerk of Federal Court if there is no passport office in your community.

American Wilderness Experience, Inc., 753 Paragon Drive, Boulder, Colorado 80303 or Outward Bound, Inc., 165 W. Putnam Avenue, Greenwich, Connecticut 06830, will provide additional information on camping excursions.

Back to School

Books

Elinor Lenz and Marjorie Hansen Shaevitz. *So You Want to Go Back to School: Facing the Realities of Reentry.* McGraw-Hill, 1977. Excellent coverage of the issues involved in this all-important venture.

Sarah Splaver. *Nontraditional College Routes to Careers.* Simon and Schuster, 1975. Worth exploring for innovative ideas.

James Cass and Max Birnbaum. *Comparative Guide to American Colleges* (Ninth Edition). Harper and Row, 1979. The most complete guide to all accredited four-year colleges in America. In-depth profiles and data

192 THE WIDOW'S GUIDE TO LIFE

on admission requirements, costs, faculty, special programs, campus life, social and cultural environment.

Marjorie Ewing Aghassi. *Getting Good Grades: How to Succeed in College.* Prentice-Hall, 1980. Valuable tips from a college adviser on how to improve study habits, score high on aptitude tests and exams, budget study time, utilize test-taking time efficiently.

Pamphlets

Write the National Association for Public Continuing and Adult Education, 1201 16th Street, N.W., Washington, D.C. 20026 for a copy of *Public Continuing and Adult Education Almanac.*

Educational Opportunities for Older Persons #541G, is available free from the Department of Consumer Information, Pueblo, Colorado 81009. It lists resources for loans, scholarships, and grants for adult education.

Guide to Independent Study ($1.00) available from National University Extension Association, 1 Dupont Circle, Suite 360, Washington, D.C. 20036, lists seventy-three colleges that offer independent study courses for credit toward a college degree.

The National Home Study Council, 1601 18th Street, N.W., Washington, D.C. 20009, publishes a free directory of more than 135 accredited private schools with data on courses offered and costs.

Learning Opportunities for Older Persons, available free from Institute of Lifetime Learning, NRTA/AARP, P.O. Box 2400, Long Beach, California 90801. Describes a number of traditional and nontraditional educational options, including credit by examination, financial aid information, and discussion groups.

General Information

Call or write your local high school, community college, junior college, college, or university for their bulletins, both adult school/extension and regular program.

College credits may be obtained through examination. Write CLEP Test Centers, c/o the College Board Publication Orders, Box 2815, Princeton, New York 08541 for information.

Free or reduced tuition to older persons is available in 1500 colleges and universities. A state-by-state listing is available from the Institute of Lifetime Learning, Department TS, 1909 K Street, N.W., Washington, D.C. 20049. You may request information on institutions in any three states.

Elderhostel residential academic programs for older adults are offered in all fifty states. For information and a free catalog contact: Elderhostel, 100 Boylston Street, Suite 200X, Boston, Massachusetts 02116.

Information on how to apply and eligibility requirements for federal financial aid can be obtained by sending for *Student Guide—Six Federal Financial Aid Programs.* #543G, available from the Department of Consumer Information, Pueblo, Colorado 81009.

Volunteer Work

Book

Julietta K. Arthur. *Retire to Action: A Guide to Voluntary Service.* Abingdon, 1969. Describes a variety of volunteer jobs with suggestions for keeping active or opening the way to a business of your own.

Organizations to Contact

ACTION, 806 Connecticut Avenue, N.W., Room M1006, Department NB, Washington, D.C. 20525, or call toll-free 800-424-8580. This is the federal volunteer service agency which administers the Peace Corps, VISTA (Volunteers in Service to America), Foster Grandparents, Senior Companions, and Retired Senior Volunteer Program (RSVP).

United Way, Community Chest, Red Cross use volunteers in a variety of ways.

Your local hospital's Volunteer Services office.

The League of Women Voters.

Girl Scouts or Campfire Girls. Work with the girls on sewing, cooking, music, dance, etc.

Hot Lines—Crisis Centers, Guidance Clinics, etc.

Senior Citizens Center

Board of Education for teacher's aide or tutoring opportunities.

Career Planning Centers need volunteers to do library work and job development.

Traveler's Aid Society volunteers provide information and direction for travelers.

Retarded Children's Centers volunteers provide transportation and assist with all kinds of instruction on homemaking, crafts, woodworking, gardening, sewing, etc.

"Recording for the Blind," an organization that makes audiotape recordings of educational books.

Your museum, ballet company, little theater, symphony, library, or other cultural organization.

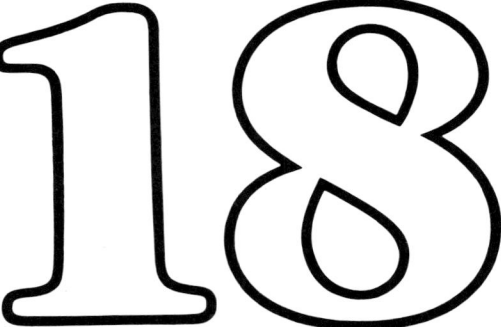

Support Systems

One of the most pervasive of all human needs is to share deep feelings with another person. Given the opportunity and some form of permission, people of all ages and all backgrounds will seek to relate to each other at meaningful levels. Clinical psychologists utilize this search for intimacy as the foundation of group psychotherapy. In our experience, whenever we bring widows together in groups, they become deeply personal almost from the outset. It is as if, simply by being together, they have been given "permission" to share. There is no one who understands in quite the same way as another widow. All of the superficial explanations become unnecessary—to speak is to be understood.

Since we know that at a basic level all people desire intimacy with others, isn't it a wonder that our national tradition reveres *Annie Oakley, True Grit,* and the stiff upper lip? We have common sayings like "save face," "chin up," "knuckle down," "shoulder your burden," "grin and bear it." These are meant to convey the importance of stoicism, of acceptance without complaining. We are creators of the great macho tradition that, among other things, says a man should not cry. The assumption is that a woman who teams with such a man should also bear her sorrow without tears.

In pioneer days, it may have served women well to bury their scalped menfolk without shedding a tear, then return to the home on the prairie to face the future courageously and alone. There wasn't much else they could do. If you've seen pictures of these women, you'll remember the suffering etched into their faces. It's interesting to note that their average life span was about forty-five years.

Now, over 150 years later, most Americans live a sophisticated, urban lifestyle, surrounded by the comforts of an advanced technology. Our lives are completely different, but most of us continue to behave in the same way, believing that what we need is to hold ourselves tightly together and display an ever-stiffening upper lip.

It's clear that trying to be totally self-contained is out of date, serves no purpose whatever, and succeeds only in creating the most agonizing conflict with your inner self.

That's a pretty harsh reality to face, particularly if you've been led to believe all your life that standing on your own two feet is gold medal behavior. So, in order to benefit from your support systems, you'll need to make some changes. *You'll need to learn to ask for help.* For many women, that is the most difficult thing imaginable.

The life benefits to be obtained from giving up rugged individualism in favor of interacting with others at a deep level have been proven over and over. We're certain that after some thought and study you'll want to join the thousands of widows who are finding that one of the most important ways to reorient their lives is through maximum utilization of the support systems at their disposal.

In our frame of reference, your support systems are all the people and places where you can find aid and comfort, acceptance and understanding. Many are well known to you, others must be sought out or created. When the person or group is the right one, you'll know it. You'll feel free to be who you are, say what you want, and ask for help freely, knowing you'll get it. When you have arrived at the right place, just let go and soak up as much goodness as you can stand. There'll be a time in the future when you can replenish the system by giving love and caring to others.

INDIVIDUAL PERSON SUPPORT

By now, the first rush of volunteer helpers has tapered off. Once they've seen you through the time of crisis, they'll move back into their own life patterns, which means you'll have to articulate your needs and ask for what you want. Try to pick people who can support you in differing ways. If you ask someone close to you for help and they refuse, it's well to remember that they're rejecting the helper role, not you, so don't be personally hurt. Simply ask someone else and move on.

Your loving friends, children, and others in your family can be helpful. Don't lean on any one of them totally; have a variety of people so each can provide their best. Pehaps you have one friend you can talk to at any hour of the night or day, and know that she will be there for you without it being a chore. A sister or close relative can be called to your aid if you're ill. If you have a grown child, allow her or him to assist with the physical aspects of your changing life—cleaning out the garage or closets, going through books and records. Little children can be wonderful solace and comfort. Don't push them away, and don't underestimate the extent of their understanding. Parents never stop parenting, so allow them to help you. They'll get as much benefit from the helping as you will.

Begin to add new people to your support system. There are many other women like you who would love to share a meal, go to a movie or play, or just take a walk and talk. How do you know that such a person is not your next door neighbor?

You may find it difficult to even know what you want. There may be an undefined longing that you can't understand or express to another. That may be the signal to get some "professional" help. Knowing that you need psychological help is actually a sign of good psychological health. Today, there are countless numbers of people in the "helping professions" working with people who are usually functioning quite well but for a variety of reasons need temporary help to get them over rough spots. Their life work is helping people, and this is one place you can let yourself go completely without the feeling that you are using someone, or that it is inappropriate.

The professional helper comes in many versions: male or female, psychologist, psychiatrist, social worker, counselor, minister, priest, or rabbi. There is a growing group of therapists who specialize in grief counseling (working through the pain of a loss). The choice is yours, and you may even want to work with more than one person concurrently.

Seeking professional help does not mean that you are "going crazy." Going for therapy is no longer a stigma. In many circles, it has the opposite connotation and is viewed as a status symbol. Don't wait to seek help until you're feeling desperate. Do it as a conscious effort at obtaining relief from the strain and pressures surrounding your bereavement. View your counseling sessions as contributing to your personal growth and helping you to move sooner into your new life.

Professionals in the counseling field have a broad range of competence, so you'll want to select carefully. You can be your own best guide. If you like the counselor as a person and feel helped by what he or she is doing, you'll know you're in good hands. If you feel uncomfortable, find someone else.

Don't let cost deter you. While good professionals come high on a per-visit basis, you may not need many sessions. In every community, there are social agencies that provide excellent counselors for modest fees; and there are often free clinics as well.

If you are deeply connected to a religious philosophy, this is a good time to reaffirm that faith. A religious philosophy can be quite apart from an established religious affiliation. You can explore your spirituality in traditional ways or with many of the new-age people who are looking at new concepts in their connectedness with a higher power.

While it's true that friendships do change after a death, don't be put off by being dropped from the couples list. You can develop new and even more important relationships. Relationships with grown children change too, often for the better. You can be seen in a new light that confirms your individuality. Whatever your choice, find ways to be with gentle people who will accept you as you are and support the method and timing that is best for you in making your transition.

SUPPORT PLACES

If you are living alone, establish a network of support places that can serve you in an illness or when you just don't feel like going out. (Watch that you don't use such a network regularly to avoid people contacts.) Begin by locating a grocery market that will deliver. There may be a minimum charge, and it will be more expensive; but if you use it only in need, it will be a handy support addition. If you're in one of those areas without such markets, in an emergency, explore the local liquor store. They often carry an amazing array of cheeses, juices, canned goods, and milk. They'll deliver, but you may have to include a bottle of sherry, which may not be all that bad either.

Line up a drugstore that will deliver phone orders. That's usually less difficult to find because they're serving the ill. Find financial institutions where you can bank by mail, or transfer funds from your savings to your checking account by phone. Get to know the local auto service station. In need, they'll pick up your sick car and return it well. Join an automobile club, and avoid being stuck at off-hours.

Hopefully, you'll never get in prolonged stuck-at-home trouble; but it's well to know that there are home nursing services available. Typically privately owned and operated, they do work with Medicare, Medicaid, and private insurance companies. In addition to licensed nurses, they provide a wide range of at-home services including physical and speech therapy, health aides, and social work. Beyond the immediate medical care, they work as a referral service to connect their patients with other community services. Public assistance offices provide help to low-income people. A few phone calls will line up some of these helpers should you require them. Even with physical problems, there are ways of remaining independent and staying in your own environment.

SUPPORT GROUPS

Of all the avenues open to you in finding your way to a new life, support groups may well be the most valuable. Their importance can be easily seen in the rapid proliferation of specialized groups of all kinds. Countless thousands of women have found their lives enriched, their life transition eased, their circle of friends enlarged, and their ways of relating to others improved through participation in a self-help group.

Widow-to-Widow Groups

Widow-to-widow programs are springing up all over the country. Many are sponsored by churches and synagogues, but in most cases there is no denominational restriction on membership. Some programs for the widowed are open to men as well as women. New on the scene are widow's programs sponsored by mortuaries. They have the first contact with widows, and in exchange for the help they give, they have an opportunity to improve their public image.

All widow-to-widow groups are well intentioned, but they vary in quality. Those that are dependent on a leader could have problems if the leader's ego or the sponsor's image gets in the way. Many leader-conducted groups are simply excellent. You can sit in on a session or two before making an extended commitment. There's an alternative to leader groups in *leaderless* groups that we think offers a viable option.

Women's Groups

There's probably less aloneness in being a woman alone now than at any time in history. The feminist movement, really a people's liberation movement, is trying to improve women's legal rights, improve conditions at the workplace, reform social inequities, and abolish the discrimination that has plagued women through the ages.

One of the most active and militant feminist groups is NOW, National Organization for Women. NOW has chapters all over the country. If there is one in your local community, why not join? Even if you don't subscribe to all of their goals, remember that their primary aim is to see that women get their fair share financially.

The Women's Action Alliance is a national clearinghouse on information for individuals and organizations who are interested in improving life for women in this country. Check with them on ways to get funding for a work or study project, how to deal with sex discrimination on the job, in housing, or in any aspect of your living.

Many areas have women's centers, self-help clinics, emergency hot lines and other services. For the older widow, there are services offered through senior citizen organizations and centers. A bit of searching, a phone call or two, and you are bound to find just the type of help you want.

A new phenomenon is the consciousness raising groups. Although they do not focus on the problems of widowhood, they do deal with issues of how our culture has indoctrinated us with rigid role concepts; and they cover ways of breaking out of them. Since widowhood dissolves the married role, some of the work done in these groups can be helpful in finding your new identity as a woman alone.

Group Therapy

Many psychologists, psychiatrists, and marriage and family counselors hold groups that are centered around the alone person and her needs. Group therapy can be potent medicine in the relief of tension through honest expression of grief.

Self-Help Groups

A Widowed Person's Service is operated by the American Association of Retired Persons. Volunteer counselors give individual and group guidance in coping with grief, dealing with financial matters, making important decisions, confronting loneliness and fears, and finding employment.

Groups serving special needs are available in nearly every category. You may want to join one in an area of interest not connected with your widow's status. See listing of resources at chapter's end.

Beyond Widowhood Groups

As you've journeyed with us through the chapters of this book, you've probably realized the importance of our major premise that widowhood, far from being an ending, can be the springboard into a new and rewarding life. We hope this book has opened your eyes to this possibility. The most powerful way we know to bring widows back into the mainstream of life is by banding together in mutual support, mutual consciousness raising, mutual exchange of information and, most important of all, simply mutual sharing. There is nothing in the world like being with others who are sharing the same experiences. And there's nothing as supportive as one widow who has healed being with another in her healing.

One of the most important things you can do for yourself is to belong to such a group. If there's not one available, start one yourself. Call two widows and tell them you're going to start a widow's mutual support group. Let them know that they must each bring another widow, and so on. A good group will have between ten and fifteen women, although larger or smaller ones should not be ruled out. Start by deciding on a regular meeting day, and have everyone make a deep commitment to be there regularly. You can have time for planned discussions on specific topics important to a widow's adjustment, sharing of individual problems, and a search for solutions.

You'll find that as each week goes by you will form a deeper bond with the other women, you'll become more informed, you'll have friends to be with between meetings, and you will continue to feel better and better about yourself and your life. That's the magic of truly being with others. And that's the magic in a group that comes together with the leader function being shared. We deeply believe that the potential of leaderless widows' groups is among the most important messages we have to deliver.

Now we've reached an ending and a beginning. You've struggled with constructive grieving, taking care of your personal affairs, and your financial affairs. You've dealt with the tax man, the legal system, the federal bureaucrats, and the local bureaucrats. Through it all, you're learning and growing more autonomous. You are on your way to achieving full health, a productive career, joy in both your solitude and in relating to others. It is clear that, through your own efforts, you can go beyond *widowhood* to a vibrant, self-reliant, totally fulfilled *personhood*.

ADDITIONAL INFORMATION

Book

Alan Gartner and Frank Riessman. *Help: A Working Guide to Self-Help Groups.* New Viewpoints/Vision Books, 1980. Provides information on how to form groups and how to improve their operation. Also lists the major self-help groups throughout the U.S.

Support Groups

The following organizations are national in scope. Write for information on chapters in your locale. There are also individual groups in various parts of the country; inquire locally.

The Widowed Persons Service, 1909 K Street, N.W., Washington, D.C. 20049. A public service program offered by American Association of Retired Persons (AARP), Action for Independent Maturity (AIM), and the National Retired Teachers Association (NRTA).

THEOS Foundation, The Penn Hills Mall Office Bldg., Room 306, Pittsburgh, Pennsylvania 15235. (Seventy chapters) A Christian nondenominational mutual self-help fellowship for young and middle-aged widows.

NAIM Conference, 721 North LaSalle Street, Chicago, Illinois 60610. (26 chapters) An organization for Catholic widows and the spouses of deceased Catholics.

Parents Without Partners, 7910 Woodmont Avenue, Washington, D.C. 20014. (1000 chapters) Serves as a way station for single parents and their children by aiding in the adjustment period that follows widowhood, divorce, or separation.

National Organization for Women (NOW), national headquarters, 425 13th Street, N.W., Suite 1048, Washington, D.C. 20004.

The Women's Action Alliance, Inc., 370 Lexington Avenue, New York, New York 10017, information on organizations in your community working to improve the quality of life for women.

Index

Accountants, 72–74
  Certified Financial Planners, 73
  Certified Public Accountants, 73
  Enrolled Agents, 74
  in IRS, 74
  public accountants, 74
  use of, 73
  volunteer groups, 74
Aloneness, contrasted to loneliness, 7–8, 101–02
  and half-filled glass analogy, 7
  and self-fulfilling prophecy in, 102
Annuities, 76–77
Apartment, rental of, 170–71
  advantages, 170–71
  disadvantages, 172
Attorneys, 35–38
  fee agreement, 37
  in modern U.S., 36
  selection of, 36–38
Automobile, insurance of, 75–76
  collision, 76
  comprehensive coverage, 76
  minimum, 75–76

Banks, insurance of:
  FDIC, 86
  FSLIC, 86

Banks, services of:
  convenience features, 90–91
  insurance, 91
  investment and retirement fund assistance, 90
  loans, 89–90
  special services, 90
Bills, 18–19
  checks for, 19
  estate vs. personal, assignment of, 19
  and insurances for, 18
  points to remember, 18
  system for, 18
Budgets (See Controlled budgeting, Prebudgeting)

Car (See Automobile, insurance of)
Careers:
  attainment fantasy, 161–62
  general fantasy, 162
Checking accounts, 88–89
  fees on, 89
Children, effects on, 8–9
  and courses in schools, 9
  honesty with about death, 8–9
Clothes, of women, points to remember, 156–57

203

Con artists, and widows, caution about, 132–33
Condominiums and cooperatives, 173
  condominium, ownership in, 173
  cooperative, ownership in, 173
Controlled budgeting, 28–31
  cycles, 28
  goals, 28
  planner, 30–31
  planner, use of, 28–29
  points to remember, 29

Dating, 108–09
Disability insurance, 78
Documents, obtaining, 70

Employment, 24–26
  general discussion, 24–25
  private employers, benefits from, 25–26
  public employers, benefits from, 25
Entertaining, 181
  all-female, 181
  interests, 181
Estate planning, 133–34 (*See also* Legal procedures, widow's part in)
  estate, nature of, 133
  points to remember, 133–34
  revocable living trust, 134
Exercise, 114–15
  aerobics, 115
  amounts of, 114–15
  running, 114
  stretching, 115
  Tai Chi Chuan, 115
  walking, 115

Financial institutions, human side of, 92
  and branch managers, 92
  and tellers, 92
Form 706 (estate tax):
  date of valuation, 63
  discussion, 63
  and inflation, 62
  and marital deductions, 62
  present limits, 62
Form 1040 (personal income tax), 58–61
  children, 59
  and energy credits, 60
  filing, 59
  and home business, 60–61
  husband, property of, 59
  joint return, 59
  older persons, notes for, 60
  records, 58
  and sale of home, 60

Form 1041 (fiduciary income tax):
  discussion, 61
  identification, number of estate, 61
  partial payments, 61–62
  points to remember, 61–62
Funerals, 15–18
  expenses, 16
  and gadgetry of, 16
  and 'grief counselors,' 16
  issues, 17–18
  memorial societies, 16–17
  reasons for, 16

Goals, setting of, 103
  plans, 103
Grief, 4–6
  aloneness, 6
  anger, 6
  disbelief and denial, 5
  depression, 6
  disorganization and forgetfulness, 5
  guilt, 6
  idealizing, 6
  and need for transition, 4
  numbness, 5
  other feelings, 6
  repression of, 4
  in U.S., 4

Health, insurance of, 77
  group plans, 77
  Health Maintenance Organizations, 77
Holistic health:
  Chinese adage on, 114
  discussion, 113–14
  defined, 114
  and mental force, 113
Holmes, Dr. Thomas H., 8
Home, insurance of, 77–78
  homeowners, 78
  inventory, 78
  liability, 77–78
  and renters, 77
  and travel, 77
  valuables, 78
Home, ownership of, 171–73
  reasons to keep, 172
  reasons to sell, 172
  Reverse Annuity Mortgage, 172
Housing options, discussed, 166–67

Inflation, 135
  future effects of, 135
  reduction of expenses, 135
  work, 135

Insurance, claims for, 19–21
  life insurance, 19–20
  Major Medical, 21
  medical insurance, 20–21
  Medicare, 21
  persistence, 21
  points to remember, 19–20
  procedure, 20
  reimbursement, hazards of, 20–21
  rules, 19
  tax forms, 20
Insurance personnel, 74–75
  agent vs. broker, contrast, 75
Insurance, points to remember, 78–79
  payments for, 79
Interior, of housing, as personal environment, 168
  and bedroom, 168
Intimacy, need to share, discussion, 194–95
  and American traditions, 194
  in modern U.S., 195
Investments, 128–32
  annuities, 130
  art and collectibles, 131–32
  government obligations, 130–31
  money market funds, 131
  money market investments, 131
  precious metals, 131
  real estate, income producing, 129
  real estate, undeveloped, 129
  REITs, 129
  retirement plans, tax-free, 132
  saving accounts, 128–29
  second trust deeds, 129
  securities, 130
  venture capital investment, 131

Job market, data sources of, 160–61
Job market, entry to, 151–52
  example, 152
  functional résumé, 152
  and self-concept, 151
Jobs, finding of, 158–60
  discussion, 158
  interviews, 159
  referrals, 158–59
  résumés, 159
  salary, questions to ask in interview, 160
Jobs, self-created, 154–56
  business plan, 156
  examples, 155
  small business, 154
  and Small Business Administration, 156
  steps to start, 155–56

Lawyers (*See* Attorneys)
Legal assistance, alternate forms of, 38

Legal procedures, widow's part in, 38–40
  and estate, entity of, 39
  property, transfer of, 40
  taxes on estate, 40
  and will, filing of, 39
  and will, probate of, 39
Leisure and retirement communities, 173–74
Life, insurance of, 76
Life, planning of, 138–49
  abilities, 143
  checklist, 140
  and early childhood, conditioning in, 140
  eulogy and epitaph exercise, 146–47
  faults, 144
  future life inventory, 147
  general discussion, 139
  guidelines, 141–42
  love, importance of, 142
  next two years, 148–49
  personal workshop, overview, 140–42
  positive experiences, 143
  rhythm, 141
  self-image, 142–43
  Shedlin, Arthur J., work of, 138
  strengths, 143
  'who am I?' exercise, 145–46
Living alone, 168–69
Living with others, 169–70
  communal living, 170
  example, 169
  and nonmarried couples, 170
  room rentals, 169
Location, choice of, 167
  to new state, 167
  points to remember, 167
  and Sunbelt, 167

Marriage, alternatives to, 110–11
  economic independence, 111
  living together, 110–11
  vulnerability of widow, caution about, 110
Masturbation, 107–08
Medicaid, 49–50
Medicare:
  carriers of, 48
  and catastrophic illness, 48
  discussion, 47
  Health Maintenance Organizations, 49
  Part A, 47
  Part B, 47
  points to remember, 47–49
  supplemental coverage, 47–49
Men, attraction of, 108
Mobile homes, 174–75
  Gadabout Granny, example, 175
Mortgage insurance, 78
Mothers, single working, 157–58
  childcare center, starting of, 158

Mothers, single working *(continued)*
    and children, 157
    and daycare, 157

Net worth, 126–28
    assets, types of, 126
    future earning power, 127–28
    house, and interest on value of, 127
    house, value of, 127
    liabilities, 126–27
Nutrition, 115–16
    meals, timing of, 116
    and sugar, 116
    vitamins, 116

Personal credit, 22–24
    credit cards, 23–24
    Equal Credit Opportunity Act of 1974, 23
    Fair Credit Reporting Act, 23
    loans, 24
    and name change, 23
Personal effects, 21–22
Prebudgeting, 27
    expense records, 28
    income categories, 27
    temptations to resist, 27
Private practice (*See* Self-employment and private practice)
Property (*See* Home, insurance of)

Rahe, Dr. Richard H., 8
Recordkeeping, 31–32
    files, 32
    safe deposit box, 32
    wallet contents, record of, 32
Recreation and travel:
    adjusting to singleness, 177–78
    going alone, advantages of, 178
    and pairing with other women, 178
    points to remember, 178
    restaurants, points to remember, 178–79
Recreational activities, 181–83
Reed, Myrtle, 3
Regulations, information about, 65–66
Relaxation, 116–18
    autogenics, 117
    biofeedback, 117–18
    meditation, 11
Remarriage, 111–12
    and children, 111
    legal planning, 111
    Mead, Margaret, quoted on, 112
    qualities sought, 112
Retirement homes, 174
    test of, 174
    warning about, 174

Rituals, 6–7
    Jewish (shiva), 7
Roles, freedom from, 98
    and wife/mother paradigm, 98

Saving accounts, interest on, 87–88
    certificates, 87
    joint tenancy account, 88
    and loans, 87
    and type of account, 87
Saving accounts, ownership of, 88
    individual, 88
    individual revocable, 88
    joint tenancy, 88
School, return to, 183–87
    for aged, 187
    and choice of school, 185
    in colleges, 184
    degree programs, 184–85
    expenses, 185
    for fun and fantasy, 186–87
    scenario, 183–84
    vocational courses, 185–86
Securities:
    alternate investment in, 81–82
    documents for, 82
    information about, 81
    transfer of title on, 82
Self-employment and private practice, 26
    closed corporation, 26
    partnership, 26
    points to remember, 26
    problems with, 26
Selfness, contrasted with selfishness, 101
Sex, common attitudes toward, 107
Sex, outside marriage, 109–10
    for itself, 110
    and old ideas, 110
Shock, response to, 97–98
    automatic, 97
    and self-affirmation, 98
    and self-responsibility, 97
Social Security:
    application, 43–44
    benefits, eligibility for, 44–45
    and children, 44–45
    problems with, 43
    proposed reductions, 46
    tips, 45–46
Spinster's Book, The, Reed, 3
Stockbrokers, 80
    recommendations, 80
    and regulation of, 80
    widows, caution to, 80
Stress, 8
    and drugs, 8
    Holmes and Rahe, work of, 8
Supplemental Security Income, 50

Support, groups for, 197–200
consciousness raising groups, 198–99
group therapy, 199
local centers, 198
National Organization for Women, 198
of other widows, for mainstreaming, 199–200
self-help groups, 199
widow-to-widow, 198
Women's Action Alliance, 198
Support, personal, 195–97
costs, 196
family, 195–96
and friendships, 197
and professional help, 196
and religion, 196–97
Support, places for, 197
food delivery, 197
medical services, 197

Taxes (*See also* Form 706, Form 1040, Form 1041)
discussion, 57
fiduciary state income, 66–67
three forms, simultaneous work on, 58
Taxes, property, 67–68
appraisal, 67
reassessment, 67
relief for elderly, 68
and relocating, 68
Taxes, state inheritance and estate, 67
Taxes, state income, 66
Temporary agency employment, 153
Thought, positive, effect of in health, 102–03
points to remember, 103
research, 102
and visualization, 102
Time-sharing jobs, 153–54
and flextime, 154
nature of, 153
as partnership, 154
Titles, transfer of, 68–69
documents, 69
questions to ask, 69
and statutory lien, 69
and tenants in common, 68
and tenants by entirety, 68
Transition, 98–101
examples, 100
Graham, Catherine Meyer, 100–01
groups, 99
Humphrey, Muriel, 100
Huxley, Laura, 100
King, Coretta, 100
Molly, experience of with repairs, 99
personal interests, 99
Roosevelt, Eleanor, 100
Smith, Margaret Chase, 101

Transition, checklist for:
in first four weeks, 14
after first month, 14
in first two weeks, 13
immediate, 13
learning of, 13
after six months, 15
within six months, 14–15
Travel, 179–80
points to remember, 179–80
saving money in, tips, 180
widows' travel club, 180
Trust departments, 91

Veterans Administration, benefits from, 53–55
burial, 54
documents, 54
National Service Life Insurance, 55
points to remember, 54
tips, 55
and wartime service, 54
and widows, 54–55
Volunteer work, 187–89
Caress, 188
for children, 188
discussion, 187
Doves, 188
in hospital, 187–88
Meals on Wheels, 188–89
in school districts, 188
School Volunteer Grandparents, 188
Vista and Peace Corps, 188

Well-being, psychological, 118–19
and cancer, 119
therapy, 119
and wellness, 118
Wellness, 119–22
general discussion, 119
hallmarks of, 120–22
ordinary standards, 119
Widowhood:
and American women, 3–4
early 20th Century view of, 3
at present, 3
and suttee, 3
Will, preparation of new, 40–41
Wills, filing and probate of (*See* Legal procedures, widow's part in)
Women:
and life flow, 151
and men's jobs, 152–53
statistics on in modern U.S., 150
work of, 150–51

```
                    23339
HQ
1058.5          Fisher, Ida
.U5
F53                The widow's guide to
                life
```